The Second
Socialist Revolution

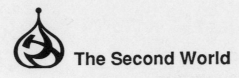 **The Second World**

TEODOR SHANIN *Series Editor*

Already published

The Economic Challenge of Perestroika
Abel Aganbegyan

Rural Russia Under the New Regime
V.P. Danilov

The Peoples of the Soviet Union
Viktor Kozlov

Five Days Which Transformed Russia
Sergei Mstislavskii

Tatyana Zaslavskaya

The Second Socialist Revolution

AN ALTERNATIVE SOVIET STRATEGY

Foreword by Teodor Shanin

*Translated by Susan M. Davies
with Jenny Warren*

INDIANA UNIVERSITY PRESS

Bloomington and Indianapolis

U.S. edition published by
Indiana University Press
Bloomington, Indiana 47405

Published by arrangement with I.B. Tauris & Co Ltd, London

The paper used in this publication meets the minimum requirements of
American National Standard for Information Sciences —Permanence of
Paper for Printed Library Materials, ANSI Z39.48-1984.

Manufactured in the United States of America

Library of Congress Cataloging-in-Publication Data

Zaslavskaia, T. I.
   The second socialist revolution : an alternative Soviet strategy /
Tatyana Zaslavskaya ; introduction by Teodor Shanin ; translation
by Susan M. Davies with Jenny Warren.
        p.   cm. -- (The Second World)
   Translated from Russian.
   ISBN 0-253-36860-X. -- ISBN 0-253-20614-6 (pbk.)
   1. Soviet Union--Politics and government--1985- 2. Soviet Union-
Economic policy--1986- 3. Soviet Union--Social conditions--1970-
4. Perestroika. I. Warren, Jenny. II. Title. III. Series.
DK288.Z37   1990
947.085'4--dc20   90-34127
                                                             CIP

1 2 3 4 5 94 93 92 91 90

Contents

The Second World Series

'In the West they simply do not know Russia . . . Russia
in its germination.'

Alexander Hertzen

As a publication project *The Second World* pursues an explicit goal,
admits to a bias and proceeds on a number of assumptions. This
should be stated at the outset. The series will aim to let the Soviet
authors and their historical predecessors in tsarist Russia speak with
their own voices about issues of major significance to us and to
them. It will focus particularly on their explorations of their own
society and culture, past and present, but set no rigid boundaries to
these; some of the texts will be more general while others will carry
primary evidence, for example, memoirs, documents, etc. Many of
the texts have been commissioned to reflect the most recent issues
and controversies of Gorbachev's *perestroika*.

To bridge differences of culture and experience each of the books
will carry a substantial introduction by a Western scholar within
the field. Particular care will also be taken to maintain satisfactory
standards of translation and editing.

A word about words. A generation ago the term 'Third World'
was coined in its current meaning, to indicate a somewhat imprecise
combination of societal characteristics – the post-colonial experience, under-industrialization, relative poverty and the effort to
establish an identity separate from the superpowers, the 'Bandung
camp'. This left implicit yet clear which were the other two 'worlds'.
It was 'us' and 'them', those best represented by the USA and those
best represented by the USSR. Much has changed since, giving the
lie to crude categorizations. But in research and the media, at the
UN and on television, the words and the meanings established in the
1960s are still very much with us. This makes the title of our project
intelligible to all, yet, hopefully, should also make the reader pause
for a moment of reflection.

Turning to the invisible rules and boundaries behind the editorial
selection let us stress first the assumption of considerable social
continuity between pre-revolutionary and post-revolutionary societies. Present without past is absurd (as is, of course, the treatment

of the USSR as simply the Russia of old). Next, to talk of pre-revolutionary Russia/USSR is not simply to talk of the Russians. The country is multi-ethnic, as have been its intellectual achievements and self-evaluations. Yet all the books presented are deeply embedded in Russian language and cultural traditions. Lastly, we shall aim to show Russia/USSR neither as the 'goody' nor as the 'baddy' but focus attention on the characteristics particular to it.

The Second World is biased insofar as its choice of titles and authors consistently refuses the bureaucratized scholarship and paralytic tongue which has characterized much of the Soviet writing. In other words, it will prefer authors who have shown originality and courage of content and form.

Western perceptions of the Soviet scholarly achievement, especially of its social self-analysis, have been usually negative in the extreme. This was often enough justifiable. Heavy censorship stopped or biased much Soviet research and publication. 'Purges' have destroyed many of the best Soviet scholars, with whole disciplines closed on orders from above. The Soviet establishment has excelled in the promotion of safe scholars – the more unimaginative and obedient, the faster many made it into the limelight. However, much of the hostile detachment of the Anglo-Saxon scholarship and the media originated in its own ideological bias, linguistic incompetence and a deeper still layer of mutual miscomprehension. To understand the human experience and thought in a particular social world, one must view it on its own terms – that is, with full awareness of its context – of history, political experience, culture and symbolic meanings. This necessitates the overcoming of stereotypes rooted in one's own experience and a challenge to that most persistent prejudice of all – the belief that everybody (and everything) is naturally 'like us', but somewhat less so (and that the best future mankind can have is to be like us but even more so).

The bafflement of the mainstream of Western scholarship at the dawn of Gorbachev's reforms has accentuated the collective miscomprehensions of Soviet society. On the one hand stand those who see nothing happening because nothing can happen: 'totalitarianism' is not open to any transformation from within. On the other hand stand those to whom the USSR is at long last becoming 'like us'. Both views miss the most important point, that Soviet society is moving along its own trajectory which can be understood only on its own terms. This makes the need to allow this society and its scholars to speak to us in their own voice, an urgent one.

Uniformity and uniformization are false as perceptions of history and wrong as social goals, but so also is any effort at keeping human worlds apart. This is true for international politics, scholarly endeavour and daily life. Half a century ago a Soviet diplomat,

Maxim Litvinov, a survivor of the revolutionary generation which was then going under, addressed the League of Nations to say: 'Peace is indivisible'. The World War to follow did not falsify this statement, but amended it. Peace proved divisible but only at the heavy price of human peril. The same holds for knowledge.

Teodor Shanin
University of Manchester

Foreword

A major characteristic of Mikhail Gorbachev's *perestroika* has been the overwhelming surprise at its depth, speed, and remorseless advance despite the overwhelming odds. Whatever the explanations or excuses, the fact remains that none of the Western Sovietologists deemed anything like it possible, while to the Soviet citizenry the surprise was equally great. As this experience unfolds further, still outrunning all efforts at its analytical digestion, something can be said about what its substantive analysis will entail. It will have to be less deterministic and accept that there are tides of historical 'alternativity' in which the extrapolating trends are punctured by 'moments of truth' when, for a while, different 'roads' can be taken. It will also have to incorporate the historical role of accident. Most importantly, it will have to reassert the significance of new images and concepts, i.e. words which are more than commonsense routine or propaganda slogans, for human history is a dialectical loop of collective perceptions and collective preceptors in action. Accordingly, it will have to re-accentuate what stands behind the statistics – the significance of individual men and women, especially those capable of generating new ideas and fighting for them against the continuity of the self-evident, the established dogmas, the grim bureaucracies, and popular prejudice parading as common sense.

Tatyana Zaslavskaya has been one such generator of new ideas. She has coined some of the major perceptions, images, and 'words which matter' for *perestroika*. Often (as with the term, 'the human factor'), those words existed before, but became attached to Zaslavskaya's intervention in debate, taking on a new colour and an interpretation which was very much her own. Even her name has become a symbol for good and ill. Some use it as a signal of belonging to a brotherhood of radical supporters of reform. To others it is equally recognizable and significant in its notoriety – a way of personifying what they are determined to resist.

A question which should be tackled even before one considers Zaslavskaya's views and impact is the question where did people like her come from – what 'made them' humanly and socially? A biographical supplement to her own introductory note in this book may help to give meaning to Zaslavskaya's views and also present a generation of Russian intelligentsia without whom *perestroika* would never have happened the way it did.

A BIOGRAPHICAL SKETCH: THE PERSONAL AND THE PUBLIC

Zaslavskaya's personal story is one of the Russian intelligentsia at its core and at its best. Her mother was the fourth generation in an unbroken line of intellectuals. Her father was a university professor of peasant stock – the first generation of his family to make it into academia. Tatyana Zaslavskaya grew up particularly close to the family of her maternal grandfather, a professor and dean of physics at the University of Kiev. Throughout her early years and later this family and its intellectual and ethical environment formed her main reference point. In her own words 'those were the real people'.

Tatyana grew up very much as 'her mother's daughter' – bright, affectionate, deeply involved in her studies, very literate, the typical top girl of her class. Childhood came to an abrupt end as her biography linked up with her country's history at its most dramatic point. The war began in 1941 when Tatyana was fourteen, and her mother was killed in the first air raid on Moscow. Next came evacuation and its hardships, followed by a return to Moscow when the Germans were driven back. Having missed a year of her studies she still managed to complete her secondary schooling at the age of sixteen. The Faculty of Physics of the excellent University of Moscow followed as a matter of course. For three years Tatyana proceeded with her studies as one of the top students of her class. But doubts set in from the very beginning; she was not sure that she actually wanted to study the natural sciences. Eventually she broke the news at home that she would like to switch over to the social sciences. The family, and especially her stepmother, objected to such a move as irresponsible, inconsiderate, indeed frivolous. A family battle followed; the parents opposed her move while her older sister defended her right to do so. Tatyana went her own way, beginning afresh at the Faculty of Economics. She also threw herself whole-heartedly into the work of the Komsomol – the Young Communist League. For a time she was the toast of her new Faculty – an activist, a loyalist, with marks which once again put her at the top of her class, a student 'with excellent prospects'.

This did not last; Tatyana Zaslavskaya was to get her first taste of political infighting, malicious whispers, crumbling loyalties and straightforward envy. She was accused of bourgeois ideological deviation because she quoted the works of Trakhtenberg, a gifted economist whose turn it was then to become the whipping boy. A

proper witch-hunt followed. A gap opened up around the bright
student with a black mark against her. Some of her friends stopped
recognizing her in the corridors of the university. When graduation
came and most of her peers proceeded to post-graduate studies at
the Faculty, she was not offered the opportunity to do so but was
assigned to a glass factory in an essentially pen-pushing job. But a
teacher, who had become a friend, refused to accept this, and it was
through her extraordinary (and, in the circumstances, courageous)
effort that Tatyana found herself in a research job after all, at the
agricultural division of the Institute of Economics. In 1950 she
also began work on a Ph.D. under the supervision of Professor
V. Venzher – a major figure in Soviet economic thought, an old
man who had fought in the Civil War and remained true to himself
through the often terrible times. Even in the eyes of his enemies
he was recognized as a man of exceptional integrity. In the 1950s
he represented for many a human bridge between the revolutionary era and the Khruschev period – a grandparents/grandchildren
alliance against a Stalinist middle generation. It is Venzher whom
Zaslavskaya still considers her main teacher and inspiration within
the social sciences.

Fieldwork for the Institute and for her next degree brought
Zaslavskaya, the city girl from the intellectual middle classes, into
her first extensive contact with the Soviet countryside and Soviet
agriculture. The topic of her thesis was the methods of income
assessment in the collective farms. Her encounter with village life
as it really was shocked and horrified her. Those were the post-
collectivization and post-war days. The destitution of the villagers
was staggering, their prospects dim. It was an experience never to
be forgotten by her in the times that followed.

Meanwhile, Zaslavskaya's academic career was moving on. She
received her degree of *Kandidat* in 1956, published extensively and
established a reputation as a very bright agrarian economist. In
1963 she met Abel Aganbegyan who promptly 'drafted' her into
the Institute of Economics in Novosibirsk. She was offered better
working conditions and leadership of a team of young people ready
and keen to study the transformation of rural Siberia. In 1965 she
gained her degree of Doctor of Economics and in 1968 was elected
an Associate Member of the Academy of Sciences of the USSR. By
that time she already had 40 major works to her name.

There was another dimension of life which she shared with many
Soviet professional women, the problem of combining professional
work and family obligations. By this time she was married and had
two small daughters who needed her care. As an Academician she
now had privileged access to supplies and services but things were
never easy. She could not even dream of many of the goods and

services which professional women in Western Europe take for granted.

As the years of academic success and daily chores went by, Zaslavskaya became increasingly dissatisfied with her work. She began to feel that she had little more to say in the academic field she had made her own, the rest was mostly repetition and routine. Methods of agrarian economics did not give a sufficient answer to many of her queries. Following a study of the problems of geographical mobility of the labour force, where rural-urban migration was concerned, she began to read increasingly the works of sociologists of her own Institute such as V. Shlyapentokh and V. Shubkin, and to discuss matters with them. In 1966 she attended the World Congress of Sociology in Evian. When in 1967 Aganbegyan was appointed director of the Institute of Economics he suggested appointing her as head of a sociology division within it. She was doubtful but eventually accepted and threw herself with enthusiasm into a world of new disciplinary ideas, methods and research. She established a friendship and a research as well as writing partnership with Inna Ryvkina, and brought together a team of committed sociologists. She searched through the literature and found herself particularly interested by the work then being done by Polish sociologists. All this was a far cry from what was happening throughout the USSR where a veritable purge of the best and the brightest within the field of sociology was taking place. Moscow's Institute of Sociology was in decline, Leningrad's Institute of Sociology had its best members dismissed and dispersed. Novosibirsk, however, mercifully far away from 'the centre', kept its team and advanced its own sociological tradition, thus becoming a major 'exception to the rule'. It was rural sociology in which they excelled.

In 1973 Zaslavskaya was asked to take the chair of a national Committee for the Development of Soviet Villages consisting of an interdisciplinary galaxy of scholars. A statistical model was set up of villages as socio-economic units, with 300 variables to the complex interdependence of characteristics and dynamics involved. When in 1977 Zaslavskaya and her colleagues had worked the material out in full and came to look at the long-term conclusions indicated by the model, they were shaken by their own results. They tried out a number of variations. It became clear that if development were to proceed along the lines of the 1970s, this extrapolation of the basic dynamics of the Soviet countryside would produce an acute crisis of falling supplies from an agriculture which 'devoured' national economic resources, while the whole economic system declined. Any more optimistic scenario had to assume a doubling of the increase in productivity of Soviet agriculture and a sharp increase in production (of up to 8 per cent per year). This could be provided only by a 'qualitative leap forward', i.e. a major transformation in the way Soviet agriculture operated. To Zaslavskaya it was patently clear that no purely economic methods could secure such a change, and that beneath the approaching economic crisis lay social problems which must be urgently investigated and addressed.

For this purpose Zaslavskaya's team turned to a region in central Siberia which lies within striking distance of Novosibirsk. The mountainous area of Altaiskii Krai is one of the world's beauty spots, while for a century its plains provided an area of settlement for peasants moving from European Russia, an emigration cum colonization which reached its peak at the turn of the century. The local Party leadership was sympathetic to the social scientists' work and offered the necessary facilities. In 1979 the region became the focus of extensive empirical studies which uncovered numerous crisis points in the rural society and what amounted to a deepening 'freezing' of the whole agricultural system. By the early 1980s the need for fundamental change was clear to all those involved in the study of Altai and specific projects tantamount to a socio-economic '*perestroika*' of its agriculture were being debated. Much of what was being considered then forms part and parcel of Gorbachevian reforms in agriculture legislated in 1986–8.

In the early 1980s more was actually happening 'at the top' than met the eye. A new and surprisingly young man was brought into Moscow to join the Politburo and to take charge of the country's agriculture. Mikhail Gorbachev had shown a particular liking for intellectuals and a wish to listen to what they had to say. In April 1982 he called a meeting of senior social scientists to discuss the problems of Soviet agriculture and the food production programme he was to preside over. Zaslavskaya was there – her first meeting with Gorbachev. She recollects it as being surprisingly informal. Gorbachev was a good listener, open to argument and friendly towards her views. He summed up his own view of the food programme as representing 'big ideas but unsatisfactory methods' and when challenged as to the inbuilt limitations of the broad economic structure he answered with an 'If only I could . . .' – as surprising as the whole critical yet relaxed atmosphere of the meeting. Zaslavskaya met Gorbachev a few more times (and was later asked to join the team preparing his report to the Party Congress he was to address as its newly established leader).

For Zaslavskaya the 1982/3 period was in fact to be one of an exceptional 'high' and of a testing 'low'. In September 1982 she participated in the meeting of the Academy of Sciences of the USSR together with the Academy of Agricultural Sciences and spoke about the social crisis in agriculture – out of 35 speakers the only one to do so. In her own recollection it is one of the moments when life peaked: a mercilessly open description of the countryside's ills to a tense, totally silent audience and then a storm of applause.

Zaslavskaya's academic effort and growing eminence were being increasingly recognized at the official level. In 1981 she had been elected a full member of the Academy of Sciences. She was now in favour with academic officialdom, increasingly sent abroad on delegations, and awarded a variety of extra privileges. Then the thunderbolt of official displeasure struck again when in 1983 a colloquium met in Novosibirsk that was to make Zaslavskaya famous, or notorious, the world over.

Zaslavskaya's sociology unit was preparing a new ten-year research project aiming to study the social mechanisms of economic development as exemplified in Siberian agriculture. In 1982, a 100-page initial draft of the project had been dispatched to ten major institutes in the country for comment. In April 1983 about 50 social scientists from all over the Soviet Union were to meet in Novosibirsk to discuss it. In view of the sharply critical and controversial nature of the draft the censorship authorities (the *Glavlit*) refused permission for its publication as an open text, but after some pulling and shoving Aganbegyan used his powers as the institute's director to get it published 'for internal use only' – without the need for the censorship's blessing. This meant, however, that every participant at the conference on receiving the text had to sign for it and to take responsibility for its staying 'internal'.

The colloquium met and turned into an intellectual feast. The participants were mainly those who had shared for years the most invisible political outlook in the country – that of internal 'loyal' dissent, without which the whole Gorbachev phenomenon would be inexplicable. They refused to accept the policies of the political leadership, while at the same time refusing to join the 'open dissent' of those who, before the era of *glasnost*, published underground leaflets, briefed Western newsmen and found themselves rapidly marginalized within Soviet academic institutions, often suffering arrest or emigrating and being forced into exile. Those who met in Novosibirsk chose a path which could best be described by a saying originating in the Spanish colonial empire: 'I obey, but I do not comply'. At the core of 'not complying' lay the analytical effort of establishing alternative models of thought and perceptions of reality, as well as the defensive ethic of small circles of friends. For theirs was not the pure intellectuality of an enlightened group of critically minded individuals. They signed collectively a number of 'non-public' yet widely known letters of protest against particularly outrageous deeds on the part of Brezhnev's government: ecological destruction, political irresponsibility, arrests of good people, etc.

Despite considerable pressures they on the whole stood by these documents and paid the usual price of some privileges withdrawn, prospects lost, etc. But, significantly, they also expressed obedience through silence in public, even though anybody who was somebody in the Soviet establishment knew that they did not actually comply.

Consideration of what was said at the 1983 colloquium in Novosibirsk makes some of the surprises of Gorbachev's *perestroika* less surprising after all. Much of what was to be introduced in the USSR after 1985 was actually debated at Novosibirsk. The meeting was opened by a paper from Zaslavskaya, once again 'for internal use only', which challenged the whole structure of the organization of the Soviet economy by pointing to its increasingly restrictive character. The view that simple extrapolation of the existing model of agrarian development would lead to economic crisis and disaster, and that only massive structural changes could bring the country back on course, was central to what Zaslavskaya had to say. This message was presented in a way which made it particularly dramatic to all those trained in the 'orthodox' Marxist language of perception common to the Soviet establishment. She said that, while the USSR's 'forces of production' had moved very far indeed from the early 1930s, the 'relations of production' established then were still intact. This was creating a rapidly growing gap between the level of the forces of production and that of the relations of production. To those trained in the conceptual language used by Zaslavskaya the conclusion was self-evident. All of those assembled would have been able to quote by heart the words of the master: 'At a certain stage of their development, the material productive forces of society come into conflict with the existing relations of production. . . From forms of development of the productive forces these relations turn into their fetters. Then begins an epoch of social revolution.' (Karl Marx in K. Marx and F. Engels, *Selected Works*, (Moscow, 1973) Vol. 1, pp. 503–4).

The colloquium was being closely watched by hostile eyes. The forces of order were growing impatient with half-loyalties. As the participants returned to their posts the debate spread. Within weeks of the conference, the *Washington Post* published extracts from Zaslavskaya's paper and all hell broke loose. An investigation by the KGB was launched to discover the source of the leak and charges were made against participants in the colloquium who came from Leningrad. Aganbegyan and Zaslavskaya were charged with irresponsibility and deviation, dragged through endless investigating committees, subjected to a barrage of abuse, and eventually given a formal Party reprimand. Their scholarly reputations were also dragged in the mud by the establishment's 'good boys and girls'. At the same time, they were now more noticed, indeed were coming to eminence, in Western scholarly circles and public media. Overnight Tatyana Zaslavskaya became one of the better known names in the West and, via Western radio stations beaming into the USSR, more and more visible also in the circle of those in the USSR who found Brezhnev's management of the country incompetent and increasingly intolerable. The scandal became so topical that the whole of the Soviet political high command was obliged to look at the offending document.

Zaslavskaya herself responded to the viciousness of the slander used against her by the Soviet establishment of the day, the harshness of pressures she did not expect and found deeply offensive, as well as her own surprising new eminence, by deep depression. She had tried her best to warn her country about the impending crisis. She had done it 'by the book', never breaking any laws. As a result she was facing persecution – what can one do at all in such a society? After a spell of dismay, apathy and silence came an effort to shake it all off by turning to sociological theory. Together with Inna Ryvkina she began to work out the basic parameters and concepts of an Economic Sociology as a sub-discipline of sociology still to be fully established. Two years were devoted to this project and a book was written to expound the paradigm (it is still to be published). Zaslavskaya's attention was increasingly given to what she described as the social mechanisms and impediments of economic development.

The 1985 launch of *perestroika,* and its rapid 'deepening' from an effort at effective economic reform to a massive overhaul of Soviet society *in toto*, the opening up of the nation-wide debate about all and sundry, and the new basic sources of information, were once again to put Zaslavskaya's life-story in direct relation with her country's history. She responded vigorously, rapidly becoming one of the most effective spokesmen for *perestroika.* She was elected President of the Soviet Sociological Association. She helped to draft the 1987 official decision to enhance, in fact to re-establish, sociology as an academic discipline. Moscow was the place where she was spending more and more time. In 1987 she accepted the task of setting up a National Public Opinion Research Centre there and became its first director. She suffered a heart attack but she refused her doctor's orders to take things easy. Her eminence and her impact grew. So did opposition to her views. She was both praised and vilified in the press. In 1989 a conservative presidium of the Academy of Sciences refused her a place on the list of candidates for the Congress of Soviet Deputies. She was elected all the same and made history when her demand that the Congress legislate the abolition of police rights to disperse demonstrations while a Congress is in session was supported by more than 800 deputies while the obedient majority shrank for once to only 1400. She was blackballed together with most of the radicals in the election of the (permanent) Supreme Soviet but elected to serve on the Congress's Standing Committee for Social Problems. A life of intense activity continues. In her own view political work is hard but to a committed social scientist it is a duty to be carried out all the same.

A SOCIOLOGIST IN A REVOLUTIONARY ERA

This brief biographical sketch has shown Tatyana Zaslavskaya to be a person vivid enough in her individuality. However, most significantly she is also representative of a generation of Soviet intelligentsia which finds its origins in the Khrushchevite 1960s. In the 1980s she also became the personification of sociology or, to be more precise, of a particular type of radical Soviet sociology in transition. This discipline had shared with genetics and with Albert Einstein's Theory of Relativity the honour of being singled out for damnation and banned altogether as bourgeois inventions under Stalin. All were recognized anew under Khrushchev but sociology once more fell foul of the government in Brezhnev's self-congratulatory era. This time it was not banned altogether but simply left to wilt, starved of its budget, excluded from university curricula, and purged of critical ideas and of its brightest representatives (who often drifted away to safer tasks). Far enough from Moscow the Department of Sociology in Novosibirsk was to survive as a group of scholars and as a tradition. It therefore became central to the resurrection of the discipline under Gorbachev. There were, of course, other 'pockets of resistance' spread throughout the country – single sociologists and small bands of those who refused to give way. In the face of the still mainly conservative Institutes and the continuous open hostility of the Ministry for Higher Education (in control of the universities) it was the Soviet Sociological Association which in the-mid 1980s came to lead the discipline and its regeneration effort by giving more voice to sociologists of radical persuasion. Zaslavskaya's election to its presidency represented this symbolically as well as politically.

It was the critical potential of Soviet sociology and its tendency to look for 'deeper', i.e. more comprehensive, explanations which had made for its banning and/or repression before Gorbachev. These characteristics now provided for sociology's new status in the Soviet Union of the Gorbachev era. To Zaslavskaya these were the very reasons which had made her initially move across from economics to sociology and now were to prove her point of strength in a rapidly developing debate.

Zaslavskaya was one of the small group of people who established and popularized the basic new interpretations defining the outlook of *perestroika*'s radical wing. The Soviet media were quick to christen her one of the *Prorabs* (engineer in charge, spokesperson) of *perestroika*, while the conservatives learned equally rapidly to reproduce her name with a sneer or associate it with treason. Accordingly, as political confrontations advanced, she became the favourite of such publications as *Moscow News, Ogonek* and *Izvestiya* and, equally, the scapegoat of the conservative and nationalist *Literaturnaya Rossiya*. She came to receive a massive fan mail of admiration as well as violent abuse and threats. In the face of all this, Zaslavskaya continues to speak her mind as each of her articles elicits a massive response, and her many public appearances draw large audiences.

Central to Zaslavskaya's position have been three arguments she has offered, each of them dramatic in its far-reaching consequences and its vigour of presentation. They were set out as a simple restoration of common sense and instantly adopted as elements of scholarly discourse as well as of public speech. First, that beneath the growing signs of economic disintegration lies a crisis of social structure and human behavioural patterns; one can not cure 'the economic' without 'the social' and 'the human factor'. Second, that there is no way of understanding social relations without empirical investigation; nothing can be taken for granted; this is especially true for perceptions rooted in the ideologies and the logical constructions of the previous era. Third, that real socialism is humanism; there is no other way to judge the existing regime's achievements, failures and modes of operation than through the application of a socialist humanism as a measuring stick.

Soviet bureaucrats and US corporations, COMECON and the IMF all share a belief in the supremacy of the accountants' balance-sheets over everything else. The immediacy of profits or gross production figures controls all other considerations. The use and growth of 'resources' is the one thing which defines 'progress', while all the rest is sentimental trash. As for actual human beings, these are kept outside the basic equations; they will naturally benefit somewhere, sometime, from the economy's progress as charted by its planners and whizz kids. Or, as put in Lenin's most unfortunate of slogans: 'Communism is Soviet power plus electrification' i.e., with Soviet power already in place, Communism is to be measured by the kilowatts of the extra power stations (and, by now, there are plenty of them around).

Such economistic-cum-bureaucratic intuitions of the development specialists have been challenged in the West for a number
of reasons. Changes in the balance-sheet of states and of corporations did not correspond in any direct way with the wellbeing
of majorities and/or their will, when democratically expressed.
'Electrification' does not as a matter of course produce communism (or democracy, or popular welfare). 'Input' or 'balance' do
not necessarily produce 'output' and 'growth'. None of these can
be understood if we exclude power relations, ideas and complex
human motivations. It was the voice of Zaslavskaya, the trained
economist who moved on, which sounded a forceful challenge to
economistic views in the USSR. In her view, the social structure, the
organization of power and the 'human factor' had to be brought
into the picture in any meaningful discussion of economic processes,
present or future.

The accepted knowledge of social structure, politics and human
behaviour was for half a century kept in official and academic circles in the USSR at the level of general platitudes of a dogmatic,
brash and crude philosophy of history. These combined with an
increasingly cynical pragmatism in actual daily life. 'Everybody
knew' that Soviet society was one of non-conflict between social
classes. Equally self-evidently, power was 'held by the working class'
and/or 'the Soviet people' bound by the 'proletarian international-
ism' of mutual affection. Human beings were quite simply the
products of an 'advanced socialism' and therefore advanced social-
ists to boot. The few exceptions still in evidence were being ironed
out by the vigilant effort of those to whom the making of vigilant
efforts was entrusted. And, of course, while all this was endlessly
repeated, the actual bulk of the Soviet people proceeded to seek
out their particular dodges in order to scrape a living or grab a
privilege.

In the face of the combination of increasingly worn platitudes
and daily cynicism, Soviet sociologists began to ask actual workers
and executives questions about actual conflicts and perceptions,
problems they encountered, powers they faced and inequalities
they laboured under. New pictures of reality rapidly began to
emerge as the gap between experience and the formal images of
society began to close. The vision of the new sociologists centred
on social contradictions. Their new president emerged as a crucial
spokesperson of new and uncensored evidence exercising a growing
impact on Soviet public opinion while studying the changes within
it.

But what seemed to have provided the broadest response to
Zaslavskaya's views was her moral appeal – intellectual as much
as emotional. A language of applied humanism drew a response well

outside the narrow circles of social scientists and the political elite. She spoke of justice as an immediate goal of any socialist project, of human alienation as a yardstick of government's failure, of truth as the sole target of scholarship. There could be no mistake – she meant it. In the face of the tradition of cynical rhetoric claiming the absolute 'unity of the people and the party', Zaslavskaya spoke also of social diversity and conflict as proof of society's health and the need for their full recognition, representation and political acculturation.

Zaslavskaya's article in *Kommunist* of September 1986 entitled 'The Human Factor, Economic Development and Social Justice' became a minor classic and so did her interviews and lectures explaining its analytical and ethical roots. Zaslavskaya asked the deceptively simple question: what permits the bureaucratic management of Soviet economy and society, by now blamed for all the country's ills? Her answer lay in public apathy expressed in the total lack of real political involvement on the part of the majority. But, she persisted, what stood behind public apathy? Her answer lay in institutionalized social injustice, alienation and a tissue of official lies. She also offered proof from sociological evidence gathered in her rural studies of Siberia – the two-thirds of employees who reported not working at full strength, the lack of desire for promotion which involves extra responsibility expressed by nine-tenths of directors of farming units and so on. What struck her readers much more sharply than any statistics was the knowledge of its truth in their own personal experience.

Zaslavskaya's significance, and her intellectual roots within her country's tradition, can be defined in yet another way. We know a scholar and public figure by their enemies and can define their significance by the intensity of dislike and slander they arouse. The fury of personal attacks on Zaslavskaya – innuendoes and threatening calls, demands for her resignation and election anti-meetings by the crypto-fascists of the *Pamyat* – have been as extensive as the loyalty she arouses. To know her by her enemies, there are three major tendencies which unite against her in a classic anti-Gorbachevian alliance: the Party bosses in defence of the right to privilege and corruption, the Stalinist old hands in defence of their dreams of a past which never was, and the xenophobic Russian nationalists. It adds to the honour of Zaslavskaya and helps to define her that she is hated by all three. The noisiest of them, the Russian xenophobes, speak about Zaslavskaya very much in the language of the fascistic Black Hundreds of 1905–7 with their Great-Russian pomposity, their 'we are not intellectuals but common people' pretence, their demogogic clamour against the privileges of the elite, and their

actual defence of bureaucratic rule. Their hatred of the enlightened intelligentsia is matched by the claim that these are not
really pure Russians but ethnic aliens (*inorodtsy*) – Jews, Poles,
Germans, Georgians etc. It came therefore as no great surprise
when Zaslavskaya née Karpova, the granddaughter of a peasant
and as Russian as they come, was recently declared by *Pamyat*
to be 'a Jewess who helps other Jews to destroy our economy',
while at the same time a conservative newspaper was describing
this major scholar who exposed the poverty and backwardness of
Russian villages as the author of a programme leading to village
destruction.

In her analytical contributions to *perestroika* the real Zaslavskaya
benefited from and expressed the collective and personal experience
and the rich traditions at the intersection of which she stands.
Her basic experience as a rural sociologist reinforced her grasp
of social diversity, of parallel realities and of the human agents of
production. It also made her face misery and injustice in all their
starkness, in contrast to the glib reports, official falsifications and
colourful posters of universal cheer. A golden chain of the tradition
of the Russian intelligentsia played its role as well: the crusading for
truth, the service to the people, the being true to oneself come what
may, linked her to images of her childhood in Kiev but also to past
generations of rural economists cum sociologists cum reformers like
Venzher and Nemchinov, Chayanov and Groman and still further
back to the Zemstvo statisticians of the 1890s, and to the populist
radicals who went 'to the people', to the Siberian prisons and to
the gallows in the 1870s and 1880s. All these gave substance to
the humanist interpretation of socialism which she expounds. The
presidency of the Soviet Sociological Association at a crucial stage of
development made her personal experience and preferences colour
the discipline at large. A different breed of sociologist has been coming to the fore and, hopefully, a new type of young sociologist will
begin to develop: one to whom sociology is not just an occupation
but a vocation and a public stance.

As against the hullabaloo of praise and hate, three recent major
contributions which Zaslavskaya authored or co-authored represent well her actual stance and professional achievements of the last
decade. These begin with the *Socio-Economic Development of the
Siberian Village* (Moscow, 1987) written by a team of twenty-five
sociologists in Novosibirsk and summing up their substantive and
methodological work. Next comes the not-yet-published *Economic
Sociology* written together with I. Ryvkina as a major text to define
a system of analysis of the social structure of economics in the USSR.
The third is the one we publish here. This, under Zaslavskaya's sole
signature and responsibility, sets out her views concerning the social

structure, characteristics and goals of what is to her the necessary revolutionary restructuring of her country – a radical interpretation of *perestroika* by its leading intellectual.

Its characteristics are once again those of *perestroika*'s intellectual elite and Zaslavskaya's personality. They combine the public with the personal, for detachment is clearly not Zaslavskaya's idea of scholarly virtue. The narrative brings together history, life history, analysis and political argument. Indeed, *perestroika* itself is treated as history, i.e. not as a view or a programme to be executed but as a process of self-clarification in the face of rapidly changing reality, of failures, of endless search in response to endless surprises as to the results of the policies adopted. The analysis links the Soviet economy to the Soviet social structure both by outlining the historical and social roots of the current economic crisis and by displaying the increasingly severe economic impact on the country's welfare systems, consumer markets and social reproduction. It then proceeds to a political sociology of the forces which support and oppose *perestroika* within a growing confrontation. Finally it defines the fundamental goal of *perestroika*'s radicals – a second socialist revolution aiming to bring to fruition the hopes of 1905, of 1917 and of the 1920s, enhanced by learning from Soviet and global experience ever since.

There has been recently a fundamental shift in Western perceptions of the USSR. The question is no longer: 'Will the Soviet Union change?' It is changing. The question is: What is it to become?'. The issue of alternatives as seen by the Soviet people, by their analytical guides and ideological forerunners, is central to the way questions about the future will be answered. This book carries a masterview of society and a manifesto of goals and preferences which principally reflect the collective intuition of the radicals of *perestroika*. It is also a very personal view by a fascinating person whose own life story is linked closely with *perestroika*'s titanic effort at social transformation and with Soviet sociology's coming of age. I think it does them proud.

Teodor Shanin
Manchester University, 1989

Introduction

This book, like most of the others in the *Second World* series, is about the restructuring of society in the Soviet Union. The interest in this process shown by Western readers is understandable. The word *perestroika* – restructuring – can be heard today in almost every language, and attention throughout the world is focused on what is going on in the Soviet Union. It would hardly be an exaggeration to say that not only the historical destiny of our country but in many ways the future of the entire world community depends on the outcome of this process. Restructuring comprises a series of such wide-ranging and radical transformations of the economic, political and social areas in Soviet society, involving as it does qualitative change in its most important features, that it can rightly be called a 'revolution'. On the one hand, it offers the hope of a more just and happy life and, on the other, confronts us with tasks of hitherto unknown complexity. Social restructuring at one and the same time entails both the possibility and the necessity of intense political activity on the part of the Soviet people, and the resolution of a host of problems that affect their vital interests. Before addressing these problems in detail, however, I should like to tell the reader something about myself and my own attitude to restructuring as there are quite a number of stories written about me in the West.

By an irony of fate, I became a 'supporter of restructuring' several years before the word *perestroika* was uttered for the first time and I shared Gorbachev's views long before he became General Secretary of the Soviet Communist Party and made his political programme public. After leaving university, I worked for thirty years in economic institutes attached to the USSR Academy of Sciences, first in Moscow and then in Novosibirsk. I studied the socio-economic problems of the Soviet countryside, taught students and post-graduates, wrote articles and books and acquired academic degrees. In 1968 I was elected a full Member and in 1981 an Associate of the USSR Academy of Sciences. Considering that among the 220 Soviet Academicians there were only five women, this was no mean achievement. I often went abroad, took part in international conferences and congresses, and maintained contact with professional colleagues in various foreign countries. Nevertheless, I was known to at most only a hundred specialists outside the Soviet Union.

With the passage of time my circle of interests widened but the problems I was studying not only remained unresolved, they became even more acute. This made me take up the study of a more general and complex problem – the social mechanism for developing the agrarian sector of the Soviet economy. It took two years' collective work to formulate the research project. Towards the end of 1982 its authors decided to put it forward for discussion by a group of highly-qualified economists, lawyers and sociologists studying associated problems. The project was circulated to ten academic institutes for preliminary discussion, while I produced a more concise paper summarizing its principal ideas. This was circulated to members of a seminar, and became the subject of lively and creative debate. Arguments and discussions continued far into the night – in hotel rooms and foyers and colleagues' flats. Those who could not get hold of the paper – only a small number of copies had been printed for restricted circulation – wrote it out by hand.

When the participants went home, some of them photocopied the paper and passed it on. By accident or design, two copies (without naming the author) fell into the hands of foreign correspondents and were published in the Western press under the heading 'Novosibirsk Manifesto'. So it was that in the fifty-seventh year of my life and the thirty-third year of my academic work, literally on one day and quite unexpectedly, I became the centre of attention of an extremely broad international community. And the most surprising thing is that this sudden interest has turned out to be long-lasting and has become stronger rather than weaker over the past five years.

It is now usual to regard the 'Novosibirsk Manifesto' as the 'first swallow' of restructuring, flying high in the sky while the weather was still freezing. The ideas I put forward in 1983 have, in fact, much in common with Gorbachev's ideas for reform. This, of course, is not because one of us borrowed ideas from the other, but because we were students at the same university at almost the same time, and both studied agricultural economy and sought ways of raising its efficiency, particularly with regard to the human factor, i.e. by overcoming workers' alienation from their labour. Our first meeting took place in April 1982, when Mikhail Gorbachev was a member of the Political Bureau and secretary for agriculture in the Central Committee of the Communist Party while I was a member of the Economics Section of the Academy of Sciences. I believe we quickly realized that we thought the same way about the main fundamental questions.

In the West the press often calls me 'Gorbachev's personal adviser'. This is not true. In the six years and more that we have known each other, we have not met more than five or six times, and always in the presence of others. Nevertheless, our assessments of most of the key questions of restructuring do coincide. Of course, I study Gorbachev's statements on socio-economic questions very carefully, and I believe my own do not go unnoticed by him, and this is important in itself. For, under the conditions of radical restructuring, increasing demands are being made on specialists studying social development. The 'trial and error' method is becoming not only inefficient but impossible. What is needed now is a scientifically-based concept of the paths already trodden, the substance of the present stage of development, and the long-term aims of society and ways of achieving them. For this reason the importance that Gorbachev and his close associates attach to maintaining close links with the academic world and to trusting and listening to specialist opinion seems the only correct approach.

Unfortunately, the current state of Soviet research does not measure up to the demands made upon it. History, political economy, law, sociology, and political studies are not yet providing answers to most of the questions addressed to them and cannot therefore give sufficiently effective help in the implementation of restructuring. This is the inevitable result of decades of bureaucratic control of academic institutions. It is no secret that for a long time the Party leadership allocated to specialists the role of mere admiring commentators on decisions that had already been taken. The creative formulation of questions, new ideas and original approaches to research problems, far from being supported, was punished, sometimes by administrative methods. The more courageous and innovatory research results were, the less likely they were to be published. Mediocrity prevailed, while talented experts had to stay in the background, doing minor work just to exist.

Of course, no bureaucracy could completely prevent intellectuals from thinking creatively. These people carried on independent research relying on the fact that eventually they would be required to provide, not sunshine stories about universal prosperity and happiness, but 'the truth, the whole truth and nothing but the truth'. Now, that time has arrived and works are beginning to be published based on fundamentally new approaches and giving new results. It will take some time for society to come to terms with the often contradictory ideas, assimilate them and reconcile them with formerly known truths, and integrate them into the general picture of present-day reality.

The most important thing, of course, is to carry out research directly orientated towards formulating an integral conception of restructuring as a specific stage in the development of Soviet society. Social thought today must work on untrodden paths, participate in the formulation of new decisions, lay the foundations for the strategy and tactics of restructuring and smoothe its progress. The task of social scientists is simultaneously to reveal emerging contradictions and difficulties, expose mistakes that are being allowed to be made in the practice of government, and see that they are put right as quickly as possible.

Free discussion of any and every difficult issue is an essential condition for the creative development of knowledge. Although in principle this is elementary, in the Soviet Union the creation of an atmosphere of free discussion is still something to be fought for – and not only in regard to administrative bodies and controlling authorities, but in the face of inertia on the part of academics and scientists themselves, their innate paralysis of thought and ingrained self-censorship, the power of ideological dogmas, and readiness to comply with orders 'from above'. Above all, if our social science is to develop freely, new 'human material' is needed, a new generation of academics and practitioners, unburdened with the hard experience that we had to go through. But there is no time to wait for this to happen. Beginning with ourselves, therefore, we must fight for the emancipation of our own thinking processes. This is what I am trying to do when examining the problems to which this book is dedicated.

Some years have gone by since April 1985 when Mikhail Gorbachev became our country's leader. Historically speaking, this is a short length of time, but on the scale of a human life it is not inconsiderable. During this period the concept of *perestroika* has entered the lives of tens of millions of people. It is always in the papers or on the television screens, heard on the Underground and in shops, and is the subject of discussions in the family and among colleagues. But does everybody understand the concept in the same way? Sociological research shows that this is not so. In reply to the question 'What is restructuring?', most people either pick out certain random features of the present period or quote specific Party slogans (e.g. 'increasing production efficiency' or 'democratizing society'). It seems that people are incapable of defining the social substance of the changes taking place.

One of the reasons for this 'hazy' understanding of the substance of restructuring is the fact that the attitudes of politicians and scientists themselves towards this question have gone through several stages over the past four years.

The first task proposed was to speed up social and economic development which in practice would have entailed even more rapid consumption of natural, productive and human resources and a further sharpening of contradictions. At the time, however, it seemed fairly natural to put forward this aim.

It was soon realized how extremely limited it was. It became clear that more rapid economic development requires changes in the mechanisms for managing the economy, the activation of its social factors, and an end to workers' alienation from the means of production and the final outcome of their labour. As a result, at the official level there was a considerably deeper understanding of the aims and substance of the projected reforms. The conclusion was drawn that *radical economic reform* was essential since it would both accelerate growth rates and make the economy more responsive to scientific and technological progress, more rational, flexible and modern. The basic direction of reform was now *restructuring the mechanism for managing the economy*, a change-over from administrative-command methods to economic ones, and the development of automatic regulators associated with market relations. This was a big step forward in the understanding of what tasks had to be undertaken. At this stage the correctness of the direction in which Soviet society had been moving over the past decades was not yet in doubt.

The next stage was recognition of the necessity for *radical changes* not only in economic but in all associated *socio-economic relationships* (social, legal, etc). This arose from a realization that the economic and social aspects of socio-economic relations were inseparable and, in particular, that the social structure is formed above all by the system of economic relations, while the roots of people's economic behaviour usually lie in the relations between social strata and groups. Any serious changes in economic mechanisms give rise to corresponding changes in social structure – the development and growth of some strata, the contraction and disappearance of others, and a change in their relationships with one another. A radical restructuring of economic relations must therefore by definition be an element in a more complex and wide-ranging reform affecting the qualitative social characteristics of society.

Awareness of this fact demanded a redefinition of the substance and aims of restructuring. Academics and politicians put forward slogans concerning the development and improvement of socialism, the strengthening of social justice and the democratization of social life. They were, however, unco-ordinated and amorphous and did not amount to an integral system. It was essential to bring out the fundamental substance of the projected transformation of social relations, to determine who would gain from it and who would lose, and what connection there is between the content of restructuring and the development of socialism.

However, restructuring was progressing at a slower pace and with greater difficulty than had originally been expected. It encountered, on the one hand, conservatism and inertia on the part of the mass of working people and, on the other, deliberate opposition from the Party-Soviet apparatus, which was concerned with retaining the previous order of things. The difficulties encountered by restructuring could be seen in inconsistencies and contradictions in the new laws which were bound about with so many instructions that the legislators' original intention was watered down or lost. They were also evident in the poor on-the-spot implementation of decisions taken at the centre, and the retention of administrative-command methods of managing the economy and other areas of society. A prime example of the latter is that telephone calls from the offices of Party or Soviet officials continued (and still continue to this day) to carry more weight than either an enterprise's economic accounting and profits or the social interests of working people. It gradually became obvious that, so long as the existing political power system was retained, socio-economic reform could have no positive results and that the key to its success lay not in the economic sphere but in the Party's management of society and the economy. For economic and social restructuring to be successful, the basic political structures have to be changed and authority has to be redistributed between socio-political institutions and administrative organizations and therefore between different social groups.

It was against this background that Mikhail Gorbachev put forward and argued the idea that, owing to its complexity and far-reaching consequences, the restructuring of social relations represented a *social revolution*. It is clear from the General Secretary's book that he does not use the concept 'revolution' simply as a metaphor designed to emphasize the radical nature of the changes that are taking place but in the literal sense of the word. This idea represents a qualitative leap forward in the conceptualization of the social substance of restructuring. However, it has not yet been taken up by Soviet politicians and academics: despite its fundamental novelty, it seems to have gone unremarked by the press. There must be a reason for this. It seems that most people are not prepared to accept the idea and, since they do not have the arguments to declare themselves 'for' or 'against', they prefer to avoid the issue. The transformation that is now being implemented is, therefore, most often referred to in the press and the specialist literature simply as 'restructuring' (without explaining the term), often as 'reform' and only very rarely as 'revolution'. Putting forward the concept of restructuring as a revolution gives rise to a number of important questions. Firstly, what grounds are there for regarding restructuring as a revolution, not a reform? Secondly, is it in fact already a revolution or is it more a question of its developing into one? Thirdly, what is the social substance of the revolution and in or against whose interests is it directed? Finally, can a revolutionary restructuring of social relations be carried out by peaceful means or is it likely to take violent forms?

These questions have not only remained unanswered in Soviet literature, they have not even been widely discussed and they have been avoided in most writings about restructuring. In my opinion they are vitally important and need to be openly debated.

Clearly, revolution and reform are fundamentally different things. Reforms, including the most radical, are usually implemented 'from above', even if they are the result of pressure 'from below'. They do not affect the fundamental questions of power and do not alter its character. They merely modernize and adapt outmoded administrative and social structures to new social requirements and conditions. The following are examples of this kind of reform: the 1861 Reform in Russia which abolished serfdom and laid the basis for the development of capitalism; the Stolypin Reform of 1906–7 which radically changed agrarian relations; and the Kosygin Reform of 1965 which for the first time tackled the job of changing administrative-command methods of economic management in the Soviet Union.

In contrast to this, it is the question of power that is crucial to a revolution. It is therefore usually implemented 'from below' by the forces of progressive social groups that break down the opposition of those in power and of their conservative and reactionary supporters. Thus, the February Revolution of 1917 overthrew the autocratic power of the tsar and his ruling clique and replaced the monarchy by a bourgeois democratic republic, while the Socialist Revolution of October 1917 brought to power the proletariat in alliance with the peasantry.

The present situation has little in common with what existed in 1917. We do not have the sort of 'revolutionary situation' when, in the words of Lenin, the 'top' cannot go on ruling in the old way and those 'below' will no longer submit to them. As I understand it, therefore, the term 'socialist revolution' represents not the present state of society but the direction restructuring is to take, its inherent socio-political potential.

Within the classic framework of reform, restructuring often 'marks time' and does not achieve the goals that have been set for it. What happens in practice is not a complex and radical reform, but a contradictory, faltering, 'cut-down' reform that encounters deliberate and constant opposition from the all-powerful state monopolies of ministries and government departments. Examples are not difficult to find. The Ministry of Water Resources whose chief activity has been the construction of costly canals that destroy the natural environment has over the past few years been castigated by the press. Condemnations of this ministry are always to be found in the newspapers, its activity arouses great indignation, and the public demands that it be abolished or at least that its vast resources be used for the construction of roads or other useful projects. The ministry, however, with its two-million-strong workforce, calmly continues to squander tens of thousands of roubles of public money for the sole reason that this is to its own advantage. And the public can do nothing about it.

Industrial ministries are obstructing the change-over by enter-prises to self-financing and self-management by swamping them with compulsory state orders. In 1988 the Ministry of Communications restricted subscriptions to several dozens of popular newspapers and journals, most of which are generally considered to be the mouthpieces of restructuring. In the six weeks following the date when subscriptions are accepted, only 27 per cent of those wishing to subscribe to *Ogonek* were successful, 39 per cent to *Znamya*, 45 per cent to *Novyi mir*, and 49 per cent to *Literaturnaya gazeta* and *Druzhba narodov*. These severe restrictions which were contrary to the policy of openness aroused a public storm of protest and an endless stream of letters from ordinary members of the public to different offices, newspapers and magazines. In spite of this, it took more than two months' hard struggle to get the restrictions lifted.

These examples are enough to illustrate that the framework of reform carried out exclusively 'from above' is too narrow to deal with all the tasks that have to be undertaken. Great social goals need corresponding means to achieve them. In particular, an aim that has been impossible to achieve by reform may be achieved in a more radical revolutionary way as a result of restructuring the political system.

The specific directions of this restructuring were laid down by the 19th All-Union Party Conference, further developed in the course of a wide-ranging discussion by working people, and embodied in decisions adopted at the Extraordinary Session of the Supreme Soviet in December 1988. This session passed the following laws: 'Amendments and Additions to the Constitution of the USSR', and 'Elections of People's Deputies of the USSR'. These represented the first practical steps in implementing the comprehen-sive programme of democratizing Soviet society. This programme includes a clear and consistent demarcation of functions between Party and state management bodies, the transformation of Soviets into democratically elected representative bodies with the power to make decisions on basic social issues, and a change of Party function from the direct management of society to a concentration of effort on political and ideological matters and on the radical restructuring of relations within the Party and Soviet system with a view to its democratization.

Implementation of the projected restructuring of the country's political structure will entail the transfer of a significant part of the authority and powers of Party organizations to the Soviets, those of central government to republican and local authorities and those of executive bodies to elected ones. From the social point of view, this means the handing-over of power by the comparatively narrow, privileged and bureaucratic stratum of officials nominated by the Party apparatus (the *nomenklatura* system) to the people who democratically elect and control the activity of their deputies. The socio-political direction of these transformations is expressed in the October Revolution slogan which has recently achieved a new popularity – 'All power to the Soviets!'.

The overwhelming majority of revolutions have either a national liberation or a social and class character. This prompts the question as to whether the stratum comprising Party and Soviet officials nominated by the Party apparatus constitute a social class. Lenin defined as classes large groups of people distinguished by their relation to the means of production and their role in the organization of social labour, and the magnitude and structure of the part of social wealth they appropriate, and connected to each other by relations of exploitation. For a long time Soviet social science has maintained that the October Revolution put an end once and for all to the exploitation of man by man and that now all strata of society are linked together by relations of comradely co-operation and mutual assistance.

No account has been taken of such blatantly obvious facts as the yearly extraction from the countryside of thousands of millions of roubles that have been used for urban development; the extremely low pay for mental as opposed to physical work; or the ever-growing gulf between the living standards of the 'managed' and the 'managers'. However, what theoretical writings wished to overlook has been imprinted on the public mind. Despite protestations of official ideologists to the contrary, it was not factory workers and collective farmers, not manual workers and the intelligentsia who acted as socially conflicting groups, but the 'managers' and the 'managed', the 'bosses' and the mass of working people, i.e. groups primarily distinguished by their position in the political power system and the system of distribution of the social product and accordingly by their way of life, their social circles, and their value systems and interests. When conducting sociological research in Siberia, we discovered as long ago as the 1970s that a trend towards social distinctions between 'bosses' and 'workers' was recognized by both sides. When workers referred to managers and managers referred to workers, they habitually used the word 'they'. This indicated the alienation of workers from power and the alienation of those who held power from those whose activity they had to direct. I think the class consciousness of the 'managed' was more quickly formed than that of the 'managers' since the latter were more strongly under the influence of official ideology. However, trends towards greater social exclusiveness on the part of the Party-nominated stratum were fairly obvious.

The idea – generally accepted, often repeated, and deeply etched on our consciousness – that our society has completely abolished all forms of economic exploitation of some groups by others has prevented a correct evaluation of the relations that actually exist. During the period of restructuring and openness, however, we have learned more truths about our society, past and present, than ever before. People have been presented with a picture of shameless theft of public property by the ruling stratum, colossal swindles, systematic use of office for personal enrichment and the accumulation of multi-million rouble family fortunes, the unjustifiable and illegal acquisition of privileges and advantages. Moreover, the social mechanism of all this 'activity' was primarily based on the coalescence of the Party and Soviet apparatus with operators in the shadow economy and the criminal world. Since the only source of enrichment for these shadow operators and ruling groups is the consumption of working people and the lowering of their living standards, it is difficult to call the system of relations that has developed anything other than exploitation. All this leads to the conclusion that the socially degenerate stratum of officials nominated by the Party apparatus has a definite tendency to turn into a ruling class, exploiting the rest of the people.

Restructuring has put an end to this tendency and to a certain extent reversed the process. A number of hardened mafiosi, bribe-takers and thieves have been exposed and sentenced, while others continue to be exposed, expelled from the Party and are undergoing criminal prosecution. The property that they did not conceal is being confiscated by the state. The investigation into the 'cotton swindle' in Uzbekistan is now in its fifth year and hundreds of senior Soviet and Party officials are implicated in the case. The privileges of officials in the Party apparatus are being systematically reduced or removed and the special channels for supplying them with food and other goods are being closed. Some of the sanatoria and rest homes, formerly used exclusively by the Party-nominated section of the apparatus, have been converted into rehabilitation centres for soldiers back from Afghanistan or are to be run by trade unions. Measures are also being taken to bridge the psychological gulf between leading officials in the apparatus and the public: the new generation of leaders who have emerged as a result of restructuring are in regular touch with working people, take part in meetings on important issues, and carry on a permanent dialogue with the general public.

All this is extremely important. These measures are, however, not enough to change the situation radically: political power has to be transferred, in deeds not words, to representative bodies of working people so that apparatus officials come to occupy the social position that accords with their undoubtedly important, but not exceptional, role in society. In my opinion, such a change in the actual power structure would signify a genuine social revolution.

Considering that our society has experienced two bourgeois-democratic and one socialist revolution, it is clear that in the present circumstances we can only talk of a second socialist revolution. This sounds strange but actually there is nothing extraordinary about it. The transition from a feudal to a bourgeois system took many decades and in a number of countries there have been several bourgeois revolutions. Social and class struggle is not straightforward. Revolutionary classes are not always victorious – they also suffer defeat. When this happens, for a time they gather new forces and return to the attack to complete the transformation and provide full scope for social development. So a second socialist revolution which has the objective of completing the work begun by the first is historically not only possible, but justified.

However, before one can call restructuring a second socialist revolution (even if only in intent) a serious analysis must be made of the historical road already travelled by our society. There must be a clear understanding of when this society was moving towards socialist goals and when it lost ground. Soviet historians are actively seeking the answer to this question. With the collaboration of economists and sociologists, they are studying the social substance of such stages of development as War Communism, the New Economic Policy, Stalinism, the Khrushchevian 'thaw' and the Brezhnevian 'stagnation'. The place in history, the point on the 'scale' of socialist development, occupied by our society at the present time is also the subject of study. Most historians agree that a counter-revolutionary coup d'état took place in the second half of the 1920s, resulting in the degeneration of socialist relations which replaced the construction of socialism that had been started at an earlier stage. In the Stalinist period, with its mass repression and the annihilation of millions of people, the appeal to socialist aims and values was an effective means of controlling the way working people behaved, but it was only a fig-leaf covering the real nature of the regime. The brief Khrushchevian 'thaw' was a clumsy and inconsistent attempt at returning the country to the road of socialist construction. Historically speaking, it was ill-prepared and had little chance of success, although it can be said that without it there would have been no restructuring today. The stagnation period that followed signified a return to the previous track of the degeneration of socialism. Propagandist assertions that in the mid-1970s a 'developed socialist society' had been created in the USSR were as poor a reflection of reality as was the Stalinist thesis of the building of socialism in the mid-1930s.

Restructuring, begun in 1985, is the second and most decisive attempt to return Soviet society to the road of socialist development from which it has managed to diverge a fair distance. For precisely this reason, in order to accomplish the tasks it has been set, restructuring must develop into a second socialist revolution.

Is it obvious, however, that the projected and current changes are socialist in character? At mass meetings, in readers' letters, and sometimes in the press, two sorts of objections to this view are encountered. The first is usually put forward by people who are still loyal to the traditional ideology and the second by intellectuals who tend not to take any statements on trust, without convincing proof.

Representatives of the first group are often of the opinion that, if the ideas of restructuring are put into practice, society will not in fact get closer to the socialist road but further away from it. They put forward as arguments what Marx and Engels had to say about the incompatibility of socialism and the market, the bourgeois nature of small-scale entrepreneurial activity, etc. They maintain that the objective of raising the economic efficiency of production and increasing material incentives at work contradicts such socialist values as the social equality of all members of society and the creation of social guarantees for people with limited working capacity. They assert that introducing such new forms of organizing production as sub-contracting to a particular workforce or family or leasing state enterprises to groups of workers amounts to the privatization of social ownership of the means of production and is equivalent to the rejection of socialism.

As for intellectuals, their thoughts tend to run along the following lines: if our society has already unwittingly deviated from the socialist road, is there any guarantee that in the course of time someone won't tell us that restructuring was a mistake and that the true road to socialism lies in a quite different direction?

Such arguments cannot just be brushed aside; they deserve attention and an answer. The very fact that doubts about the correctness of the official viewpoint are expressed at all is a new phenomenon, indirectly confirming the development of restructuring and openness and people's growing involvement in their outcome. In order to demonstrate the socialist character of restructuring, however, an answer must be given to the main question – what is socialism?

Only a few years ago any Soviet student could have given the answer. 'Socialism is workers' power, social ownership of the means of production, and planned management of the national economy. It is the absence of exploitation and unemployment, a strictly regulated and limited market, the distribution of incomes according to the quantity and quality of work done, and the provision of a wide range of social guarantees. And at the basis of all this, an advanced way of life and favourable conditions for the all-round development of every individual.' The definition of socialism in the majority of social science textbooks went roughly like that. Under the new conditions, however, it is becoming unsatisfactory, because it does not separate the essential features and goals that are intended to make socialism progressive and socially attractive from the instrumental features that ensure that those intended goals are achieved.

Nevertheless, in today's conditions these are the essential features of socialism, for which our fathers and grandfathers fought on the battlefields of the Civil War and which make socialism a more progressive system than capitalism, that are moving into the foreground. The principal and most general of these characteristics is the fact that socialism is orientated not towards profit maximization or more rapid economic development but towards optimal prosperity, good living conditions and development of the human personality. In this connection it should be pointed out that Lenin did not consider socialism merely as the planned organization of social production, irrespective of its social characteristics. He stressed that the planned organization of socialist production must necessarily be aimed at achieving high living standards and the free and all-round development of all members of society. In Lenin's opinion, 'Only socialism provides the real possibility of subordinating social production and the distribution of output to scientific considerations about how to make the life of all workers as easy as possible and offer them the possibility of living well'.[1]

Without claiming that this is an exhaustive definition, I would list the essential features and goals of socialism as follows:

- the absence of any significant measure of exploitation of some social groups by others, the reduction of unearned income to a minimum, the regular and just distribution of income and consumer goods according to work done;
- a steady rise in living standards and the elimination of poverty;
- workers' political power, the possibility of free expression and the protection of the interests of all social groups, a high level of democracy, and the extensive development of all forms of self-management;
- political and cultural equality among nations, the overcoming of chauvinism in large nations and nationalism in small ones, an internationalist character in relations between peoples;
- inalienable and diverse human rights, strict observance of the law, equitable and uncorruptible exercise of justice;
- a high level of morality, humanity in social relations, the creation of favourable conditions for development of the human personality.

If, in the course of social development, these features become stronger, then one can talk about the strengthening of socialism. If, however, they become weaker or are replaced by their opposites, then socialism does not develop but becomes corrupted and distorted.

But where do social ownership of the means of production, the predominance of planned economic relations over market ones, etc. figure in these generally accepted features of socialism? I suggest that they are important, not in themselves, but in the extent to which they are necessary for achieving the essential characteristics of socialism. If private ownership of the means of production had not been abolished (or at least restricted), it would have been impossible to end exploitation. Socialization of the means of production, therefore, is an indispensable precondition of socialism. But a precondition, or the condition on which a phenomenon emerges, must not be confused with the phenomenon itself. Thus, social (or, to be more precise, state) ownership of the means of production is of itself far from being a guarantee that socialism will be built. Unfortunately, it rules out neither poverty nor the exclusion of ordinary people from active political life nor even the mass annihilation of human beings. This all leads one to the conclusion that socialism is far from having been built in our country. In this respect I am in complete agreement with the opinions expressed by Yuri Afanasev in his article 'Reply to the historian', published in *Pravda* on 18 July 1988.

The tasks now being laid down by the Party leadership are fully in keeping with the essential features of socialism. This is absolute proof of the socialist character of restructuring. Restructuring, however, does not mean that the building of socialism has been completed: the process will take much longer, probably several decades. As I see it, restructuring is significant because it sets society on the road leading to the socialist 'temple'. Restructuring is the regrouping of social forces and the redistribution of power, social wealth, rights and freedoms among social strata and groups that, although it does not in itself signify the building of socialism, provides the necessary preconditions for this to be done. Understood in this sense, restructuring is genuinely revolutionary.

What is unusual is that the revolution is being accomplished 'from above', on the initiative of the ruling party. To a certain extent this softens the conflict between those who gain power and those who lose it. The upper echelon retains its authority and regulatory powers: it is only the position of the middle and lower links in the apparatus that changes. Although initiative 'from above' is a favourable condition for revolutionary transformations, it is not, however, sufficient on its own. Without powerful support 'from below', the transformations cannot transcend the limits of reform.

This means that the essential condition for transforming restructuring into a social revolution is the active participation of broad sections of the people. As social forces are gradually becoming consolidated and organized and are better able to appreciate and pursue their own interests more intensively, then the final outcome of restructuring is above all determined by the positions taken by large social groups, their conscious activity and their resolute determination to continue to the end. In the face of such determination, any attempt by politicians to deviate from the chosen path and to return to previous methods of governing the country will provoke such a political response on the part of broad sections of the population as to ensure the irreversibility of the changes. It would seem that the reform begun by Khrushchev did not succeed primarily because it was an 'armchair' reform and not capable of developing into a social revolution with mass support.

How can intensive political activity be generated when for decades people were brought up in a spirit of fear and obedience, unquestioningly carrying out orders 'from above'? The whole life of society was permeated by hypocrisy. That is why the most thoughtful and energetic people became alienated from social values, immersed themselves in their personal lives, became engrossed in the accumulation of property, the pursuit of exciting experiences, trips abroad, etc. Our society now has to pay the price for tolerating this moral dichotomy for so long. Large numbers of people, having been offered the opportunity to participate in the life of society, seem in no hurry to take advantage of it. In their time, they have heard many tempting promises that were never kept, lived through many changes that did not lead to any appreciable improvements, and even now cannot see any improvements in their situation. In many regions people's living standards have deteriorated rather than improved and the initial enthusiasm has faded. 'Wait and see', people are saying.

We have a vicious circle here: in order to increase the efficiency of restructuring, the broad masses of the people have to be drawn into it. But before this can happen, they must be convinced in practice that restructuring will bring about an improvement in their situation. Is there a way out of this vicious circle? I suggest there is. It lies in the democratization of social relations, the development of openness and frankness about social issues, access to all channels of information, public discussion of important questions in the press and on television, and the disclosure of all official 'secrets' of public interest.

Although complete openness has not yet been achieved, it is gathering momentum, growing, and gaining new ground. What, only a year ago, many people could not bring themselves even to think about is now discussed in lecture rooms and in print. As a result people are becoming politically active. Thousands of informal organizations, social movements and associations are springing up and beginning to operate, many of them with a political complexion. In the Baltic republics, the Russian Federal Republic, Moscow, Leningrad and a number of other towns in Russia, Popular Fronts in Support of Restructuring are being formed and are drawing up political programmes. Political meetings, marches and demonstrations are taking place more often than ever before and with mass participation on a scale never before seen. National, ecological and social problems, previously driven underground, are widely discussed. In the struggle to express their interests, some working people are beginning to use such extreme methods as withdrawal of their labour, political hunger-strikes, and even self-immolation. All this is evidence of an awakening social and political consciousness and a growing desire for independent action and direct involvement in the transformation of society.

Most social movements that support restructuring have a more radical attitude than the government. They criticize the actions of the authorities 'from the left' for carrying out reforms which are not sufficiently consistent and comprehensive, and this to a certain extent balances out conservative criticism 'from the right'. Although most social movements are still taking their first tentative steps, they already represent a force to be reckoned with. The steady increase in their mass membership, their growing social and political maturity, and their firmness of principle indicate that at a certain stage broadly-based progressive public opinion will catch up with, and possibly even seize, the initiative shown by political leaders in regard to restructuring. In this event the functions of the political leadership will be, firstly, to draw up a theoretical and practical general strategy of restructuring; secondly, to implement this strategy by political and legal means (publication of laws, decisions, etc.); and, thirdly, to conduct a lively dialogue with the various social movements in order to facilitate their integration and interaction, acting as arbiter in the case of social conflicts between groups with different interests.

The question arises as to whether the development of restructuring, begun 'from above', into a social revolution 'from below' will lead to a sharp increase in social tensions and intensified conflicts between social groups to the point of violence. Does not such a danger follow from the very word 'revolution'? I think not. History has seen both bloody and peaceful revolutions. For example, the February Revolution of 1917 was bloodless, as by then the tsar had lost the solid support of society. It seems to me that no major social group would want restructuring, which is meant to democratize and improve their lives, to take on a dangerous and violent form. The public memory of the blood shed in the preceding period is too fresh. Our country's second socialist revolution must be a peaceful one. Several factors speak in favour of this being a real possibility. Firstly, the fact that the initiative for a revolutionary transformation of the political structure comes 'from above' precludes the necessity for armed seizure of power by progressive social forces. Secondly, the unjustifiable concentration of power, rights and privileges in the hands of officials nominated by the Party apparatus is unconstitutional; the task of the revolution is therefore to bring political practice into line with the constitution and the associated legislation. Thirdly, the stratum of officials nominated by the Party apparatus does not enjoy popular support and, if the public took a firm stand, it would have to back down. To paraphrase Lenin: 'No bureaucracy can withstand an alliance between political leaders and the advanced strata of the people'.

The possibility that social, political and national conflicts may arise must not, of course, be underestimated. It is, after all, evident that social tension is growing. The centres of tension are not only in the Baltic and Transcaucasian Republics but in a number of large Russian towns – Sverdlovsk, Kazan, Ufa and Irkutsk. The first steps in democratization evident in greater openness and more human rights and freedoms have encouraged the birth of chauvinist, nationalistic, anti-socialist and even fascist movements and not simply democratic ones. The leaders of these movements not only incite their followers to violence, but actually commit it. This inflicts great moral damage on the restructuring that has enabled such movements to emerge. This is true of the notorious society called *Pamyat* ('Memory') whose leaflets deliberately incite Russians against the Jewish people; of nationalistic groups which have been operating in Sumgait and are guilty of murdering several dozen Armenians; and of semi-criminal youth movements in Kazan which commit acts of violence against children and teenagers. Such organizations and movements are like the genie that has been let out of the bottle and can do great damage.

As I see it, the following factors form the basis for these phenomena: the low level of political consciousness and activity, the lack of democratic traditions, the immaturity of public consciousness which is full of prejudices and dogmas, the inadequacy of public opinion on many questions, and the low level of social morality. The last, in particular, needs elaboration. For many years hypocrisy has flourished and a dual morality has held sway throughout the country. Lofty exhortations have been addressed to the workers by those who practised a quite different morality when it came to themselves. In these circumstances protest movements often took immoral and illegal forms. The following principles were commonly applied: 'If the bosses steal, we'll steal too', 'If they only pretend to pay us, we'll only pretend to work', and so on. Moral decay ran extremely deep. The borderlines between good and evil, mercy and cruelty, human feelings and people's alienation from one another, began to disappear from public consciousness. It will take time and effort to overcome these phenomena.

For the time being, however, we have to proceed on the basis of what exists. This means, firstly, the necessity of Party and state control over the activity of the various social movements, above all, in order to ensure that they remain constitutional: and, secondly, the need for a policy that will allow for a certain compromise between the development of mass political activity and the maintenance of social order in the broadest sense of the word.

Restructuring is a vital opportunity for our people. The tasks associated with it are extremely complex. Its road is strewn with obstacles. Resolving some problems gives rise to new, often more complex, ones. The implementation of restructuring requires the painstaking formulation of political strategies and tactics but there is no time for such a formulation – it has to be done in passing, so to speak. The situation is not one of the easiest, especially considering the fast pace of events. But, as the saying goes, 'The game's worth the candle'.

Both at home and abroad, hundreds of specialists – economists, lawyers, historians, sociologists – are busy studying the problems of restructuring. Personally, I am interested in those aspects of it where the economic and social areas overlap. The following questions, for example, belong here:

- Which main characteristics (forms of politics, economic and social policy, standards of living, types of social contradiction, levels of social consciousness) defined the stages of development in Soviet society that preceded restructuring?
- Which socio-economic processes objectively prepared the ground for restructuring and made it necessary and inevitable?
- What are the social differences between the previous and the new methods for managing the economy and what influence does the change in this mechanism have on the position of different social groups?
- What are the probable social consequences of restructuring economic relations, what social problems will it cause, and how can they be dealt with?
- What is the substance of the new understanding of social policy and its ends and means, which specific problems does this policy address, and how are they being and how should they be resolved?

- What is the connection between the need to tackle urgent economic problems and the objective of strengthening social justice? What does the principle of social justice consist in, what are its specific features under socialism, and in what sense can we talk about 'socialist justice'?
- How are the policy of income distribution, methods for regulating the consumer market, and the system of social guarantees changing as a result of restructuring? Does restructuring have anything new to offer as regards the resolution of these perennial problems?
- What is the present distribution of social forces around restructuring: which circles support it, which are preventing its implementation, and why?
- What social strategy can be applied to make restructuring more effective, to increase the numbers of its supporters and reduce those of its opponents?

These questions, and others associated with them, are examined in the five chapters of this book. Chapter 1 makes a brief excursion into those stages of our history that prepared the ground for restructuring. Rather than simply listing the historical facts, I have concentrated on my own personal view of our society's stages of development in which I happened to play a conscious part.

In Chapter 2 the social aspects of restructuring the Soviet economy are examined, the previous economic mechanism is described, and the reasons for its inefficiency analysed. The main object of this chapter is to show the social content of changes that are being made in the economy and their possible social consequences.

Chapter 3 deals with the social policy associated with restructuring. The main aim of this policy is declared to be the strengthening of socialist justice. I have tried to show what this means as applied to employment, education, income distribution, housing provision, the organization of a consumer market, etc.

In Chapter 4 I have approached restructuring as a social process in which groups with different, sometimes opposing, interests take part. What types of relationship towards restructuring are common among different social groups, which particular group characteristics determine these relationships, what policy variants can be used to modify people's behaviour – those are the questions addressed in this chapter.

Chapter 5 is about the democratization of political life, since this is the main guarantee that positive changes will become irreversible. The specific content of such objectives of democratization as the further development of openness, the restructuring of political institutions, the extension of human rights, and the development of new social movements is examined. Both the achievements and the tasks that still have to be tackled are noted.

The book comes to an end with a postscript concerning the extraordinary year 1989 – the first year of radical restructuring and the year in which the severity of the crisis of our society and economy became fully apparent.

In a single book it is not, of course, possible to deal with the whole range of social problems arising as a result of restructuring, nor could I do it. This book has a much more modest aim – to share with Western readers my understanding of the important tensions and hopeful processes under way in the Soviet Union.

Brief Historical Background

1

STALINISM

The war lasted a little less than four years – 1,418 days. Military losses, the deportation to Germany of the inhabitants of enemy-occupied territories, and civilian deaths reduced the population of the country by 27 million. However, in an unbelievably hard struggle, the people held out and achieved victory. A peaceful life lay ahead. I was 18 years old, in my second year at university, and I shared the same feelings as other people: grief over the irreparable losses (I lost my mother in the bombing of Moscow) and the hope that life would become easier.

Life was very difficult, however: food was rationed, and most families were half-starved. In order to feed myself I had to combine study with work in one of the university laboratories. But everybody looked forward to a quick economic recovery and was ready to take part in it through their own individual work. The tragedies of the mid-1930s and the reverses at the beginning of the war faded into the background; people associated them with the objective difficulties of developing the country, the complexity of the international situation and the necessity of preparing for war. They believed that the past could not repeat itself.

Pride in the victory that had been achieved made the authority of Stalin almost boundless. He was depicted as the main, if not the sole, architect of victory, the leader, father and teacher of the people to whom we owed all the best aspects of our life.

The system of economic management in this period was just as rigidly centralized as it had been in wartime. A plan for an enterprise handed down from above had the force of law and non-fulfilment entailed political and criminal responsibility. Unprecedentedly harsh standards of discipline at work and with regard to production were the rule in enterprises and institutions. Being late for work, overstaying the lunch break, not to mention attempts to take home any kind of scrap products from work, were punished by imprisonment or exile to a corrective labour camp.

At the same time, postwar economic recovery went ahead comparatively quickly, which in principle made it possible to improve people's living conditions. But the state took little advantage of the opportunity. The press propagandized the idea of concentrating all efforts on reconstructing industry and continuing to 'tighten our belts'. And, it has to be said, this was received with a fair degree of understanding on the part of young people. Constantly hungry, ill-clothed, ill-shod, we were prepared to put up with the disorder of our lives patiently and to postpone the satisfaction of our most basic personal needs until such time as the problems of the nation as a whole had been solved.

The engines of economic growth were, on the one hand, people's own belief in the need to restore the economy as fast as possible but, on the other, fear of punishment for any deviation from the prescribed norms. The majority of economic administrators and managers continued to live according to a wartime regime and to work 14–15 hours a day, striving at all costs to fulfil the plan. The working week was fixed at six days or 48 hours, but in fact it was much longer. According to the Soviet Central Statistical Office, despite all the difficulties, the plans were fulfilled 100 per cent and more, which reinforced the idea of the correctness and immutability of plan fulfilment and therefore of the reigning state order. It was not until several decades later that those who had survived were to discover how these cheering results had been obtained; they had been adjusted personally by Stalin's red pencil.

The living standards of the majority of the population remained extremely low. During the war most personal possessions had been lost or destroyed, stocks of food eaten up, clothes worn out and furniture broken up for use as fuel. The housing situation was particularly bad. A huge proportion of the prewar housing stock had been destroyed and the rest had fallen into disrepair. The construction of new housing was undertaken to a limited extent, mainly in the areas liberated from enemy occupation. As a result, there was extreme overcrowding and often insanitary living conditions. The construction of public buildings to meet social or cultural needs had fallen even more behindhand and was confined in the main to the rebuilding or repair of schools.

Of course, not all groups in Soviet society had an equally bad time. Thus, collective farmers were in the most difficult situation, receiving practically nothing for their work in collective production. Not infrequently during the Stalin period agricultural prices did not even cover the costs of delivering collective-farm produce to the collection points so that it was in effect handed over to the state free of charge. As a result, the collective farms had no money for developing production or for paying members for their work. The collective-farm family's main source of livelihood was its individual holding, consisting of a small plot of land and a small number of livestock. However, this smallholding was so heavily taxed that in a number of cases the families had to give up practically everything they had produced.

In 1951, when I was looking through the aggregate annual accounts of collective farms in one of the regions of Kirghizia, I noticed that on average the collective farmers received one kopek for a day's labour, and for a year about two pre-reform roubles – today approximately 20 kopeks (the price of 1 kg of bread). In reply to my puzzled question as to what they lived on, it was explained to me that most of the families had a small flock of sheep and goats, which were pastured in the mountains, concealed from the tax authorities. So it was that I, a graduate of a university where I had been told about the advantages of the socialist distribution of income according to work done, first came up against the fact that a social class comprising about 40 per cent of the population of the country was paid practically nothing for its work.[1]

The resources extorted from the collective farms went towards the reconstruction of industry and the development of the towns. Life was much more difficult in the country than in town, but it was only possible to leave the collective farm and move to a town with the permission of a meeting of the collective-farm workers, and it was not recommended that such permission be given. In addition, moving from one part of the country to another was permitted only for people who possessed an internal passport proving their identity. The overwhelming majority of collective-farm workers did not have such a passport, and they thus found themselves caught in a trap – they had nothing to live on in the country, but they could not move away to the towns.

Life was slightly better for workers in the towns than for the peasants. They did have a regular, albeit small, money wage, they obtained goods on ration cards, and they had better medical care and better schools. At the same time, their work was very hard, their working week was longer than on the collective farms, and their meals were fairly meagre because they had no individual smallholdings. The wage level of industrial workers rose only very slowly. People were even forced to make annual loans to the state for which they had to give up one or two months' wages.

The most privileged stratum of Soviet postwar society comprised high-ranking officers and generals, senior personnel in Party and Soviet organizations, factory directors, professors, writers, artists, composers, media workers, etc. The material standard of living of this group was several times higher than that of ordinary people. They had comfortable flats and second homes in the country, official chauffeur-driven cars, high salaries, special clinics, sanatoria and rest homes. They obtained food and consumer goods through 'special' channels outside the general state retail system. Obviously, a state and Party 'elite' existed even before the war, but the public knew little about the life it led. After the war, the size of the 'social elite' increased substantially and the contrast between its situation and that of other groups became even more striking. I therefore relate the formation of an elite stratum of society, sharply differentiated by virtue of its position, to the postwar years in particular.

The emergence of this stratum created a new social situation. Firstly, the extreme difference between the level of consumption and lifestyle of the elite and that of the general public was difficult to explain by differences in the quality of their work. Secondly, the fact that special channels were organized to supply the elite stratum with high-quality goods at lower prices lessened its dependence on the economic, political and cultural development of the society as a whole. The personal situation of people who bore particular responsibility for the successful development of society could now improve even while the living conditions of ordinary people deteriorated.

However, in practice, people's living standards did improve, albeit slowly. In the early postwar years, there was an expansion of so-called 'commercial' trade in goods that were sold off the ration but at considerably higher prices, a system that had first been brought in at the end of the war. Goods were not always available in the commercial shops, of course, and not everyone could afford to buy them, but nevertheless there was some easing of the situation. In December 1947, there was a currency reform combined with the abolition of food ration cards and a rise in the retail price of food. Old money was exchanged for the new at the ratio of 10:1 and, since it was dangerous to declare any wealth acquired by dishonest work to the financial authorities, its monetary component simply vanished. The abolition of ration cards was greeted with great enthusiasm, and currency reform and price rises with understanding. For people at last had the opportunity to buy foodstuffs that were dearer than before, but in the quantity and variety that they themselves had chosen.

The high level of retail prices fixed in 1947 provided the possibility of reducing them at a later date. In the remaining period of Stalin's life, there were several price reductions, each of which increased the real income of the population by 3–5 per cent. They were therefore welcomed with open arms.

In the political sphere, the situation was rather more complex. Stalin's ideological line, which had been slightly softened during the war, began to harden immediately after victory. The 'iron curtain', which had been raised a little when the Soviet Army went into the territory of liberated countries, was lowered once again. Soviet society once more closed in on itself, cut off from the rest of the world. Listening to foreign radio broadcasts, not to mention spreading information they contained, counted as a crime and was severely punished. News filtering in from abroad was passed on in a whisper and only to the most trusted people.

The campaigns against all freedom of thought became harsher. Any creative questioning, any deviation from dogma and tradition elicited the accusation of 'bourgeois influences'. Even the sincere expression of a love of knowledge on the subject of Party history, philosophy or political economy was often treated as 'provocative behaviour' and punished, even to the extent of expulsion from college or university[2]

Every year government resolutions were published, exposing certain groups of intellectuals to harsh criticism. The work of the poet Anna Akhmatova and the writer Mikhail Zoshchenko underwent brutal and disrespectful criticism. The composers Muradeli and Shostakovich were accused of their music 'not being understood by the people'. Scientists were subjected to constant outbursts of criticism. In 1947, the so-called 'philosophical discussion' was conducted, and in 1948 the notorious 'biological discussion' devastated Soviet genetics. Many geneticists were arrested, the rest were deprived of all possibility of continuing their research. The discussion marked the complete triumph of the pseudo-academic Lysenko, who had been elevated by Stalin, and who engaged in truly criminal activity in destroying both biological science and individual scientists. Cybernetics, sociology, semiotics and a number of other disciplines were proclaimed 'bourgeois pseudo-sciences' for which there was not, nor could there be, any place in a socialist society.

Against the background of such 'ideological preparation' a new wave of repression began at the end of the 1940s with the apparent aim of preventing the return from the camps of hundreds of thousands of people who had been sentenced to ten years' imprisonment back in the 1930s. But this aim was kept secret. The most varied grounds for arrest featured on the surface: the recounting of an anecdote, a carelessly expressed doubt about the correctness of an 'ideological resolution', concealment of a biographical detail – for example, nationality, the fact of having been in occupied territory, a family relationship with 'enemies of the people'. A friend of ours was exiled to Siberia, where he died of tuberculosis, 'for dissemination of the poems of Marina Tsvetayeva'.[3]

In 1949–50 a new campaign was mounted – the fight against so-called 'cosmopolitanism' – the true purpose of which was the official propagation of anti-Semitism and the elimination of Jews from the administration, the defence industry, science and higher education. In the autumn of 1952, the well-known case of the Jewish doctors who were accused of the systematic and methodical annihilation of the Slavonic peoples, including measures to ensure that Russian children were born dead or deformed, was organized. During that period patients stood for hours in queues waiting to see Russian doctors in the clinics, but shied away from Jewish ones as from murderers. One can imagine the feelings of these people who were not guilty of anything.

Such was the situation in society shortly before the death of Stalin. How did people relate to it and what was the public frame of mind? I would say it was contradictory.

On the one hand, after decades of having it instilled in them, many people still had great faith in Stalin. The regular price cuts kept this faith alive and strengthened it. Life was improving and the material well-being of the majority of the population had risen. As regards the regular 'ideological campaigns', by no means everyone was affected. Some were dismissed and repressed, but others took their places and had a successful career. The campaign against 'cosmopolitanism' was particularly effective in this respect, freeing as it did many thousands of attractive posts for new people to fill. And those people were honestly devoted to the system that had trained and promoted them.

On the other hand, it became increasingly difficult for decent, honest people to understand what was going on. The social roots of the phenomena against which the Party was fighting were no longer clear. The reasons for the repression were inexplicable. Many people were asking themselves why, despite heroic efforts at work, life was improving so slowly and why a military style of economic management and a harsh discipline at work that was unsuitable in peacetime still persisted. This all gave rise to some intellectual ferment, but in practical terms opposition to Stalinism was very weak. I believe the bulk of the intelligentsia were perplexed and did not understand the social nature of the processes that were going on. And those who did understand preferred to keep quiet since to express one's opinions meant suffering repression and disappearing from public life. As a result, deathly silence reigned, which was brilliantly portrayed in Tvardovsky's poem, 'Tyorkin in the Other World', and in Bondarev's novel, *Silence*.

The portrait of Stalinism that I have sketched makes it fairly easy to judge in which direction Soviet society was moving in that period. In the political field, instead of the democratic management and openness that is inherent in socialism, there was a despotic concentration of power in the hands of Stalin and his close entourage, arbitrary rule, a lack of accountability to the people and extensive use of repressive powers not only against those who were beginning to act, but against those who were merely beginning to wonder.[4]

In the economic and social spheres, instead of a proper distribution of earnings according to work done, there was open exploitation of the countryside by the towns, of small towns by large ones, of outlying regions by central ones, of collective farmers by workers in the state sector of production, and so on.

In the field of national policy, instead of a harmonious combination of the interests of nations and nationalities, Russian chauvinism prevailed, combined with an anti-Semitism that was sanctified by the state and the repression of a whole number of peoples.

Finally, in the cultural and ethical field, instead of moving towards the humanization of society and moulding man as a social being, people were treated as a labour force required for 'great epoch-making feats' but without any individual value of their own. Informers and careerists were encouraged, while independent thinkers and actors were punished. Such moral qualities as devotion to family, friends, and intimates, loyalty to principles, honesty, etc., were actively discouraged.

All these interconnected features went towards making up the complete image of the system known as Stalinism. Its basis was state ownership of the means of production, used by a comparatively narrow group of top administrators by no means in the interests of the people. In the Stalin period, elements of socialist relations present in Soviet society were deformed, distorted and corrupted and this created the preconditions for the social regeneration of the system.

The death of Stalin was the first blow to Stalinism. It was, it is true, perceived by most people as a misfortune, causing confusion and perplexity. Many people honestly did not conceive how the country could continue to exist without its great teacher and friend. At memorial meetings the men were strained and grave and the women usually wept. I wept myself, although by that time my doubts about the correctness of Stalin's line were greater than my belief that he was right. This may be only a trivial personal detail, but it could be said to be important in characterizing the general immaturity of public opinion at that time. Only the most far-sighted people considered that Stalin's death could give rise to progressive changes in the development of society and open the way to the development of socialist relations. But to say such things aloud was dangerous.

THE 'THAW'

The Soviet people had not yet recovered from the shock waves produced by Stalin's death, when it was followed by the unexpected exposure of Beria, the head of the KGB. Represented as the main perpetrator of the unjust repressions of the 1930s and 40s, he was arrested, sentenced and shot. New leaders came to power – Malenkov, Khrushchev, Kosygin, Brezhnev, and others. Whereas the development of Soviet society in this period, aptly named 'the thaw' by the writer Ilya Ehrenburg, took on a high degree of dynamism, its end was unlike its beginning and that must be dealt with in more detail later.

The 20th Congress of the Party, devoted to the exposure of what was to become known as the 'cult of personality of Stalin', became the central event of the period of the 'thaw'. ('The cult of personality of Stalin' was the euphemism applied to the concept of Stalinism as an integral socio-political system.) After analysing the mistakes tolerated in the Stalinist period and revealing its nature as essentially against the people and anti-socialist, the Party prepared the ground for the democratization of social relations. Even before the 20th Congress, Khrushchev had begun the mass rehabilitation of those who had suffered unjust repression. As a result of a systematic judicial review, only a few of those sentenced were found guilty: the overwhelming majority of surviving prisoners were released from imprisonment and rehabilitated. And only when these people returned to their homes and began to tell of what they had been through, did the younger generations for the first time find out the truth about the extent of the lawlessness and the merciless cruelty of the Stalin terror. The material produced at the 20th Congress developed and strengthened these impressions which left an indelible trace in the public consciousness.

The exposure of the 'cult of personality of Stalin' created a certain split in the public psyche. The man whom people were accustomed to regard as their friend and benefactor, the architect of victories in both peace and war, had been unexpectedly transformed before their eyes into a criminal who had murdered millions of people. To experience this was not a simple thing. It was easiest for the young people, the majority of whom accepted the new truth eagerly and shared the views of the new leadership. It was more difficult for people of 30–40 years of age, of whom I was one. They had lived through part of their maturity in the Stalinist period and thus had to re-assess their actions and views and to answer their own conscience honestly as to when and how they had failed to listen to it, and shown an unforgivable conformism to Stalinism. Out of the crucible of these experiences, my generation became more mature and self-critical and, at the same time, more critical towards the country's new leadership. For whereas Stalin, who had been put forward as the 'genius of all time', had in fact turned out to be a criminal, the people who had taken his place had far more ordinary biographies, capabilities, qualifications and experience of life. There was, therefore, no reason to regard their decisions as 'the last word in truth.'

As regards the older age group, who had devoted their whole lives to putting Stalin's ideas into practice, many of them just could not understand and accept the truth about him. They perceived the exposure of the 'cult of personality of Stalin' as the libel of a great man and remained true to his memory and ideas to the last days of their lives. I knew many such people – indeed some of them are alive to this day. They do not believe that the democratization of society is either necessary or urgent and they stand wholeheartedly for the iron 'order' that existed in Stalin's time. To persuade them otherwise is not possible.[5]

An important feature of the 'thaw' period was the ending of the Soviet Union's isolation from the capitalist countries. Diplomatic ties with other countries were strengthened, mutually beneficial trade was developed, the country's leaders went on trips abroad to exchange experiences, develop cultural co-operation, etc. The press, radio and television (which had just recently started up) widely publicized these trips, enabling Soviet people to get to know about life in the West. Tourist trips abroad began to be organized. My first trip abroad took place at this time – to Sweden in 1957. It made a very great impression indeed on me; before me was another, a different way of life, people with different values, needs, opinions, and different ways of organizing the economy and solving social problems. This experience not only broadened my mental outlook, it threw additional light on our own domestic problems. My own personal impressions shattered the idea I had been given that the life of working people in the West consisted mainly of suffering. We saw that, in fact, the countries of the West had in many instances overtaken us and we had lively discussions about ways of overcoming our own weaknesses. Heated economic and political discussions took place and people including specialists began to think more freely. A relaxation of press censorship also contributed to this.

When discussing the political democratization of social relations, mention has be made of measures taken to overcome discrimination against particular groups in the population. These measures included, in particular, the issuing of internal passports to the rural population in the course of the decade (from the mid-50s to the mid-60s). This was a huge step towards making the civil rights of rural dwellers equal to those of townspeople – restoring to them, in fact, the right to move freely from one part of the country to another. Another example was the return to their homes of the Daghestanis, Chechens, Ingushes, and certain other peoples, who had been deported during the war from their previous places of residence.[6] Thus, society was gradually becoming more normal.

As regards the economy, the new leadership adopted a policy of systematically introducing economic accounting, regularizing wages and increasing material incentives for workers. They began with agriculture for whose product there was a particularly acute need. In 1953 there was a substantial rise in the prices of collective-farm produce and economic relations were normalized between collective farms and the Machine and Tractor Stations (MTSs), which had formerly made a quite inordinate charge for carrying out mechanized farm work. In 1958, the MTSs were abolished altogether and tractors and agricultural machinery were sold to the collective farmers who for the first time were able to organize their production independently. The sharp rise in the prices of agricultural produce, bringing it into line with its social cost, made most of the collective farms profitable and increased their incentive to raise production and improve the quality of output. In the years 1953–8 agricultural output rose more quickly than in all the years the collective farms had been in existence – by 8–9 per cent a year. The high growth rate was subsequently maintained by the development of virgin and fallow land in Kazakhstan, the South Urals, and Siberia.

At the beginning of the 1960s the reorganization of industrial management became an issue. Industry as a whole was now being organized on a predominantly regional basis instead of on an industry-by-industry basis. Many industrial ministries were abolished and Economic Councils (*Sovnarkhoz*) were created in major regions of the country. Enterprises enjoyed a greater degree of economic independence than before. Regional linkages between enterprises developed vigorously, and commercial contracts concluded on the initiative of enterprises themselves became more important.

All this had a quite positive result. In the years of the 'thaw' the rates of growth of industrial output and national income were the highest achieved in the postwar period. The pace of scientific and technological progress also accelerated. It is no coincidence that in 1957 Sputnik – the first artificial Earth satellite – was launched, and in 1961 the first manned space flight took place.

In this period, not only heavy industry but also light industries including food industries, showed unusually high rates of development. Goods quickly increased in variety, and the inexperienced shopper often had to ask the shop assistant what some article or other was used for. On the one hand, the much wider choice in consumer goods pleased everybody but, on the other hand, it disturbed them, even knocking them slightly off-balance. I remember going into a shop one day where they were selling several hundred different types of fabric – I came out without buying anything and felt really ill at not being able to make a choice. After long years of scarcity most of us were unaccustomed to living in conditions offering a wide choice between different options.

At the same time, people's needs grew rapidly. Incomes had risen, many people had obtained new flats, had furnished them and equipped them with domestic appliances – refrigerators, washing machines, television sets, etc. In order to satisfy these growing needs, more had to be earned, and for this, more and better work done. This created a tremendous material incentive to work, and a relative degree of satisfaction and confidence that the planned economy was working and would continue to work reliably.

Successful economic development created favourable conditions for solving social problems. One of the first measures taken by the state was to stop raising compulsory annual loans from the general public, which had reduced real incomes by 8–10 per cent. At the same time, the government promised to repay previous loans completely in 20 years' time. People greeted this measure with relief.

Accelerated economic growth enabled a series of measures to be taken to improve the wages system. For the first time a minimum wage (60 roubles per month) was fixed and low-paid groups of workers were exempted from tax. The wages of many categories of workers engaged in work that was complex, dangerous, detrimental to health or physically heavy were raised, and special bonuses ranging from 15 to 100 per cent were added to the wages of those who worked in regions with difficult climatic conditions and a poor social infrastructure.

In 1965 guaranteed wages were introduced for collective farmers. Previously their income had been distributed only at the end of the year. Collective farms were given the right to make a sizeable monthly advance to their members. Economically weak farms were given the necessary funds to do this on a long-term credit basis. All this resulted in a considerable levelling out of income differences between different groups of people. Society was becoming more egalitarian.

The creation of a universal system of pension provision, which did not exist in the Soviet Union until the mid-1950s, had the same effect. Elderly people had either put away a portion of their income 'for a rainy day', relied on help from their children or been forced to work until the last days of their lives. According to the new law of

1956, all men and women who had reached the age of 60 and 55 respectively and had worked in social production for 25 (20) years were entitled to a retirement pension. The amount varied depending on the number of years worked and the level of wages earned. Allowances were paid to mothers bringing up children without a father and to families with a large number of children. Other social benefits were expanded. Workers and employees who changed from a six-day to a five-day working week with two days off appreciably improved the way they spent their time: they were able to organize their domestic life much better, broaden their cultural pursuits, and generally improve their way of life.

The launching of a full-scale housing construction programme was even more significant. After the war, although several times more people were concentrated in the towns than before, the housing stock had considerably decreased. Multi-occupancy of flats was the rule with several different families sharing a common kitchen, bathroom and toilet. This put a strain on relations not only between neighbouring families, who often had conflicting tastes and habits, but also between members of the same family crammed into one or two rooms. The building programme demanded tremendous efforts: the allocation of large capital investments, the creation of a building materials industry, and the recruitment of a whole army of construction workers. The amount of urban living space more than doubled in the 1960s. One hundred million people improved their living conditions and about half of all families obtained separate flats. At the same time, new schools, nursery schools, hospitals, leisure centres, shops, stadiums, swimming pools, etc, were built.

All these were indisputable achievements but they still left many social problems unresolved. For example, living conditions in the rural areas lagged badly behind those in the towns. To show the degree of backwardness, I cite two facts only: a) between 1917 and 1960 the state invested less than 10 per cent of the amount invested in the towns in developing the social infrastructure in the villages (calculated on a per capita basis); b) in the early 1960s, the average earnings of a new arrival from the village in the first few months after moving to town more than trebled – so great was the difference between incomes in industry and in agriculture. Naturally, upon receipt of a passport, the rural population, especially the young people, flocked into the towns, accepting literally any work and any kind of accommodation. Consequently, in only ten years (1956–66) net losses to the rural areas amounted to 18 million people, the majority of whom constituted the most educated and forward-looking section of the population.

This process had three main consequences. Firstly, a marked change in the ratio of the population producing agricultural output to that buying it. Secondly, an 'ageing' of the rural population and a deterioration in its social structure, resulting in some regions in the complete desertion and disappearance of many villages. Thirdly, a marked change in the socio-demographic structure of the urban population – a reduction in the number of 'hereditary' workers with their own class morality, and an increase in the number of workers who were peasants by origin and who retained a peasant system of values, needs and interests. These changes exerted, I believe, no small influence on the events that were to follow.

The trend towards democratization of social relations helped to extend free speech and freedom of the press and, accordingly, the opportunity for creative work also. For the first time in many decades, the intelligentsia began to think, speak and write more or less freely.[7] This also had an effect on the social sciences. In the field of economics, creative books began to appear, written from a unorthodox standpoint, refuting the old dogmas and raising issues for discussion. Our science began to come to life. It was at this time that my first books were published.[8] In the Stalin period it was, of course, unthinkable that such books would be published. They were, after all, devoted to the most acute social problems and were written in accordance with objective reality, and not wished-for abstractions. However, even in this period, publishing works of this nature was by no means an easy matter. For example, the book that I wrote with M. I. Sidorova – *The Methodology of Comparing Labour Productivity in Agriculture in the USSR and the USA* – was never published since the application of such methods produced too pessimistic a result. It was as if two years of highly intensive work had been wiped out of my life. And this was far from being an exception. The true picture of the 'thaw' contained not a little disappointment and bitterness.

But to return to the positive features in the development of science. At the very end of the 1950s, on the initiative of Academicians M. Lavrentyev, S. Sobolev and Khristianovich, the Siberian Division of the Soviet Academy of Sciences was founded for the purpose of stimulating the establishment of science in Siberia. Twenty institutes attached to this new Division were sited in the Novosibirsk satellite town of Akademgorodok, which had been especially constructed for that purpose. A whole group of creatively-minded young Moscow economists, headed by Abel Aganbegyan, moved out there and took me along with them. The new institute entrusted me with researching the reasons for the mass migration of the rural population to the towns and I soon realized, to my surprise, that I was working in the field not so much of economics as of sociology, which was then undergoing an intense revival. Since there had been no professional sociologists working in the country for a long time, enthusiasts of the 'new' science had to teach it to themselves. But how fascinating it was, how well it met the needs of the time and how irresistibly it drew one into its whirlpool, where one got to know masses of interesting people. It was a completely different, brilliant and fascinating life.

Together with sociology, sciences such as genetics, cybernetics and semiotics which had formerly been persecuted were also developing. Cultural and spiritual life was in full swing, and this was felt much more strongly and sharply in the young Akademgorodok than in Moscow. Scientific and political discussions went on in academic staff-rooms, in the social club 'Under the Integral' and, indeed, in every flat. Concerts given by singers and poets – Vladimir Vysotsky, Bulat Okudzhava, Aleksandr Galich, Yulii Kim and many others – enjoyed particular popularity. Their songs reflected the feelings and aspirations of the progressive section of the Soviet intelligentsia, praising such eternal values as friendship, love, compassion, and hatred of lies and betrayal. The best concerts gave the listeners a feeling of spiritual freedom and unity. In this sense my generation was fortunate – the years of our youth and maturity coincided with a stage of spiritual uplift in society, the memory of which stayed with us in the darkest years of reaction.

On the whole, the Khrushchev 'thaw' represented a period of revival and democratization for Soviet society, successes in economic development, a vigorous social policy and a growth in people's spiritual freedom. However, the policy pursued by Khrushchev was not consistent and, as a result, a progressive development in society was often accompanied, or even replaced, by a retrogressive one. The introduction of economic methods of management alternated with a hardening of purely administrative ones; the development of market relations with their drastic curtailment; aid for the individual smallholdings of the rural population with the compulsory collectivization of their livestock; increased openness with stricter censorship; the democratization of political relations with heavier ideological pressure.

Policy shortcomings at that time are also attributable to a poor understanding of economics which caused imbalances between the various measures taken. In particular, personal incomes and purchasing power in the 1960s increased at a much faster rate than the corresponding supply of goods. As a result, many goods were in short supply and this, strangely enough, as the consequence not of poverty but of growing prosperity. At first, shortages were explained by slowness on the part of distributive workers, then by poor work by the State Plannning Commission, and only in time did it begin to dawn on us that shortages had come to stay 'in earnest' and that enormous efforts would have to be made to overcome them.

I think most people understood that the ambivalence and inconsistency of the policy pursued by Khrushchev could not continue for long. Sooner or later, society or its leadership would have to make the choice between two possible paths of development: either to make democratization irreversible by creating a political mechanism that ensured genuine people's power or sooner or later to return to a Stalinist 'barrack-room socialism'. Understanding that there was no third path, the intelligentsia tensely watched the government's every step, interpreting not only its obvious content but also its hidden meaning. Policy, however, continued to be ambivalent, vacillating and contradictory. As a result, the section of society that was expecting radical reforms became increasingly disillusioned.

At the same time, there was growing dissatisfaction among the most conservative stratum of society, in particular, among those working in the central administration appointed under the *nomenklatura* system – i.e. in posts subject to the approval of the Party apparatus. For Khrushchev had not only succeeded in cutting their wages but had also deprived them of a significant number of their former privileges – for example, the official cars and fully-serviced houses in the country provided by the government. This reduced the social gap between the leading functionaries and 'ordinary mortals'. The abolition of many ministries and the creation of Economic Councils forced some of their staff to move out of Moscow to distant towns and often entailed demotion. Then in 1963 Khrushchev put forward an idea that was even more dangerous from the point of view of the Party apparatus – the splitting up of district and regional committees into urban and rural committees with the aim of bringing management closer to the managed. Since this further destabilized the position of the Party apparatus, its patience ran out. In the autumn of 1964 the post of General Secretary of the Central Committee of the Communist Party was occupied not by Khrushchev but by Brezhnev.

At first, the new leader seemed to be inclined towards the further democratization of society, the development of socialist relations and the elimination of the negative consequences of the 'arbitrariness' that was a feature of the last years of the Khrushchev administration. Thus, in 1965 preparations went ahead for the so-called 'Kosygin reform' which was designed to introduce economic methods of management, extend the independence of enterprises, increase the role of profit, etc. The new leadership emphatically condemned voluntaristic methods of solving problems and took the decision that wider use should be made of expert recommendations, and so on. From the very outset, however, this line was not followed with any consistency. The economic reform had not had time to become a reality, let alone to produce practical results, when under the pretext of various amendments and clarifications to previous decisions the new leaders were beginning to put it into reverse. The independence of enterprises was curtailed; the regulation of wages 'from above' became stricter, and the number of binding planning indicators rose. The basic reason for this speedy reversal of the reform can be said to lie not in the economic, but in the socio-political sphere. The first steps taken showed that extending the economic independence of enterprises weakened the dependence of managers on the central state and Party apparatus; hence their concern to stop any further development of the reform.

The obvious divergence between word and deed in this important matter and the patent degeneration of the reform caused resentment at Brezhnev's political line among a section of the intelligentsia, workers and students. Given the relative freedom of discussion, this resentment began to grow into a ferment, capable of developing into social conflict. In order to prevent this happening, steps were taken to restrict democracy and to frighten the opposition. The trial took place in 1967 of the writers Sinyavsky and Daniel who were accused of anti-Soviet propaganda. It was held *in camera* and the majority of reporters were unable to attend. The articles appearing in the newspapers, accusing the defendants of various strange sins, did not explain what, in fact, they were, i.e. what Sinyavsky and Daniel asserted in their writings. University teachers and public lecturers angrily demanded condemnation of the 'provocative', 'anti-popular' and 'anti-Soviet' positions of the writers, the essential nature of which they were unable to explain. In these circumstances, more than a hundred academics made an official request to the government to provide full information on the substance of the judicial procedures. The letter was completely loyal in content. Before it could reach its destination, however, its text, together with the list of signatories, had been broadcast to the Soviet people by the radio station 'Voice of America'. This was enough for a political accusation to be brought against those who had signed the letter and for a campaign for them to be 'subjected to criticism' at trade union and Party meetings. The political climate of society was changing before our very eyes.

The events in Czechoslovakia and Hungary in 1968 speeded up this process still more. They showed the Soviet government of the time that the genuine development of democracy, by providing truthful economic and political information about the country's development and allowing open discussion of it, changed people's awareness and made them more critical and demanding of the political leadership and, if it displayed any weakness, threatened social excess. The conclusion was drawn that democratization of society had to be reversed and replaced by tighter ideological and political control over their minds of the people. So ended the comparatively short 'thaw', and 'winter' set in once again.

RE-STALINIZATION OR 'STAGNATION'

The first sign of the onset of a new stage was the disappearance of openness: not only the suppression of social criticism, but also an end to the flow of information about social and political questions of interest to the general public and the persecution of any kind of creative thought. All forms of censorship became stricter. Editorial, academic and artistic councils, fearful of ideological criticism 'from above', examined every phrase as if through a microscope, looking for hidden sedition. Diversity in political, economic and scientific opinions quickly disappeared, all publications took on a boring similarity, persistently 'defending' (from whom?) the views expressed in resolutions of the Party's Central Committee or the speeches of political leaders.

Social science institutes were forbidden to publish independently even limited edition monographs and the publication of collections of articles was set around with a huge number of bureaucratic conditions and stipulations. Henceforth, economists, philosophers, historians and sociologists could publish their work only with large state publishers or in centrally run journals, past whose editorial boards not even a fly, let alone unorthodox ideas, could get by unnoticed. Ideological control extended not only to content but to the form of exposition and the methods used in the argumentation of scientific ideas.

Openness within enterprises, institutions and organizations gradually disappeared. Critical contributions at meetings ceased, for as a rule they provoked either an outcry or a reprimand. Thus, step by step, by one method or another, silence was once again established in the country, outwardly reminiscent of the period of Stalinism. Nevertheless, there were at least two significant differences between the two periods. Firstly, during the Brezhnev administration which our press usually calls the period of 'stagnation', there was no mass political repression such as characterized the most important element of Stalinism. Secondly, public social and political awareness was different in principle. I mentioned above how difficult we had found the explanation of the true face of Stalin, that is, the deception of which we were the victims. Such lessons are not easily forgotten. And whereas all Stalin's actions had met with uncritical approval from the majority of people who had faith in his genius, the attitude of the ordinary people to Khrushchev, Kosygin and Brezhnev was different. Their actions were discussed (if not at meetings, then within the circle of family and friends), analysed and often disapproved of. There was practically no overt support for the suppression of openness and criticism of the government among my acquaintances. Most of the intelligentsia were in a troubled and indignant state of mind. But those who wished to live and work in that society had to adjust to it one way or another.

After the Kosygin reform had been virtually sabotaged, the mechanisms for market regulation of the economy were completely switched off and economic management once again took an administrative and bureaucratic form: the planning of 'each and everything' from the centre was revived, centrally fixed prices ceased to reflect the production costs of goods, the measure of 'gross output' that had been criticized a thousand times became the sovereign lord of the economy, and so on. The discontinuation of economic methods of management, the violation of the principle of the self-financing of enterprises, and the loss of any clear relationship between work and pay for different groups of workers in effect constituted a disregard of objective economic laws. This all led to people's alienation from their work, its reduction to a simple instrument for obtaining wages and social and professional status. It can be said that the social and moral devaluation of work became one of the harshest 'punishments' for Soviet society's disregard of economic laws and for political conformism to the leadership's reactionary policy.

The discontinuation of market mechanisms deprived management bodies of objective criteria for assessing economic and labour efficiency. Pay differentials began to depend to an increasing extent on the power and influence of government departments, personal status, and personal and family connections with local Party leaders, etc. The correlation between the labour that workers put into social production and the income they received was increasingly broken, thus correspondingly weakening their material incentive to work efficiently. As a result, economic rates of growth crept down inexorably.

Even the Central Statistical Office, with its arsenal of methods for providing whatever economic indicators were required, could not quite conceal this fact. The consistent failure to fulfil annual plans was poorly reflected in the statistics since the plans were adjusted downwards in good time.[9] Five-year plan targets, however, were published in Party Congress documents at the beginning of the five-year period. It was therefore possible to find out the real figures for economic growth at the end of the five years. Analysis has shown that, despite a systematic lowering of intensity, the degree of non-fulfilment increased with each plan. Let me illustrate this with an example from agriculture. Planned output growth in the eighth five-year plan (1966–71) was 25 per cent, in the ninth (1971–5) 20 per cent, and in the tenth (1976–80) 16 per cent. The actual figures for output growth in these five-year periods were 21, 15 and 9 per cent respectively. Therefore, in the eighth five-year plan 84 per cent of output growth was achieved, in the ninth, 75 per cent, and in the tenth, 56 per cent. Planned and actual growth indicators for the sector seemed to vie with each other in regard to rates of decline, though the actual indicators declined at a quicker rate. In explaining the reasons for non-fulfilment of the plans, each sector and enterprise pointed to poor work on the part of their suppliers who failed to deliver equipment, raw materials and other physical inputs, energy, packaging, etc. This was essentially true, but at the level of the economy it was indicative of the systemic character of its 'sickness'.

The slowing down of economic growth led to a noticeable decrease in the construction of housing and public buildings, although the demand for them remained acute. The number of flats made available, as well as their total area, decreased from one five-year plan to the next. The quality of mass housing construction deteriorated and residents increasingly began to move into virtually uncompleted homes and finish the work themselves.

Wages rose comparatively quickly while the cost of consumer goods rose much more slowly. In physical terms (items, metres, kilogrammes, etc) the quantity of many types of goods tended to fall. As a result, food shortages increased, and demand for manufactured goods and services was not satisfied. Every so often, various essential goods disappeared from the shops: now crockery, now light bulbs, bed linen, razor blades, typewriters, washing machines, ladies' toiletries, and so on. One could not speak of an improvement in real living standards in these circumstances, although the Central Statistical Office continued to record a growth in general prosperity (slower than before, it is true).

How, in concrete terms, did the decline in living standards of a significant number of people manifest itself?

Firstly, in the majority of sectors, wage rises were actively checked. Output norms were increased and piece rates were reduced on the grounds of technological progress and sometimes without any such justification.

Secondly, the prices of consumer goods rose steadily. Standard goods were, it is true, usually sold at constant unchanging prices, but their actual quality gradually deteriorated. Then better models of exactly the same goods appeared alongside them, costing correspondingly more. For some time, the consumer had the choice between cheap and dearer goods, until the first disappeared from the shops and the second replaced them. Thus, the price had not been raised officially, but it had risen in fact.

Thirdly, increasingly widespread shortages reduced the variety of goods on offer for satisfying particular needs. As a result there was less choice and less opportunity for acquiring a range of consumer goods and services and for conscious planning of the family budget.

The scarcity of consumer goods had not only economic but also important social consequences. More than anything else, there was a lack of fashionable, high-quality, imported goods which enjoyed great prestige. Gradually they came to form a special group of 'goods in great demand' and were virtually unavailable in the shops. It was simply impossible to buy them at the official price but speculators sold them at prices half as much again or twice as dear. Some of these goods found their way into the various systems for discretionary distribution by work collectives – for exceptional work, in response to particular needs and even as lottery prizes. Others were made available through special channels to 'the elite' occupying high positions in the social hierarchy – senior officials in Party and state bodies, high-ranking military personnel, members of the Academy of Sciences, leading writers, actors, painters, etc. Although the social status of these groups vis-à-vis their relationship to political power varied, they were supplied via similar channels.

The development of special channels for supplying privileged groups with scarce goods at fixed prices resulted in a situation where what was once a single nationwide consumer market, in which the purchasing power of every rouble was equal, split into at least two relatively independent markets with a different range of goods, price levels and purchasing power. At the same time, there was also a split in the channels for the concessional (or free) provision of services to different social groups. Better-equipped clinics provided with better-qualified staff and more effective drugs, comfortable sanatoria, special shops, hairdressers' salons, etc. were built for senior officials. They were offered special privileges in obtaining valuable books, and theatre and concert tickets. Their children were given priority in attending schools specializing in the teaching of physics and mathematics, biology or chemistry or where some of the subjects were taught in English, French or German. Even at airports and railway stations, VIP rooms were set aside for senior officials so that they did not have to rub shoulders with the ordinary mass of workers or share with them the hardships of the journey.

The emergence of an upper echelon of political leaders as a specific social stratum could be seen not only in its differential consumption of goods and services but also in a tendency to close ranks and in particular to marry predominantly within itself.

Entering into kinship relations with people from another social environment became increasingly undesirable and unacceptable.

The gradual transformation of senior Party and state officials from a professional into a social group led them to need a stratum of people who fully supported this order of things, shared the values of the elite, strove to join its ranks and, in expectation of this, took upon itself the task of establishing direct contacts with working people who adopted a critical attitude towards the 'bosses'. The attempt to achieve this aim contributed towards the development of an unwieldy bureaucratic administration that erected an increasingly high wall between the upper levels of political power and the mass of the people. Quite a large number of posts in this administration were occupied by the children, grandchildren and other relatives of 'the elite'. For working here ensured not only a high salary, social privileges, and preferential treatment but also good working conditions, frequent trips abroad, etc.

The shortage of production inputs that had developed – raw materials, energy, effective technology, etc, – had important social consequences in the formation and widespread development of what is known as 'shadow' economic relations, i.e. those not recorded in official statistics. Originally, these relations largely emerged under the stimulus of efforts by management to fulfil production plans which had not been backed up with centrally distributed inputs. Enterprise directors who had some supplies in stock but experienced a shortage of others tried to get hold of inputs in short supply by exchanging them among themselves. Then more complex types of 'shadow' operation appeared – for example, the temporary loan of workers 'through the back door' in exchange for absolutely essential goods, the fictitious writing-off of some finished output as rejects while actually using it to barter with suppliers, and so on. Naturally, such deals were either not recorded at all or falsely recorded. However, the managers found them very convenient and often unavoidable and they increased in volume.

In the field of 'shadow' economic relations, there was a much stricter ethical code than in the 'open' economy. Having given one's word, one had to keep it, otherwise one could be driven out of the business world through lack of trust. The fact that these 'shadow' deals were mainly carried in the heads of the participants allowed part of the proceeds to be used for personal needs, which did, indeed, often happen. As a result, a stratum of managers and economic administrators was formed who led, as it were, a double life – in the normal economy and in the 'shadow' one, operating either on the very borderline of the criminal law or beyond it. Sociologists would say that this stratum suffered from a 'divergence in status elements', meaning that according to some indices (type of post held, standard of living) it occupied a very high position, but according to others (legal position) a low one. From a luxurious office these people could well land up in the dock and even behind bars.

Another social group occupied a similar position – workers in the distributive, public catering and service sectors who had a particular relationship to the problem of consumer shortages. As we know from experience, various forms of speculation, false measures, underweighing, and fraudulent dealings with the customer and the state had, and unfortunately still have, a mass character here. Goods in short supply were sold under the counter at increased prices, low grades of goods were handed over as middle or top grades, milk was watered down, and sugar was deliberately kept in damp conditions in order to increase its weight. Top quality vegetables and fruit delivered to state warehouses for sale in the shops were replaced by poor quality produce and redirected to collective-farm markets in northern towns, to be sold at much higher prices. As a result of such operations, unearned income was acquired and shared out among various groups of workers in the distributive sector in proportions known only to them.

Curious changes in the attitudes of young people towards different types of job took place in the period. In the mid-1960s the lowest position on the scale of social prestige was occupied by work in agriculture and the next lowest by work in the distributive and service sectors. But in the 1980s that situation changed. After observing who was the quickest to buy a car, modern high-fi equipment, fashionable clothes, etc, a significant number of young people began to prefer jobs in the distributive and service sectors to more skilled but low-paid work.

However, perhaps the most dangerous phenomenon corrupting and crippling the structure of Soviet society in the period of 'stagnation' was the gradual fusion of operators in the shadow economy and the elite of the distributive sector with the corrupt section of the state and Party apparatus. All three groups needed this type of fusion since the first two had the real opportunity to line their pockets but had reason to fear control on the part of the administration and the law, while the third could safeguard the freedom and 'legality' of the actions of the first two groups, while having in their own right only a decent salary and some social privileges. When a mutually advantageous pact was made, officials 'closed their eyes' to illegal operations going on under their noses and gave managers and administrators the opportunity to 'make money out of nothing', and the latter, in their turn, allocated part of their illegal incomes to greasing the palms of those officials. As a result a powerful, stable and, it can be said, 'indestructible' mechanism was formed which extracted unearned incomes at the expense of the overwhelming mass of working people.

As a criminal activity, this mechanism should in principle have been exposed by the law. Large-scale financial operations were, after all, being carried out under the eyes and with the participation of dozens, hundreds, and sometimes thousands of people, some of whom were far from wishing to aid swindlers and tried to fight them. These people wrote to the State Procurator, to Party bodies, to the newspapers and called for help in exposing the criminals and for the necessary documents and statements to be produced. The corruption of the Party apparatus, however, was inevitably accompanied by corruption in the judicial bodies which took their cut of the profits. Prosecution of the Party and trading mafia was, therefore, mounted only in extreme circumstances, when it was unavoidable. It was, in any event, conducted without strict adherence to the law and tended towards either acquittal or a minimal sentence for the guilty parties. Even if the criminals did receive long terms of imprisonment, they were soon pardoned and released and many of them turned up at their posts again only a year or two later, at liberty to line their pockets at the expense of the public and the state.[10]

The emergence of mafioso-type groups can be likened to a cancer in the social organism. Beginning in the first instance in Georgia, Azerbaidzhan and Uzbekistan, in the course of a few years it transmitted a state of 'metastasis' throughout the whole country. As was noted at the 27th Congress of the Communist Party, large areas of the country came under the leadership of certain members of the Politburo and were therefore not subject to criticism from outside, let alone inside. Socialist legality did not operate within these areas and it was impossible to obtain justice there. People who took the risk of seeking justice by applying to higher authorities frequently became the victims of the ruthless mechanism in whose way they had stood. Today's press cites hundreds of such cases.

The majority of the general public could see what was going on before their eyes but did not believe it was possible to obtain justice. The socio-psychological result was mass alienation from society's aims and values and an indifference to the fate of public property which was more and more often seen as belonging to 'no-one' or, more precisely, to 'somebody else'. As a result, petty theft became extremely widespread, as did the practice of taking 'perks' from the job. People going home from work regularly took with them something for their own use: feed concentrates and milk from livestock farms, mineral fertilizer and part of the harvest from the fields, sausages from meat-processing plants, flour from bakeries, paint, turpentine, wallpaper and sanitary equipment from building sites, and so on and so forth. But perhaps worst of all was the fact that petty theft was becoming justified by public morality. For example, in answer to the sociologist's question, 'Why do many workers take home goods belonging to state or collective farms?', country people more often than not selected the answers: 'Because they cannot be bought anywhere', 'The prices are too high', 'They do not take much', 'The boss takes more', and so on.

It is evident that in the period of 'stagnation' certain phenomena could be observed in the economic and social fields in our society that witnessed to deep-seated social deformations and distortions of the very substance of socialism. Major social processes in that period had a negative character. The foundations of family life were being undermined, and the number of divorces was increasing more quickly than the number of marriages. The number of one-parent families, usually consisting of mother and children without the father, grew. Alcoholism and drunkenness were also gradually taking hold among women. Young people began to take drugs. The birth rate fell, mortality grew, and life expectancy decreased – particularly that of men. Adult crime and juvenile delinquency were on the increase and psychiatric illness and suicide became more frequent.

One would have thought that all this should have worried the leadership of the country, but in fact the 'high-ups' made no effort to know the truth about what was happening 'down below', while the middle ranks of the administration were reluctant to impart bad news to the 'high-ups', preferring to give the impression that everything was working well. The volume of published information on economic and especially social statistics was steadily decreasing. Whereas the figures for the All-Union Population Census of the USSR 1959 were published in dozens of volumes, in 1970 there were only five in all and in 1979 only one volume. Birth-rate, mortality and life expectancy figures disappeared from statistical reference books and the professional literature. Previously published information about migration between town and country, and different republics and regions, became 'state secrets'. The worse matters became in one or another field of activity, the larger the area of 'confidential' information.

Sociology which was intended to act as a 'feed-back' for social administration and to keep managers and those managed informed about the processes actually going on was superfluous in such a situation. More than that, it was dangerous and unpleasant. Sociologists who seemed not to understand that nobody wanted this information continued their research and demonstrated that many questions had not been solved and that social conditions in the country were deteriorating, and demanded some action from the authorities. This was the cause of some annoyance and induced the desire to stop up this source of information, which in many instances contradicted the official statistics. As a consequence, the results of objective research came to be declared 'a libel against Soviet reality' and attempts were made to discover 'gross methodological errors' and 'an uncritical attitude to bourgeois sociology' and so on and so forth. More and more areas of research were closed to sociologists, even such 'innocent' ones as marriage and divorce, the birth rate, migration of labour, and others. Many publishers began to refuse to handle sociological research.

Life was not easy at that time, particularly for the intelligentsia, and especially for creative people among them, but by no means only for them. The feeling, growing into the conviction, that society had lost its way, that everything was going wrong, that things could not go on like this for long, grew stronger among the majority of the people. Everyone expected that a turning point must be reached that would change life for the better. In moments of melancholy, we would say that our generation would be unlikely to live to see the 'dawn' but would probably just die in the dark. In our better moments, however, we did believe that there were, or would be, healthy forces in society capable of leading it on to the right path and we dreamed of taking part in the social renewal. Independently, we did what we could to bring the dawn closer, however difficult that might be. The best writers, journalists and social scientists tried hard to make the public aware, even if only in part, of their perceptions of what was happening, and to prepare it for essential changes.

The paper I gave at a seminar in Novosibirsk in 1983 on 'The social mechanism of economic development' (which later got to the West by ways unknown to me and made my name known to the Western reader) should be viewed in the context of this general process of critical re-evaluation of reality and the search for ways out of the situation that had developed.[11] In this paper I tried honestly to evaluate the economic processes taking place in our country, to define their social basis and to put forward a constructive plan of action. The seminar, which was attended by about a hundred progressive-minded academics, turned into a real feast of creative thought. We ourselves reacted to it as some sort of miracle – this was, after all, the time of 'stagnation'. However, this seminar itself demonstrated that a new stage of development was knocking at the door.

The collective 'brain storm' enabled us to understand more clearly the state of Soviet society in this period. It was characterized by i) the formation of social groups and strata whose consumption was parasitic in character and had as its source the exploitation of the major part of society; ii) the exceptionally unequal distribution of political power and the extremely low level of participation in government by the mass of working people; iii) a deterioration in people's standard of living; iv) the revival of authoritarian management methods in all areas of social life which held back the development of essential human creativity; v) extremely heavy ideological pressure on all forms of spiritual life in society; and vi) the breakdown of public ethics and a deterioration in people's social qualities. These tendencies were evidence of the decay rather than the strengthening of socialism and, essentially, of the 're-Stalinization' of society. Of course, history never repeats itself exactly but, with some adjustment to the change in conditions, the general direction taken by our society in the period of 'stagnation' can be considered to a certain extent as a move back to Stalinism.

To begin to move in the right direction, i.e. towards socialism, a sharp U-turn had to be made. Andropov made the first attempt at this but he had too little time to accomplish much. He succeeded only in engendering hope for the desired changes and creating a breath of spiritual fresh air in the stale social atmosphere. After announcing his intention of continuing Andropov's policy, which had rapidly achieved popularity, the conservatively-minded Chernenko managed in his short term of government to unleash a new attack on democracy.

After Chernenko's death in the spring of 1985, Mikhail Gorbachev was elected General Secretary of the Soviet Communist Party. Two months later, at a Plenary Session of the Central Committee, he came out with a programme for the radical restructuring of social relations in the Soviet Union, which the stratum of the intelligentsia with which I was closely associated greeted as a ray of hope.

The Sociology of Economic Reform

2

SOCIAL CONDITIONS AND PRE-ASSUMPTIONS OF REFORM

In the preceding chapter I discussed how I view the course of Soviet postwar history and which particular features of that history have, in the last analysis, made the radical restructuring of all social relations essential. However, the preconditions for the transformation of Soviet society that is taking place today are embodied not only in concrete historical reality but also in the deeper layers of social activity and in processes conditioned by the natural development of society and its technological and socio-economic progress. Three processes stand out in this respect.

The first is the development of the material and technological basis for production. This includes an increase in the quantity and complexity of applied technology, the constant replacement of successive generations of technology, and more capital-intensive production, automation and computerization. Although the pace of technological progress in our economy lags behind both the needs of the country and the pace of analagous processes in the highly developed countries, it does exert a considerable influence on our social development. One of the characteristic features of technological progress is the fact that over time the worker begins to put into action (to direct and control) an ever greater mass of labour already expended by society or, as Marxists put it, labour embodied in the conditions and means of production — factory premises, technological production lines, raw materials, other inputs, energy, etc. In the most developed economic sectors the value of the means of production is significantly higher than the income the worker stands to receive for the rest of his working life. Moreover, a worker's professionalism, sense of responsibility and quality of work determine not only the value of output but, what is scarcely less important, the efficiency (and even simply the state of maintenance) of the equipment in use. The cost of an explosion in a nuclear power station pile, a wrecked ship, or dozens of goods wagons carrying valuable freight destroyed in a train crash, cannot be paid back to society even by the most exemplary work of those whose negligence caused the accidents. It need only be recalled that the direct economic loss alone incurred by the accident at the Chernobyl Nuclear Power Station, which was the fault of members of staff, is estimated at 2,000 million roubles while the damage to human lives and health is incalculable in economic terms. This event, which shocked many countries, is a striking example of the increasing role of the human factor in production under conditions of technological progress.

Another factor that has the same effect is the ever grow-ing structural complexity of the economy and the increasing interdependency of its linkages. In the Soviet Union today there are more than 100 million different types of enterprise producing more than 20 million products. Supply lines between enterprises number many thousands of millions; the most important of them are established under planning procedures and are thus organized and regulated from the centre. This means that to a significant and growing extent the ultimate efficiency of the economy depends upon how skilfully, reliably and responsibly planning and finance officers are working, and whose interests they are serving.

The third factor, which must not be left out of account, is the increasing complexity of external control over work quality. The growing division and specialization of labour leads to a situation in which certain production, design and research teams become almost the only ones carrying out important economic functions. There is virtually nobody whose job it is to carry out on-line quality control and the product is in fact only tested in use. In essence, the whole of society comes to depend on the activity of such 'micro-monopolies'.

To take the activities of just one design institute, which 20 years ago confirmed the advisability and safety of locating a pulp and paper mill on the banks of Lake Baikal: the designers' calculations looked convincing enough on paper and the strong objections of many scientists, warning of probable pollution of the lake, were ignored. Years passed, the plant was built and production began. It soon became apparent that the lake was being polluted and a significant proportion of its fauna were dying. The plant is now being refitted for the production of an ecologically cleaner output (furniture) at a cost to the public of tens of millions of roubles.

A similar situation occurred with the project to divert part of the waters of Siberian rivers to Central Asia. Experts at the State Planning Commission exposed the inadequate socio-economic and technological basis of this scheme. It became clear that putting it into practice would not only have caused irreparable damage to the natural environment of Siberia but would also have had little effect on solving the really acute problems facing Central Asia. Work on the scheme was stopped in time, and the public breathed a sigh of relief. Once again, it was the 'human factor' that lay at the root of this near-disaster – this time in the form of irresponsible professional experts who approached the problem not from a social standpoint but from that of their own egotistical interests.

Quality control over physical output is made more difficult by the growing specialization and spatial division of labour, both in agriculture and industry. Nowadays a whole army of inspectors is needed to carry out operational supervision of quality. Moreover, since inspectors are human, have their own interests and do not always carry out their duties well enough, 'second-tier inspectors' must be placed over them, and so on. The result is an essentially bureaucratic system of control that is, firstly, expensive and unwieldy and, secondly, ineffective, for people adapt to even the cleverest forms of external control and learn to get round them. Not unnaturally, in many cases the percentage of faulty goods produced far exceeds intelligent guesses as to what is the normal quality of output.

Existing data reveal the poor quality of work by technologists and designers which is reflected in inefficient new technology. Frequently, under the guise of new technology, slight modifications of obsolescent equipment are produced that do not meet the needs of technological progress. The introduction in many enterprises in 1986 of a system of state quality control of output did at first produce a noticeable improvement in quality. It cannot, however, be regarded as a definitive solution of the problem. It is only a temporary measure operating in the period of transition to new methods of economic management. A genuinely forward-looking process, and one that is in keeping with the real spirit of socialism, is to change over from external control by specially appointed staff to, firstly, automatic quality control by special instruments and, secondly, control by the workers themselves with a personal interest in high quality work. The necessity for such a change is one more indication of the enhanced role of the human factor in the economy.

The second process which has indirectly prepared the ground for social restructuring consists in gradual changes in the quality of people engaged in social production. Under conditions of technological progress the 'human factor' in production should in principle become more manageable, more flexible, more responsive to management, more disciplined and dependable. In practice, however, in the opinion of most managers, people are becoming more difficult to manage. In the early 1980s this was the opinion of practically all state-farm directors and about 90 per cent of collective-farm chairpersons in West Siberia. This observation related not only to the ten years preceding the questionnaire but to the three years immediately preceding it, i.e. from their point of view the difficulties of personnel management were increasing 'before their very eyes'.

What was the matter? Why had this happened? It would seem that two basic principles were in operation here. The first was the constant rise in workers' educational and cultural levels and their knowledge of current events and developments both at home and abroad. People's personal self-awareness and awareness of their legal rights was developing together with an independence and critical quality of opinion, while their working and intellectual potential was growing, and their values and needs were becoming more complex and varied.

These changes were based on such fundamental processes as the constantly rising level of comprehensive education throughout the country, increased social, professional and regional mobility, the rapid urbanization of Soviet society, and the development of a mass communications network including television which could be relied upon to keep people living in remote areas in touch with the whole of Soviet society and the rest of the world. In 1939 out of every thousand in the working population, only 110 people had received secondary education up to between seven and ten years and 13 had received further education up to between 14 and 15 years. In 1987 the corresponding figures were 764 and 125. The number of workers with schooling of less than seven classes decreased in the same period from 877 to 111 per thousand. The urban population in the period 1939–86 increased from 32.5 per cent to 66.2 per cent, turning a predominantly rural and agricultural country into an urban and industrial one. From 1960 to 1986 the number of television transmitters in the country rose from 275 to 7,401, the number of television sets from 5 million to 85 million, and the number of radios and radio-relay receivers from 59 million to 187 million. These figures say much for the qualitative change in socio-cultural conditions.

This has naturally caused a considerable increase in the social needs and interests of people engaged in social production. Culturally developed people, after all, while being potentially the best workers, are more complex as objects of management. They assess work assigned to them more critically and value more highly the opportunity to make independent decisions that particularly affect their interests, such as the choice of various ways and means of doing the work. If, however, their activity is strictly regulated and there is no real independence of action, the most developed section of workers become alienated from their jobs and switch their interests and energy to other matters.

The third process which has made a considerable impact on social restructuring consists in a gradual lessening of economic pressure on workers to work intensively and efficiently. Behind this process lies greater individual freedom of choice with regard to specific forms of behaviour in the field of employment and earnings. In fact, in the early postwar years (not to mention the war itself) the average wage in our country did not exceed subsistence level. In order to secure a normal kind of existence – to provide themselves with enough food, clothing, fuel and household goods – most adult and even some juvenile members of the family had to work extremely hard in paid employment and in individual and domestic jobs. Changing jobs at will was at that time fairly complicated. Moreover, up until the mid-1950s there was no universal retirement pension, and people had to save up the necessary means to keep themselves in old age. In 1940 only four million people were in receipt of state pensions, and the average pension was only 75 roubles a year.

Since then the situation has changed radically. From 1960 to 1987 alone, average real income per person employed increased 2.8 times, wages and salaries 2.5 times, retail sales of goods and services per head of population four times, the number of people in receipt of a pension 2.7 times, and the total paid out in pensions almost seven times. At the present time Soviet living standards, although not satisfying the needs of most social groups, significantly exceed both the physiological and socially conditioned subsistence level. Although state benefits for retirement, invalidity, and temporary incapacity for work likewise remain comparatively low, they do free most people from having to save up all their lives for a 'rainy day'. An important factor in the freedom of economic behaviour of young people is the common practice of parents giving some financial and practical help to their grown-up children and their families. According to our researches, about two-thirds of rural families provide their grown-up children living in the towns not only with money, but with meat, butter, potatoes and other vegetables, fruit, berries, etc. No less common is the help given to children by parents in the towns.

Economic pressure to work hard is also lessened by the absence of unemployment, indeed, by the large number of job vacancies in most sectors, regions and towns due to a labour shortage. More than a quarter of all industrial enterprise directors in Altai consider the main factor preventing the full utilization of their workforces to be the general shortage of labour in the towns. Sixty-three per cent actually named enterprises that systematically 'entice' workers by offering higher wages, better social and living conditions, an easier work regime, and so on. Competition between enterprises gives many workers the opportunity to earn good pay, without driving themselves too hard. In contrast, there is the recent experience of 120,000 redundant workers being dismissed from the railways. The average cut of 10–12 per cent in the total number of railway workers not only reduced freight costs but also activated the remaining section of workers, who began to work better and to show more initiative and a greater sense of responsibility.

It must be added that in the course of several five-year plan periods money income rose more rapidly than the production of consumer goods and services. The stable price level of basic food products (bread, meat, milk and other things), combined with the growing scarcity of goods and services, caused a rapid rise in savings bank deposits. From 1960 to 1986 the number of deposits increased 3.5 times, the average sum deposited nearly seven times, and the total value of savings 25 times. Today the average amount of money deposited in a savings bank is approximately seven times the monthly wage of agricultural workers, while total deposits comprise 80 per cent of the annual wage bill. A significant number of people can, therefore, afford to take a long break from work, and perhaps look for a better job.

Finally, the wages system that has been formed as a result of historical circumstance is, unfortunately, far from satisfying any criterion of social equality. Thus, different wages are paid for exactly the same work in different offices, factories, and regions, while fundamentally different skills are often paid at the same rate. This also materially weakens the economic pressure to take on intensive and skilled work and creates a certain dislocation prompting different social and demographic groups to select strategies regarding employment and earnings which are very often not in the interests of society as a whole.

Two possible extremes stand out. On the one hand, the objective is to maximize earnings through unusually intensive and highly skilled work (in agriculture, families on a team contract come into this category; in gold mining, teams of prospectors operating on an economic accounting basis; in construction, seasonal casual labour (the 'tent-dwellers') who come to the Urals, Siberia and the Far East from regions of labour surplus and who work seven to eight months, seven days a week and 13–14 hours a day). On the other hand, there is the aim of maximizing the pursuit of personal well-being and leisure by keeping paid employment to a minimum and accepting a comparatively low wage. This strategy is characteristic of young people living in comfort with their parents or in receipt of their support, of women with young children, people in poor health, the older section of the population, and others. Of course, between these two extremes there is a wide range of intermediate strategies.

In so far as objective economic pressures to work are at the moment comparatively weak, the choice of a specific type of behaviour with regard to employment and earnings depends in the first instance on a person's value system, and, in particular, the relative value attached either to higher earnings or to more free time. Sociological research shows that for many social groups in our society these values are close or at least comparable to each other. For example, in one survey of Moscow workers commended for their high levels of productivity, they were asked to rank incentives for improving their work in order of the value they attached to them. The top position was given to financial reward – all the workers pointed to its powerful effect as an incentive. The second place was given to the granting of extra long holidays (83 per cent). The average increase in the length of time between jobs reflects the increasing importance attached to free time; whereas in 1970 the average interval between jobs was 28 days, by the 1980s it was 40 days.

The above remarks indicate that technological progress, specialization and co-operation in production considerably increase the role played by the 'human factor' in the economy. At the same time, the rapid social and cultural development of workers and the weakening economic pressures on them to work make management of the 'human factor' in production more complex or, to be more precise, make it less responsive to administrative and bureaucratic methods of management. This gives rise to many acute contradictions and leads to a loss of efficiency in the economy.

The only genuinely efficient management system possible today is one based on knowledge and consideration of the values, needs and interests of people taking part in economic activity or, in other words, one that is capable of regulating their behaviour by influencing their interests. Since the interests of different demographic, national and regional, professional and other groups of people are not only not identical but are in a constant state of change, the system for managing economic behaviour must also be flexible, adaptable, diverse, and sensitive to the changing circumstances and conditions of working people's lives. The inflexibility of previously accepted forms between which there gushes a constant flow of uncontrollable economic activity dictated by vital interests is categorically contra-indicated for such a system.

Workers' interests take many forms today. Along with adequate wages, most of them want to do work that is useful and interesting and which provides moral satisfaction and self-respect in comfortable working conditions; they want to be able to work with developed technology and enjoy convenient work schedules; and they want regular holidays which they can make good use of. Many want to take an active part in workers' management. There is an extremely high level of interest in receiving housing accommodation from the state, skilled medical care, places in creches and day nurseries, and free vouchers to stay in holiday sanatoria and rest homes. Reliable organization of the supply of fresh foodstuffs and manufactured goods – fashionable and attractive clothes, shoes, furniture, and scarce consumer durables – is highly valued. The younger section of the population aims for higher qualifications, more knowledge and skills, promotion up the career ladder, and greater professionalism in management. In those enterprises, therefore, where incentives are only offered in the form of 'roubles', a significant part of human interests remains untouched, and managerial efforts do not bring the expected results.

The system of management that was in operation until 1987 and in many respects still survives to this day was characterized by excessive centralization, extreme rigidity, and poor adaptability to different and changing conditions of place and time. Although economic administrators did try, by one method or another, to struggle against obsolete instructions, the potential of most workforces has been utilized rather inefficiently. This applies to manpower resources, the means of production, and to natural resources, which are still being wastefully used.

Let us begin with manpower. Most workers point to the fact that their working and intellectual potential is being considerably under-utilized. According to sociological research carried out in towns and villages in various parts of the country, only about a quarter (at the most, a third) of those questioned considered that they were working to their full potential. The remainder considered that they were doing only a fraction of what they could do, given a better organization of production and a creative search for ways to increase production efficiency. For example, in 1984 in villages in Altai this opinion was expressed by 80 per cent of agronomists and veterinary surgeons, 78 per cent of section and unit managers and 79 per cent of state-farm workers and collective farmers.

On the best farms the labour potential of the workforce was more fully utilized than on the poorest ones. Whereas on the latter, 83 per cent of the workers were, in their own estimation, working below their capacity, on the former the figure was 68 per cent. Essentially, however, the difference is not great, and utilization of the workforce's potential capabilities on the best farms is also very low. The chief factors preventing good work were named by the majority of respondents as poor organization of production, inadequate work incentives, inefficient management, stupid and petty supervision by Soviet and Party administrative bodies, and so on. A lot of working time was consistently lost, for example, through lengthy hold-ups on assembly lines due to organizational or technical reasons or to undisciplined workers not turning up for work. Some working time was spent unproductively in the performance of social duties and assignments which are more often than not a mere concession to formalism and bureaucracy. According to a number of studies, approximately 20 per cent of working time in the Soviet economy is used unproductively.

The following finding also testifies to the under-utilization of our workforce potential. Heads of sections, farms and workteams on state and collective farms in Altai were asked whether they had enough workers to do the work that had to be done. Sixty-five per cent replied that there were not enough workers, 32 per cent that there were sufficient and 3 per cent that there were too many. The question was then asked: how would they estimate the number of people they needed, if they were allowed independently to set the level of wages, the workload and the composition of the workforce within the constraints of the same wage bill. Forty per cent replied that there would still be insufficient workers, 18 per cent that there would be enough, and 42 per cent that there would be 15–20 per cent more than necessary.

For many years the natural desire of some groups of people to augment their income by working overtime has also been under-exploited. In 1982 in towns in West Siberia additional paid work was performed by only 18 per cent of such persons, whereas another 27 per cent expressed the desire to obtain such work. And although industry was experiencing an appreciable manpower shortage, legal restrictions in operation did not permit people, who were willing to work more in order to earn more, to satisfy the demand for labour. To some extent this reflects a certain wariness evident in Soviet society towards people wishing to achieve a substantial increase in their earnings by working overtime, as though they were thus expressing a non-socialist ideology.

This is probably inexplicable to the Western reader. After all, the very principle of socialism states: 'From each according to his ability, to each according to his work', thus, as it were, urging all members of society to work more and better, with the promise that life will be better for them as a result. What's going on then? How is it possible that an article by a well-known publicist, G. S Lisichkin, under the heading 'Is it shameful to earn a lot?' uses now this argument, now that, to prove that to have a high income is not in itself shameful – it is shameful only if it is not earned by working. Here, it seems to me, we are dealing with a sort of mass 'aberration' from a socialist viewpoint, with a widely held conviction that 'you don't get rich by honest labour' and that, therefore, anyone living well and not in want is to some degree a cheat, swindler or bribe-taker.

This feature of present-day social consciousness makes any restructuring of economic relations more difficult. Many people not only do not themselves try to work more intensively and efficiently and to show initiative at work, and not only have a judgmental attitude towards those who are trying to, but obstruct such efforts as best they may.

For example, family contract teams in agriculture have achieved a sharp rise in labour productivity and an increase in food production. At the same time, the opinion that this way of organizing production should be developed was expressed by only 42 per cent of the rural population. About 30 per cent of those questioned did not declare either for or against these family teams, but 11 per cent actually thought that they encouraged 'self-seeking and greed, and made people work for their own benefit only' and were therefore out of tune with our society. This shows that many Soviet people quite simply regard a high income as a negative phenomenon irrespective of whether serious and creative work was done to obtain it and whether it brought great benefit to society. As a survival of the ideology of the 1920s and 1930s, this kind of wariness in respect of high earnings does not reflect the interests of our society today and undermines the possibility of a more rapid pace of social and economic development.

The serious under-utilization of the creative, intellectual and, I would say, entrepreneurial potential of our workers is clearly demonstrated when a workforce changes over to contractual payment, family contract work, or small-scale co-operative and individual forms of production, where pay is directly related to output. A change in economic relations radically changes the attitude of workers to work, develops their creative and entrepreneurial activity, and raises their productivity substantially (often several times over).

Where families work on contractual terms they are paid for their output and they make all production and management decisions themselves. The Soviet press abounds with examples of the high level of efficiency of the family form of work organization. The following is just one example (from the newspaper *Sovetskaya Rossiya*, 10 December 1987). The Glushkov family, having contracted for the care of 150 collective-farm cows, obtain on average 5,219kg of milk per cow per year, while the corresponding figure for the collective farm is only 3,175kg. Their total earnings over the previous year averaged about 1,000 roubles per month, while the average for the collective farm was approximately half that figure. This, together with many other examples, shows that under normal conditions the majority of workers consistently under-utilize their potential.

When discussing the under-utilization of society's intellectual and professional potential, mention must be made of such an 'unnatural' phenomenon as the desire of some highly-skilled workers to do simple manual work that does not correspond to their professional qualifications. In the mid-1980s, the number of persons with engineering degrees and diplomas among ordinary production workers in the oil and gas industries and a number of other sectors was more than 10 per cent, and sometimes even up to 15 per cent. The reason was simple; at that time unskilled workers received much higher wages than engineers, although their work was considerably easier and involved less responsibility and nervous tension. Workers who had qualified as engineers through correspondence courses put their diplomas away in a drawer and remained in the same jobs, rarely agreeing to take on what one would have thought was a more interesting and prestigious position as a foreman or engineer. In fact, a special government decision was taken forbidding people with higher education to take the jobs of unskilled workers, but it was not in fact observed and was rescinded altogether in 1987.

The shortage of high-quality food products and other consumer goods, the difficulty of converting earnings into useful goods and services, the possibility of considerably increasing personal income not by increasing 'labour output' but by a simple change of job and/or place of residence, the curtailment of any initiative, the predominance of anti-democratic organizational structures and the command style and methods of management even among the best workers – all these undermined the emphasis on intensive, creative work. The majority of people were in fact completely alienated from social values, lost the desire to work hard, and to look after and use public property as their own. A situation had developed of utter indifference to the common good.

Long years of a passive alienated existence have undoubtedly left their mark not only on the present behaviour of people as regards the economy but also on their habits and values – in other words on their social quality as workers. Once they had become accustomed to an irresponsible attitude to their jobs, workers gradually lost all their professionalism and habits of intensive, purposeful work and became used to being idle and showing no initiative. Alienation and indifference, irresponsibility and sluggishness, scepticism and cynicism became the norms of social conduct and were accepted as received standards of behaviour. Throughout the economy, increasingly wasteful use was made not only of labour but of technology, energy, fuel, raw materials, and so on.

Innumerable examples of great losses of valuable materials can be found in the Soviet press. For example, on average 20 per cent of cement is wasted, more than a quarter of agricultural produce, and more than a half of all timber, etc. New machines and equipment are piling up in many factories which are in no hurry to instal them. Kept in completely unsuitable conditions, equipment gradually becomes unfit for use and is often thrown out as scrap without ever having been used. It is particularly painful when this happens in the case of imported equipment that has been acquired with foreign currency. Thus, on 1 October 1987, stocks of uninstalled equipment kept in warehouses belonging to ministries and government departments throughout the country totalled, according to the State Statistical Committee, almost 15,000 million roubles, including imported equipment valued at 4,800 million roubles, and these stocks were increasing in volume year by year. A rise in economic growth rates is hardly to be expected when such an attitude to public property exists.

Public alienation from the interests of society has also led, and is still leading, to irreparable destruction of the natural environment. The Aral Sea is under threat of extinction; the possibility of saving it is extremely problematical. Long-term neglect of ecological problems and the drive by agricultural enterprises to maximize current harvests have resulted in a marked deterioration in the natural environment of the countryside, above all the impoverishment of the soil and the depletion of local water resources, including small rivers and underground waters. The creation of large numbers of small ponds for breeding fish has led to excessive evaporation of water, the raising of subsoil waters and the consequent warming up of significant areas of agricultural land and sometimes of populated areas as well. Uncontrolled and in many ways unwise channelling of water for the irrigation of fields has diminished the flow of many rivers and created an extremely complex situation in nearly all interior reservoirs and basins. All this has now made it essential to adopt a strategy of water use that is new in principle.

In many regions in the European part of the country, which have a low percentage of woodland, an extremely serious situation has arisen regarding the conservation of existing forests. As a result, rivers are becoming shallower, the condition of the soil is deteriorating, and there is a reduction in the size of the forest belt as a result of which ravines are created and crop yields decrease. Government departments have attempted to explain this away by claiming that crop rotations based on the chemicalization of agriculture do not need the forest belt. However, in the steppe zone of the country, the afforestation of arable land is far below the level needed to ensure the relative independence of the harvest from weather conditions.

The not always rational intensification of farming frequently leads to soil erosion as a result of which agriculture suffers great damage. The once extremely rich Black Earth regions of the Central Russian Plain have, over the past three decades, lost a significant amount of humus, i.e., its fertile stratum has become considerably thinner. Every year, when the snow melts, a great deal of fertile earth is washed away because the structure of the land has been weakened by unwise cultivation. Agriculture suffers colossal damage from dust storms which lift the weakened soil into the air and carry away the most fertile top stratum. The use of an ever-increasing amount of chemical fertilizers and herbicides results in an accumulation of chemically harmful substances in the soil, water and agricultural produce. The press has systematically published reports about the destruction or depletion of the country's fish resources and the felling of valuable forest massifs, including those situated on watersheds, which leads to the rapid destruction of natural ecological systems.

At first glance, all these phenomena are different in nature and bring different consequences. In fact, however, they have one basic cause – the existing system of economic management does not meet present requirements. Hence, in particular, the steady decrease in general economic growth rates and national income growth which has attracted the attention of both politicians and economists. Thus the average annual rate of growth of national income in 1966–70 was 7.8 per cent, in 1971–5 5.7 per cent, in 1976–80 4.3 per cent and in 1981–5 only 3.6 per cent. The growth rates of gross agricultural output for the same period were as follows: 3.9, 3.5, 1.7 and 1.1 per cent. The trend of most other principal economic indicators was of a similar order. For example, the average annual rate of growth of real income per head of population decreased from 5.9 per cent in 1966–70 to 2.1 per cent in 1981–5. Things were no better, if not worse, with regard to qualitative indicators of social development. Thus, the Soviet economy's technological lag behind the world's most developed states increased while Soviet products became less competitive in the world market, thus forcing the country to increase its export of raw unprocessed materials and natural resources.

In his assessment of these trends, Mikhail Gorbachev rightly described the Soviet economy in the mid-1980s as being in a pre-crisis situation. The radical restructuring of the whole system of the management of society was called for, beginning with the economy. Before discussing such a restructuring, however, we must briefly examine the system of economic management that was in operation in the first half of the 1980s.

ECONOMIC MANAGEMENT ON THE EVE OF REFORM

Marx and Engels, looking into the distant future, conceived of a socialist economy as a kind of 'single factory' directly managed from the centre and requiring neither money nor market. This concept was mistaken. In fact, a socialist economy can function only when enterprises are economically autonomous, both from one another and from the main agent of social ownership – the state. In these circumstances, their integration, i.e. the co-ordinated interaction of all the elements of the economy, is secured through a combination of the 'vertical' linkages of state economic management with the 'horizontal' linkages between enterprises.

The first type of linkage is evident in direct orders, regulations and instructions to enterprises from state organizations. For example, compulsory plans for the production of certain types of output are handed down to enterprises, financial and material resources are allocated to them (the 'funding system'), they are attached by the centre to specific equipment suppliers, and their 'surplus' profits have to be paid into the state budget. Another aspect of this type of linkage is the response of enterprises to state organizations – for example, suggestions that some items in the output production plan be replaced by others, consent or refusal to carry out various instructions, requests for the allocation of additional resources, suggestions that new technology be introduced, etc. As regards 'horizontal' linkages, their chief purpose is the exchange between enterprises of finished output, production inputs, services and information. 'Vertical' linkages reflect in the first instance the relations of centralized planning, whereas 'horizontal' linkages reflect market relations.

Not a single economy in the modern world is based exclusively on either 'horizontal' or 'vertical' linkages, i.e. is either a purely market or a completely planned economy. Each of the two economic systems – centralized planning and free enterprise – to some extent makes use of both types of linkage, although their role and relationship do vary. Market relations play the decisive role in the operation and development of a capitalist economy, extending not only to final output, but also to manpower, financial resources, etc. State intervention has in this case an auxiliary function. Conversely, in a socialist economy the chief role is played by centralized planning and administration, while a more modest role is assigned to market relations. However, the common view in Soviet society that a socialist economy should preclude the action of market mechanisms in principle (as 'contradictory to its character') has no foundation in fact. This has caused, and is still causing, great damage to the country's economic development.

The fundamental characteristic of a socialist economy is the social ownership of the means of production. However, the socialization of production is by no means an end in itself, but merely the most efficient way of achieving the social aims of socialism. It does not in itself strictly predetermine the forms of organizing production, but leaves plenty of scope for searching out, testing and selecting types of linkage most appropriate to the level of economic development, social structure, and the nature of the problems to be solved. The principal function of social ownership is to create the economic basis for the democratic organization of society. This can be achieved in practice, however, only when there is a democratic organization of the whole 'chain' of property relations: ownership, distribution and use of the components of property, with self-management by the workforce and a position of equality in their economic relations one with another. As a rule, the level of democratization in the utilization of socialist property is greater, the more pluralistic the forms of ownership and distribution of the means of production, the broader the range of economic linkages, and the wider the selection of economic structures. The whole path of development of our economy shows that a high level of efficiency and the balanced planning of production are achieved not by restriction and uniformity but, on the contrary, through diversification of the forms of economic linkage and not least by the development of market relations.

It must not be thought that the state has to be the only owner of socialist property. In fact, its owners can and should be state enterprises, collective farms, local authorities (Soviets), social organizations (the Communist Party, the Communist Youth League, trade unions, and so on), trust funds (such as the Cultural Fund, the Children's Fund, the Fund for the Protection of Nature, and so on), small co-operatives and associations, small sub-contractors, etc. All these economic agents must be linked through business partnerships and friendly competition, not subordinate one to another but occupying positions of equality. The network of linkages can in practice develop in two different ways. If the linkages used by planning and regulatory bodies are dominant, the network becomes purely administrative and bureaucratic. If, however, direct linkages between producers in the form of the market exchange of goods and services have a leading role, the system becomes more democratic, flexible and efficient.

Despite all its limitations, the 'classical' market is, in fact, a democratic (and therefore anti-bureaucratic) economic institution. Within the framework of its exchange relationships, all participants are at least formally equal, no-one is subordinate to anyone else. Buyers and sellers act in their own interests and nobody can make them conclude deals they do not want to conclude. The buyers are free to select sellers who will let them have goods on the most advantageous terms, but the sellers too can choose buyers offering the best price. Of course, the apparent democracy and fairness of the market makes for a great deal of harshness: the market enriches some and ruins others, by no means always in accordance with genuinely efficient economic performance. Here the spontaneity of the market is demonstrated, its characteristic element of chance. There is a general tendency, however, for those enterprises, workforces and individuals to succeed that work better, run their operations more intelligently and prudently, are more aware of technological progress and the changeability of consumer demand, etc. As a result, despite its social costs, the market mechanism does promote efficient economic growth.

The task of a socialist society is to retain the advantages of centralized economic management, while at the same time finding ways of combining it with a greater stimulation of market mechanisms – in other words to reinforce the network of vertical economic linkages with highly developed horizontal ones. Of course, this by no means implies that the planned economy will be replaced by a market economy, as commentators in the West sometimes claim. A socialist market, even at the highest level of development, will remain regulated in the sense that it will be subject to strong direction in keeping with the state economic strategy. Nevertheless – and this needs to be emphasized – this same strategy must without fail be based on knowledge of the objective laws of the market and must not merely refrain from acting against these laws but, on the contrary, must apply them in the interests of society. Only then can the combination of planned economic management and socialist market activity be more efficient than the predominance of either planned or market relations.

How to achieve the necessary combination of these mechanisms, retaining the positive features of each without at the same time allowing them to come into conflict and permitting insoluble contradictions to develop, is an extremely complex matter. So far not a single country with a centrally planned economy has successfully solved this problem, although a certain amount of useful experience has been gained. One need only refer to the successful growth of the Hungarian economy in the 1970s and the Chinese economy in the early 1980s.

As regards the Soviet Union, the system of economic management in operation until very recently was not designed to combine market and planning mechanisms. 'Vertical' command linkages managed by bureaucratic structures completely stifled the 'horizontal' linkages between producers which only formally had a market character.

Different groups of Soviet experts, while agreeing that this system has had its day and requires changing, nevertheless diverge in their concrete evaluations of its essential nature and origin. Some of them consider that the creation of the administrative-command model of economic management in the 1930s was natural, necessary and progressive. Thus, they underline the virtues of this model, such as the possibility of achieving major strategic objectives through a concentration of resources, the rapid development of new sectors and types of production, the effective redistribution of a significant proportion of national income through the state budget, etc. The successful industrialization of the economy in a historically short space of time and the rapid development of a defence industry in the war years are put forward, inter alia, to substantiate the efficiency of this management model in the conditions of the 1930s. Other experts, however, whose opinion I share, believe that a continuation of Lenin's New Economic Policy (NEP) combining centralized planning with development of the market would have allowed the same problems to be solved with greater economic success and incomparably fewer social and political sacrifices.

Experts are also discussing whether it is correct to identify the present-day system of economic management with that formed and operated in the 1930s. Originally, the thesis that the two systems are essentially identical, i.e. that they coincide in all major features and differ only in unimportant detail, was widespread. However, more in-depth analysis has led some researchers to conclude that the similarity is superficial rather than genuine. Thus, B. P. Kurashvili demonstrates that the economic mechanism of the 1930s was a systemic, integral and sufficiently effective means of achieving the aims set in that period. Over many decades, however, it became overlaid with additional bureaucratic regulations and norms and this, combined with a fundamental change in the conditions of economic development, has led to the internal dislocation and disintegration of today's administrative system. While outwardly remaining the same, the economic mechanism of the 1980s has in practice changed into an internally disintegrated look-alike of the 1930s mechanism, which has lost the ability to secure effective economic development and acts as a brake on technological and socio-economic progress. In the same way, a tree that is rotten on the inside looks normal from the outside but is in fact incapable of bearing either flowers or fruit.

If, however, it is only the outward form of the previous mechanism that has survived, how then is the Soviet economy managed, consisting as it does of hundreds of industries, many thousands of product lines, and hundreds of thousands of enterprises? The fact that it is not only not falling apart but is developing, however inefficiently, indicates that under the cover of relations dating back to the 1930s a new system of linkages and economic levers has formed and gradually replaced the previous one. Using this hypothesis, two young Soviet economists, P. O. Aven and V. M. Shironin, set out to explain the real social character of the present system of Soviet economic management. By applying economic and sociological analysis, they came to the conclusion that the present-day variant is not so much a 'command economy', as is usually supposed, as an 'economy of bargaining and deals' among vertical linkages.

In fact, in their opinion, three main features distinguish a genuine command economy: a) fairly complete and sound knowledge by senior management of the potential at the lower level; b) the formulation of instructions and orders by senior management on the basis of this knowledge; and c) strict accountability by lower levels for the non-fulfilment of instructions and orders from above.

In the early 1930s these conditions were more or less met. In the last fifty years, however, the complexity of the economy has increased manifold. Central economic and industrial management bodies therefore have an extremely vague idea of the actual potential and resources of enterprises for which they are responsible. However, if the first condition is not fulfilled, the others cannot be fulfilled either. This means that the command system of management in its previous 'classical' form cannot exist in present-day conditions. Nevertheless, management bodies must carry out their functions at least to some acceptable level. They are therefore forced, consciously or unconsciously, openly or behind closed doors, to take on a new form – namely, a management system based on 'bargaining and deals'.

Within this kind of system senior levels do not simply command lower ones (although administrative commands do continue to exist in a 'pure' form) but enter into a strange sort of dialogue, leading to the conclusion of an agreement between the two parties. In the course of reaching an agreement, the participants operate with the particular bargaining counters that they have at their disposal. For top management these are, above all, the allocation of material resources, finance, centralized investments, prices for new products, the share-out of profits between enterprise and state, various incentives for managers, their promotion, etc. By using these 'arguments', senior officials can encourage those under them who meet them halfway and punish those who are obstinate and do not want to submit to orders.

As regards lower levels of management especially in enterprises, in bargaining with the boss they use such 'arguments' as acceptance/non-acceptance of output plans from above, acceptance of a heavier workload and the working out of extra commitments by way of response, i.e. agreement to participate in periodic campaigns such as helping with the harvest, voluntary work on building sites, etc. Curiously, not only deeds but empty words can be used as 'arguments', in particular, promises made at the highest level about unprecedented harvests, the introduction of advanced technology, the commissioning of long-delayed projects, etc. In so far as 'bargaining' around production plans and the supply of inputs is conducted in conditions of inadequate managerial information about potential capacity, the relationships established as a result are vague and flexible and do not entail any very strict accountability for failure to meet obligations.

This system is a special type of 'hybrid' of centralized planning and the market, one which is, however, specific, even, it could be said, 'transformed', where the parties do not operate with such classical concepts as goods, their quality and price, but with the possibilities that exist for affecting their partner's ability to function. There is still very little research or writing about the real economic and social characteristics of this odd 'hybrid'. Its analysis is an important task facing the scientific discipline – new to the Soviet Union – of economic sociology. However, even without special study it is clear that the 'economy of bargains and deals' of the 1980s, just like the 'command economy' of the 1930s, is based to a decisive extent on vertical linkages between bosses and their subordinates and takes no account of horizontal relations between economic units of equal standing.

The specific features of the system of economic management now undergoing reform have frequently been described at home and abroad. A detailed analysis does not come within the scope of this book. However, so that the reader may have a more precise idea about the social problems of restructuring, it is necessary at least briefly to describe the system and its salient features.

In my opinion, the main contradiction within this system lies in the mix of economic and legal autonomy enjoyed by enterprises and the predominance of administrative and bureaucratic methods of management by the state. In essence, the economic autonomy of production units, the fact that each of them has the use of certain public assets and is obliged to use them efficiently, assumes the existence of a dense network of direct economic linkages between producers, i.e. the functioning of a market. The administrative method of running the economy on the basis of detailed targeted planning is, however, by its very nature bound to ignore objective economic laws, including the laws of the market. As a result, the economic system finds itself 'falling between two stools' which clearly cannot lead to positive results. Let us examine the concrete forms taken by this contradiction.

i). One of the most important ways of increasing economic efficiency is for producers to try and select the range of output that allows them to make the best use of resources and to satisfy public demand for goods in short supply. However, in the Soviet Union the volume, variety, delivery dates and technology of production of the bulk of output are fixed for enterprises in the form of compulsory state plans having the force of law. The central planning bodies and their local departments do not possess sufficiently comprehensive and reliable information about enterprise operations, particularly their resources. They also have only an approximate idea of actual demand for various types of equipment, raw materials, intermediate products, consumer goods and foodstuffs. In these circumstances, the only reliable way of setting planning targets is the notorious 'benchmark planning' when a 2–4 per cent growth is added on to the estimated volume of output achieved the previous year. This method of planning assumes that an enterprise only has to make a little more effort to achieve similar targets under any economic circumstances and that a comparatively slight increase in volume will always find a customer. The impact of consumers and their real purchasing power on the structure of production is almost completely disregarded. True, enterprise demand for production resources is formally reflected in their orders to planning bodies, but it is reflected in a distorted form. On the one hand, this demand is exaggerated in the expectation that in conditions of shortage the order will be only partially fulfilled. On the other hand, consumers are often ill-informed about new equipment which they could have ordered and so cannot provide any economic stimulus to ensure the rapid production of equipment that they need. As regards public demand for consumer goods, it was hardly studied at all and for years the selection of goods produced by the light industries, including food industries, remained almost unchanged.

Since they are strictly bound by the plan, enterprises do not have the right to change the volume or the variety of output even if they have the resources to produce goods in great demand on the most favourable terms. They have for that matter no particular incentive to do so, since their performance is evaluated almost exclusively on the basis of percentage of plan fulfilment (as a rule expressed in volume, the so-called 'gross' indicators – roubles, tons, metres, etc). This percentage is a far more important criterion for awarding incentives or penalizing workforces than are economic results – the amount of profit, for example, or greater or less profitability. The functioning of such a planning system gives rise to the notorious drive by enterprises for 'gross' production (regardless of variety and quality) and leads on the one hand to the production of a large quantity of goods for which there is no demand and on the other to an even greater shortage of many essential goods so that public demand for modern and high-quality goods is not satisfied.

ii). Goods produced in socialist enterprises are disposed of on the basis of relations of exchange, i.e. they are either sold for money to other enterprises (machinery, equipment, energy, raw materials) or to the wholesale trade. Formally, then, buyer-seller relations, i.e. a market, do exist. Prices, however, are fixed not by the negotiating parties but centrally. They are worked out and confirmed by the State Price Committee, which was specifically created for this purpose. True, it manages to set 'only' a few tens of thousands of prices annually, while the total number of prices of various types of goods amounts to millions. But centrally-priced goods make up the greater part of gross output.

What methodology is used to fix prices? In principle prices should take into account the level of socially necessary expenditure on the production of each type of goods, the comparative usefulness of goods in satisfying demand, and also the relationship of supply to demand. The State Price Committee does not have the information necessary to do this, however, especially because the extent to which demand for a particular product is satisfied varies considerably from region to region, between town and country, etc. The way out of this situation is simple: the enterprise producing the new output presents to the State Price Committee a unit cost calculation, this is 'checked' (although the necessary data for this do not exist) and confirmed, a certain fixed percentage of profit is then added to the cost of production and . . . the pricing exercise is completed. Under this pricing system high-quality and scarce goods often turn out cheaper than second-grade and old stock. Enterprises thus have an incentive not to cut but to increase production costs since profit is calculated as a percentage of costs.

An important feature of this system of setting prices is the importance attached to maintaining price stability. The motivation is quite understandable: the suppression of inflationary tendencies. In practice, however, they do even so appear, as it were by-passing fixed prices. This is done through the formal updating of a range of goods, the replacement of some models, types and sizes of goods by others which allows new prices to be fixed. This practice gives rise to unjustifiable differences in profitability. As a rule, the older the product line, the more unprofitable it is, despite the fact that it could be badly needed by the public or by industry. Thus the necessary connection is lost between the quality of production and the demand for goods which may even be in short supply, on the one hand, and the level of economic achievements, on the other. The general price index of both capital and consumer goods is climbing and more quickly than if prices had been established by agreement between buyers and sellers.

iii). By the very act of setting enterprises a plan for the production of specific types of output, the state undertakes to guarantee its sale. To this end each enterprise is handed a list of the organizations which it must supply with its output. This precludes any sort of competition between enterprises producing similar products. The enterprise cannot select the cheapest and most reliable supplier but is obliged to take whichever it is given. The situation is made still worse by the fact that payment for goods to be delivered is usually made by the bank as soon as the despatch notes are received, i.e. even before the recipient can check that the quality of the goods received is satisfactory, that all the parts have been supplied, that complex equipment is properly assembled, etc. As a result a significant amount of equipment turns out not to be ready for use and has to be brought up to standard by the purchasing enterprise. This happens particularly often in agriculture, where workers are as a general rule obliged to dismantle equipment, replace missing parts, do repairs, and bring up to the necessary standard new tractors and combines just delivered from the factory.

Of course, the all-Union and Republican State Planning Commissions do not, and cannot, know the raw material needs of each and every enterprise. Deliberately exaggerated orders are not believed and there would not in any case be sufficient resources to satisfy them. Orders are therefore only partially satisfied and it is a rare coincidence when the resources allocated (making up part of the order) coincide with the actual demand (also making up a part of it). Much more often too much of some resources and too little or none of others is supplied. Under conditions of general scarcity enterprises take everything they are given, accumulating large stocks in order to insure themselves against delivery failures and also to use them as barter for goods in short supply.

As a result there develops an uncontrollably anarchic market which is called upon to compensate for the failures of the centralized supply mechanism. In this market enterprises exchange machinery, equipment, and raw materials they do not need without using money for these operations and without recording them in their accounts. Bricks are exchanged for cement, sheep for coal, timber for fuel, etc. For many enterprises producing scarce raw materials and intermediate products it has become common practice to use spare labour from enterprises which need their products. In order to obtain the products it needs, an enterprise is often compelled to send ten of its own workers for a month or so (to be able to do this, of course, it has to have some surplus manpower). The uncontrollability of this market and the failure to reflect these operations adequately in the accounts leads to the development of a 'shadow' economy and the emergence of groups of entrepreneurs who make use of supply difficulties in order to enrich themselves. In these conditions there is also large-scale theft of socialist property including that concealed in the form of an 'exchange' of resources, economic co-operation between enterprises and so on. Thus the administrative and bureaucratic system of management closes the door to market relations while they climb in through the window, and in a very unpleasant form at that.

iv). An enterprise that is economically independent of the state and is legally and economically accountable for its use of resources should be able freely to dispose of whatever resources remain after meeting its obligations to the state. In particular, it should independently determine the size of its wage bill and how it is distributed. In fact, however, the wage bill is fixed centrally. Research has shown that the amount of planned wages largely depends on two indicators: the planned number of workers and the average wage in the preceding year. The same method of 'planning on the basis of the past' is the rule, destroying the relation between actual output and pay. The wage bill can, it is true, exceed the planned level but only in strict accordance with the growth rates of labour productivity as reflected in 'gross indicators'. As regards purely economic results – for example, increased income from the sale of output, reduced expenditure, higher rate of profit – they make practically no impact at all on the size of the wage bill.

Moreover, if an enterprise does not use up the whole of the wage bill in any one year the remainder is taken back into the state budget with no hope of its being paid out again and the following year a correspondingly smaller amount of money is allocated. There is therefore absolutely no point in economizing on wages but it becomes extremely important to wring an increase in the wage bill out of the planning bodies by fair means or foul. In this case it is not economy but a wasteful use of resources that is encouraged and the dependence of workers' pay on actual efficiency is in effect reduced to a minimum.

One consequence of this state of affairs is that most enterprises hold a certain number of workers in reserve to employ in certain circumstances. Planning the wage bill on the basis of past performance makes this possible, while there are plenty of reasons for enterprises to create a manpower reserve. To begin with, the salaries of directors and senior personnel depend on the category assigned to their enterprise and this is partly determined by the number of workers employed there. Thus if it gets rid of surplus workers an enterprise can be demoted to a lower category and lose substantial advantages. Planning instability, constant adjustments of targets, fluctuations in the supply of inputs and equipment which is planned in detail only on a quarterly basis, the necessity of constantly sending a part of the workforce to help out in agriculture, construction, vegetable storage – all this encourages enterprises to retain what are in fact superfluous workers who do not even earn their wages.

Extremely strict control over wage payments and an absolute prohibition on increasing the wage bill from other sources means, in fact, that two different, mutually non-convertible currencies operate in the Soviet economy: cash used for paying wages and non-cash money or accounting money which is used for all other needs. The rouble is regarded as the unit for both 'currencies' but 'cash' and 'accounting' monies have completely different values. The former is highly valued and carefully accounted for, while the latter is usually obtained more easily than the goods that it can buy. Accounting money is usually given by a higher-level organization which wants some essential equipment to be supplied to a factory under its control: it can also be obtained from the bank as credit at a very low rate of interest. For example, until 1988 collective and state farms could obtain practically unlimited amounts of credit from the start of the sowing season until the end of the harvest since the Soviet State Bank automatically paid for all their purchases irrespective of the availability of funds on deposit. This is another example of a mechanism that encourages the wasteful use of financial and physical resources.

v). All the features of the centralized system of economic management described above – rigidly targeted planning of production and exchange, centralized price-setting and wage regulation – inevitably cause a sharp differentiation between enterprises' actual levels of profitability. Highly profitable enterprises differ from loss-making ones not so much because they work better and more efficiently as because they produce different types of output, operate in a different natural environment, come under more privileged authorities, etc. As a result, redistribution of the bulk of enterprise profits through the state budget becomes an integral part of the system, enabling two problems to be solved: firstly, allowing loss-making and unprofitable enterprises (comprising about a quarter of all enterprises) to continue to function and, secondly, centralizing the allocation of investment in order to direct it towards solving strategic problems of the economy.

This would seem to be both just and correct since the majority of loss-making enterprises, especially those in the extractive industries, are not responsible for the fact that fixed prices for coal, timber or ore have fallen far below average cost levels. The same applies to farms situated on poor soils far from towns and road and rail transport. Their output may be unprofitable but, if it is needed by the state, then the state must cover its costs. In fact, however, such a practice is dangerous, as can be seen from the example of agriculture. In every region, district and republic there are specially compiled lists of farms that lag behind the rest and yet enjoy preferential treatment. The state provides them with substantial material and financial help and the local authorities give them priority in the allocation of scarce resources. And what happens? Instead of struggling to improve their efficiency, these farms do their very best to remain loss-making so as not to lose their privileges.

While absorption of the bulk of profits by the budget for the central allocation of investment solves some problems, it makes it impossible to tackle others, specifically the provision of incentives to enterprises for ensuring their own self-development, initiating technological progress and solving technical and technological problems for themselves. The almost complete fracture between economic results and investment opportunities delivers yet another blow to the system of material incentives for encouraging workers to achieve good production results. Alongside this, there is a growing and truly insatiable appetite for virtually free investments. Aggregate demand for state investments is one-and-a-half times greater than the amount available. Once again, the mechanism for the centralized allocation of scarce resources comes into play, unsupported by reliable information on the actual efficiency of investment in one or another sector.

vi). Lastly, the lack of built-in automatic regulators and the impossibility of co-ordinating from the centre all aspects of economic development result in permanent and universal imbalances. Some of these are corrected by the enterprises themselves but they cannot cope on their own with a significant number of them. This happens most frequently when production plans are inadequately backed up with material and manpower resources. In such cases enterprise directors apply to management bodies with requests for help in obtaining scarce resources, in putting pressure on unpunctual suppliers and frequently even in getting unreasonably high plan targets reduced. With the economic mechanism until recently in operation it was simply impossible to get by without active intervention by management bodies in the day-to-day work of enterprises. However, the borderline of such intervention is a difficult one to define rationally and it was in fact overstepped on many occasions. Intervention in the daily running of enterprises on the part of both industry and local management bodies was unwarrantably widespread. For instance, Party rural district committees considered it a duty to control not only the volume and efficiency of agricultural production, not only the area sown with different crops and the number of cattle, but also the length of time taken to perform certain agro-technological operations, the kind of technology used on the farms, the channels for the distribution of produce, and much else besides. Directors of factories and combines have a much greater degree of autonomy than collective-farm chairpersons but even they complain that they cannot make a single move without permission 'from above'.

The economic environment for enterprises is highly unstable. A production plan that more or less balances available resources can be changed several times in the course of a year. Even 'final' planning norms are changed in accordance with the boss's wishes – for example, the share of profits deducted by the state. In these circumstances operational planning is reduced to a mere formality, the plan as such disappears and is replaced with administration from above. It is important to note that state and Party management bodies intervening in enterprise operations are not accountable financially for the consequences of their instructions being carried out, particularly when this incurs losses. In these circumstances enterprises themselves do not accept accountability either for the outcome of their economic activity since they can always say they were carrying out orders. So there develops a general lack of accountability, buck-passing and cover-up in which society can suffer enormous losses and it proves impossible to find the guilty parties.

Of course, alongside its weaknesses, the system of economic management until recently in operation also had its positive qualities. By now, however, its failings far outweighed its merits. They were the main reason for the restructuring of economic relations and gave it its direction. I therefore intend to concentrate on them specifically.

To sum up this section, the economic mechanism that was in operation until 1988 was not effective in implementing either the democratic or the centralized principle of socialist economic management. The lack of economic regulators in production, above all, market mechanisms and economic competition, has turned workers in socialist enterprises into impersonal and indifferent executors of other people's will, with no interest in increased efficiency and incapable of showing any initiative. Since most decisions relating to the development of production were in fact taken outside the enterprise, there has been no point in talking about a widespread development of the principles of self-management. People not only did not feel themselves to be masters of their own factories, workshops, or collective farms but had become accustomed to poor-quality work, a low level of work discipline, wasteful use of resources, opportunities for appropriating public property, and so forth.[1] They became deprofessionalized and suffered a loss in their social status as workers. It was symptomatic that people who had worked particularly well and obtained good results inspired in their colleagues not so much a desire for emulation as a feeling of annoyance, accusations of careerism, toadying to the boss, etc. As a result of all these circumstances a large part of people's working, intellectual and creative potential remained 'unclaimed', that is, it was not developed or applied in practice. This was evidence of the extremely weak implementation of democratic principles in economic management.

It would seem that this should have been balanced by a particularly high level of development of the centralized planning principle of economic management. However, as the reader has seen, this did not occur. While attempting to solve the insoluble (and unnecessary) problem of managing from the centre all ground-level economic processes without exception, planning bodies cannot fulfil their main function which is the strategic management of economic development. Such objectives in long-term centralized planning as the improved efficiency of the economy's sectoral structure, rapid development of new-technology industries including engineering, implementation of a uniform policy on technology in major industries and enterprises, achievement of a proper balance between supply and demand, consumption and accumulation, exports and imports – all these and more have disappeared from view. As I mentioned earlier, the extent of actual, rather than merely formal, planned economic development has been decreasing for decades.

Awareness of all these circumstances has firmly convinced Soviet experts and politicians of the necessity for a carefully thought out restructuring of the whole system of economic relations that must also be rapid and radical.

THE SOCIO-ECONOMIC BASIS OF RESTRUCTURING

The key directions of restructuring in the Soviet Union are, on the one hand, the democratization of economic relations by extending the rights of enterprises, the development of worker self-management, the regeneration of market relations, and the development of economic competitiveness and, on the other, the improvement of centralized planning management with the aim of achieving the urgent and effective resolution of basic economic problems.

It has to be said that it is not the first time that these tasks have been laid down. As early as the February 1957 Plenary Session of the Party Central Committee it was noted that the 'organizational structure of the management of industry and construction must be based on a combination of centralized state management and the increasing role of local . . . economic management bodies. The centre of gravity of the operational management of industry must be moved out to the localities.'

The aims of the 1965 economic reform included 'increasing the leading role of centralized economic planning, raising the quality of planning and at the same time extending the rights and independence of enterprises on the basis of full economic accounting; strengthening economic methods of management . . .'

The resolution of the Party Central Committee and the Council of Ministers on 12 June 1979, 'On improving planning and strengthening the impact of the economic mechanism in raising production efficiency and the quality of work', contained a whole series of measures directed towards the 'development of workers' initiative and the extension of the rights of production units (enterprises)'.

Speaking at the November 1982 Plenary Session of the Party Central Committee, General Secretary Andropov again stressed the necessity of decisively increasing the autonomy of production units and enterprises. 'It appears', he added, 'that the time has come to tackle this problem in practice.' Thus, the basic directions for restructuring economic relations, put forward by the 27th Congress, have existed for a fairly long time.

Reviewing the series of government decisions concerning the key problems of economic development, S. Andreyev correctly observed:[2]

> Each successive one, together with its concrete regulations, clearly states that the general situation, which the previous decisions on this matter were designed to improve, has not changed (and has sometimes even deteriorated) . . . One has the feeling that the most serious government regulations are completely forgotten after a fairly short space of time – and not because they have been fully implemented. The government is therefore forced to adopt another lot of similar regulations as a reminder of the need to carry them out.

In this connection the question arises as to whether the present restructuring of economic relations differs from the reforms that were drawn up in previous decades, embodied in government decisions and then came to a standstill. In the fullness of time history will provide the complete answer to that question. As I see it, however, the reform being carried out today differs from past ones in a number of respects.

Firstly, it is significantly more complex and systemic, i.e. it covers, on the one hand, all components of economic management (organization, planning, incentives) and, on the other, inter-sectoral linkages, including agro-industrial, fuel and energy, transport, investment, social welfare, etc.

Secondly, the projected reforms have a significantly deeper, more radical and fundamental character and are being pushed further and more consistently than ever before.

Thirdly, this time the transformation of economic relations is looked upon not as an end in itself but as the essential pre-condition for the democratization of the whole system of social relations. Reform in the economic sphere is reinforced by concurrent or preceding advances in the ideological, political, cultural and ethical spheres which facilitate its implementation.

Fourthly, the Party Central Committee is pursuing the policy of unity of word and deed more forcefully than ever before; it is exercising very strict control over the practical implementation of decisions, developing and improving managerial feed-back and in every possible way broadening contacts with workers.

Lastly, the leaders of the current reform clearly understand the crucial role played by the human factor in the transformation of social relations. They regard restructuring not as an organizational but as a social process that affects people's vital interests, attracting the approval and support of some groups and the hostility and opposition of others. To overcome the braking effect that the bureaucratic apparatus has on restructuring, a social strategy is being worked out and employed that advances society towards the desired goals, not perhaps very quickly but all the more steadily.

This combination of factors leads one to believe that restructuring has a better chance of success than previous attempts at reform.

What then is the socio-economic basis of the transformation being carried out at the present time? How exactly is it intended to change economic relations, and how in fact are they being changed? The fullest answer to these questions may be found in the documents of the June 1987 Plenary Session of the Party Central Committee and the subsequent resolutions of the Central Committee and the Council of Ministers. I think the best way to summarize as precisely and briefly as possible the ideas contained in these documents is to list the six basic directions of economic restructuring and examine the content of each one.

i)   The change-over to economic viability

Economic viability or, in other words, full economic accounting means the business practice by which an enterprise fully covers its production costs by sales revenue. The idea of economic accounting by socialist enterprises was first put forward in the 1920s and has been constantly maintained and developed ever since. In practice, however, during the 'stagnation' period economic accounting relations existed in form only since the profit from paying concerns was absorbed into the budget and loss-making enterprises were given state subsidies.

It is intended to abolish this system in the next few years. Enterprises will be able to use state funds only on repayable credit terms. Economic accounting at the level of the enterprise will be combined with economic accounting at lower levels – department, section, and team. The redistribution of resources between primary production units on the basis of administrative decisions will become rarer and relations between them will become much more strictly economic.

The change-over to economic viability is intended to strengthen and even in some cases for the first time generate material incentives prompting workforces (from team to enterprise level) to raise economic efficiency. They will be able to achieve this by improving the organization of production, matching output to demand, introducing more efficient technology and making more economic use of their own labour and material resources. In these circumstances one can expect that workers will have a more responsible and business-like attitude towards property, socialist values will thrive, and the psychology of the wasteful use of resources and pilfering will be overcome.

But can every enterprise and workforce, with just a little more effort, achieve economic viability? Unfortunately not, and not just because of a poor price structure. A fundamental reason preventing enterprises from making a valid change-over to economic viability is the maintenance of prices that do not reflect either necessary production costs or the matching of supply and demand. The reform of wholesale and retail pricing is an essential component of restructuring. It would be impossible to manage without it, but it is important not to drag out the process in isolation from the change-over to new conditions.

As regards other reasons for the unprofitability of thousands of enterprises, they run deeper and are more difficult to eliminate. They are related to low soil fertility, unfavourable climatic conditions and the isolated location of farms; obsolescent equipment used by a number of factories; underpopulation and a shortage of labour in some regions and populated centres where enterprises are sited; the exhaustion of profitable mineral deposits and change-over to the mining of lower-grade or deep strata, etc. Enterprises operating under such conditions cannot and even should not make a profit because their output costs society too much and it would be better to produce it somewhere else.

With the change-over to a self-financing system, loss-making enterprises that are a drain on society come to light like objects left on the beach when the tide has gone out. They immediately become obvious and attract public attention. At first, apparently, they try to solve their economic problems through recourse to state credit, but without the necessary material and social conditions for efficient work, they very soon fall into debt. The financial situation of such enterprises steadily worsens, affecting wages and the provision of social and cultural amenities. The workers therefore begin to move to other enterprises and other regions. The time will therefore come when it is obvious that there is no point in paying out any more to save a loss-making enterprise and it has to be closed down and declared bankrupt. The rest of the workforce will be dismissed: they will receive redundancy pay of 3–6 months' wages and must find new jobs. The buildings and other assets will be sold to organizations and other interested parties and the money received distributed among the creditors.

It has to be said that such an operation has been rare in our society, as it is in other socialist countries. It will inevitably cause social clashes and tensions and in particular require special measures to be taken to help workers find other jobs. Nevertheless it has to be done since the viability of profitable enterprises and the liquidation of loss-making ones are two sides of the same coin – one does not exist without the other.

ii)   Extending the economic rights of enterprises

Our economy has unfortunate features that are difficult to overcome: one of the most important is the deep-rooted tradition of Party and state organizations intervening as a matter of course in the operational and technological management of enterprises. In this connection, an important direction for restructuring will be the strict separation of the managerial functions of the Party and the state and the running of the economy. In so far as the ruling bodies and their officials are not, and cannot be, held accountable for the economic outcome of their instructions to enterprises, retention of their power to intervene in the organization of production could put management and workers in self-financing enterprises in an extremely difficult position. This power must therefore be removed.

This will not mean, of course, that Soviet and Party authorities will be left without any work to do. They only have to be released from inappropriate functions to enable them to do their own work better. In the case of Party organizations this includes the implementation of an effective policy of personnel management (selection, placement and job evaluation), the inculcation of socialist values among working people, and the resolution of political problems. In the case of central and local government authorities, their job is to develop and run the productive, public transport and social welfare infrastructure, co-ordinate the regional (spatial) activity of enterprises, organize the social service sector and resolve other social problems.

Conversely, it is essential to extend the economic rights of managers, from team leaders to factory directors, in such a way as to match their level of economic accountability. It is not possible to hold people responsible for the results of developing production without their having the right to take independent decisions. If we wish enterprises to achieve viability and make the best use of their resources, directors and specialists must be allowed to plan the basic range of output, introduce new technology, acquire the necessary means of production, experiment with different types of raw material and forms of energy, and reorganize production and workplace operations. Managers must be able independently to spend any income remaining after the cost of inputs has been covered and financial obligations to the state have been met, i.e. they must be managers not only in word but in deed. Only in these circumstances can the incentive to show initiative arising from this system of economic viability be realized in practice.

iii)   The democratization of enterprise management

Important changes are also taking place in the field of management relations, in particular in the selection of personnel for senior management posts. Formerly they were appointed by senior management without consultation with the workforce. The only exception to this rule was the election of collective-farm chairpersons but even this had a purely formal character. The candidates were picked by the Party district committees and presented to collective-farm meetings by the Party secretary. The farmers silently raised their hands and the chairpersons were considered elected. Both sides understood, however, who had really chosen them. As a rule, therefore, chairpersons were primarily inclined to carry out district committee orders even against the interests of the collective farmers who in turn considered such chairpersons to be 'yes-men' and very far from being their own choice.

The situation has now changed. As a result of the policy of revitalizing and democratizing all aspects of public affairs, the practice of appointing managers has been replaced by workplace elections with subsequent confirmation by the authorities. Within months of this decision being taken, the election of managers took place in many enterprises, scientific institutions, design organizations, and so on. The election organizers did their best to ensure that in every case several nominations were discussed and that candidates put forward programmes setting out how they would carry out their responsibilities.

In the majority of cases the process of democratic discussion of nominations and secret ballots led to the election of managers with a high level of professionalism and good human qualities. But in many cases proper elections did not take place as there were no alternative nominations. Decades of passivity have taken their toll; people do not push themselves forward for management posts. In other cases, some workforces voted for managers not according to any criterion of professionalism and efficiency but the criterion of an unexacting and conformist attitude towards the workers themselves. Evidently, this is the price that has to be paid during a transitional period, when the practice of economic viability has not yet had time to make itself felt and workers have as yet no real interest in having a highly competent, if more exacting, management capable of securing high levels of efficiency and hence high wages. I am convinced that, as the economic reform gathers momentum, the election of managers will have a more precise and equitable impact. As regards the social effects, the holding of elections will make managers more responsible to the workforce. Whereas before they mainly related 'upwards', now they relate not only 'upwards' but 'downwards' as well.

The first steps are also being taken towards developing self-management. To this end special bodies are being created – Workforce Councils. So far they have behaved rather passively. Here, too, the sense of alienation built up over the years is having its effect and the attitude expressed in 'It's nothing to do with me' and 'Why me?' is very prevalent. A significant number of workers are trying their best to do nothing more than the job for which they are paid and to avoid becoming involved in other matters.

I should like to emphasize here that participation in self-management depends to a great extent on working conditions and wages. If pay bears no relation to output or productivity, interest in self-management is minimal. In teams working on a workforce contract where earnings are determined by the difference between income from sales and the cost of inputs, every worker tries to contribute to increasing production efficiency. Thus, in agriculture, such teams decide among themselves when to start sowing different crops, which technology to use depending on weather conditions, how to share out the work most efficiently, how to use seed, fuel and fertilizer more economically, etc. In the autumn of 1981 one of my colleagues, Professor V. D. Smirnov, conducted a socio-economic experiment by introducing into several Altai farms the workforce contract system on a comprehensive basis, i.e. covering all groups of workers. The results he obtained showed that changing economic relations rapidly transformed the psychology of the collective farmers. From indifferent 'hired hands' concerned only with their own affairs, they were transformed into thoughtful economists capable of performing fairly complex calculations with a clear grasp of what was to their advantage and what was not. This allows one to hope that, as reform deepens, self-management will develop and become firmly established.

iv)   Changes in the wages system

I mentioned above the fact that until very recently the total amount of wages that an enterprise was allowed to pay out to its workers was centrally planned and usually based on the level and trend of growth previously achieved. Any changes were slow to happen and bore very little relation to how the enterprise was run. Apart from that, white-collar workers were paid centrally-fixed salaries while production workers were paid according to fixed wage rates (in practice, it is true, this was often circumvented).

The change-over to economic viability entails a fundamentally different approach to wages. The total amount must now be fixed not 'initially' irrespective of an enterprise's operational indicators but as part of gross income, i.e. the difference between the income received from the sale of output and the cost of inputs and financial payments to the state. In these circumstances the total wage bill will depend primarily on how much output is produced, its quality, whether it is in demand and on production costs.

Enterprises are also being given significantly greater rights regarding the choice of forms of payment for different types of work – whether it is piecework or hourly rates, simple or progressive, paid for each stage or for the whole operation.

The workforce contract is widespread in most sectors of the economy, i.e. the system of economic relations whereby a team comprising a number of people (from 3–25) accepts full responsibility for producing a certain volume of output. They conclude a contract with management which stipulates the equipment they will be allocated, standard amounts of input (with an indication of price) and the price per unit of output to be paid to the members of the team. The team's income depends on a) the quantity and quality of output and b) the level of costs. It is distributed among the members at their own discretion. When everyone participates in the work to a more or less equal extent, the income is sometimes distributed equally, but more often a Co-efficient of Participation is used to evaluate the work, and this is determined by the team itself, taking into account qualifications, skills and knowledge, conscientiousness and other qualities. The system of contractual payment of primary workforces fits in well with the viability of enterprises both economically and socially. It therefore has a promising future.

As a result of changes in the way that wage payments are made, workers' financial interest in the effective organization of production and high-quality work increases. Not only engineers but shop-floor workers too are beginning to make rationalization suggestions in an effort to improve the quality of output, achieve savings in the use of raw materials, and so on. Under the new conditions, after all, any negligence hits their own pockets.

The distribution of gross enterprise income between wage payments, material incentives, and social funds, on the one hand, and the investment fund, on the other, is not within the competence of an enterprise itself but is based on set ratios fixed by the authorities. Nevertheless, under the new conditions, the boundary between the wage bill and other enterprise funds is becoming less rigid. The 'gulf' between cash paid out in wages and that spent on purchases and credit transactions between enterprises is narrowing. The difference in their value, although it still exists, has lessened somewhat. The conditions are thus being created for the gradual re-establishment of the rouble as sound money. This is important for the development of a normal market and in time it could also be important for turning the rouble into a convertible currency.

v)   The change-over to self-financing

The three basic principles underlying the new conditions for running enterprises are economic viability, self-management and self-financing. I have already discussed the first two – it now remains to examine the third. The need for self-financing is more pressing than the need for economic viability since it represents the next step towards full economic accounting and autonomy. In fact, viability is achieved when sales revenue fully covers the costs of production and generates a surplus that is sufficient to meet the enterprise's financial obligations to the state and provide funds for material incentives and social amenities. The self-financing system requires that investments such as expenditure on the reorganization of production, building of new premises, purchase of new equipment, and the introduction of new technology are also financed from the enterprise's own income. In other words, enterprises have to build up funds not only to meet current needs but also for accumulation.

Since total available investment cannot be increased by 'waving a magic wand', it can at the present time only be a matter of redistributing it among different owners. Whereas under the previous system the State Planning Commission and its industrial departments controlled by far the greater part of investment, they will now only handle capital investment destined for the construction of new enterprises, the development of new regions and the implementation of particularly large schemes covering different sectors of the economy. Investment in the expansion of existing enterprises will be controlled by the enterprises themselves.

The decentralization of investment holds out the promise of quite a few economic and social gains. Every workforce after all knows not only its own possibilities but also those bottlenecks which, once cleared, will make it possible to achieve an optimal return on capital investments. It is important that the new system is based on the independent and creative activity of the workforce. It is not somebody in Moscow but managers, specialists and workers themselves who will decide what is to be done now and what is to be done in the future to bring their enterprise up to a modern technological standard. Does this not give full scope for collectives to develop informal but genuine self-management, and for people to have the feeling of being in charge of their own enterprises, workshops and sections? If people really feel themselves to be in control, new powers awaken in them and they can do much more than they would under somebody else's orders.

The chief way to divide total investment into its centralized and decentralized components is to establish fixed norms for the payment of taxes on profits. It may be assumed that as a result of the reform the amount of profit handed over to the state will be considerably smaller. (However, in the period of transition to new conditions of economic management another tendency now predominates, which is related to the struggle around restructuring. I shall discuss this further in Chapter Four.)

The main consequences of enterprises going over to self-financing will obviously include a faster pace of technological progress in all sectors; a significant increase in the reorganization of production by reducing the volume of new industrial construction; more capital investment in housing and social and cultural amenities; and an improvement in working conditions, etc.

vi)   Development of market relations

As has already been noted, an increase in the freedom of an enterprise to decide its own output is an important aspect of the reform, and one that presupposes a sharp reduction in the number of centrally planned and targeted indicators. The previous method of planning has been retained in some sectors of heavy industry, including defence, but in other sectors centralized targeted planning will be replaced by indicative planning. This means that the all-Union and Republican State Planning Commissions will prepare a production plan on the basis of available information regarding social needs. Enterprises, on the other hand, will begin to plan production taking into account their own possibilities, available resources, economic interests and the demand for different types of goods. These enterprise plans will be collated by administrative bodies right up to national level. The all-Union State Planning Commission will thus be able to compare the two plans drawn up at higher and lower levels in the management pyramid. Whenever the divergence between them is too great, i.e. it becomes apparent that enterprises mean to produce too small an amount of goods needed by society or intend to produce too much of certain goods, the central administration will have to adjust the imbalances by means of economic incentives, for example, by offering enterprises better terms for products in danger of becoming scarce. The results obtained so far in Hungary from the indicative planning of output show that it is justified.

The decentralization of planning also means that supplier-customer links laid down in the plan will come to an end. These inter-enterprise linkages formerly controlled by the central authorities will become more 'horizontal', i.e. they will be based on direct contracts regarding terms, prices and orders. As a result, contract prices negotiated between supplier and consumer with regard to level of demand, quality and compliance with modern standards, and thus of market mechanisms, will become common practice. To avoid market forces breaking out of planning control and disrupting the economy, the all-Union State Price Committee has devised what is known as the 'fork', i.e. the lower and upper parameters of contract prices for key products. This will be one of the regulatory indicators of the socialist market.

As shortages disappear, the practice of 'funding', i.e. the restricted distribution 'from above' of technology, equipment, raw materials and other inputs will fall into disuse. Enterprises will either place orders directly with producers or obtain them wholesale. In light industries and food industries, enterprises' main activity will be based on contracts with the wholesale and retail trades. The practice of holding industrial and trade fairs, where large-volume deals are made at negotiated prices, will become more common.

All these changes have one and the same purpose – the development of market relations and the replacement of administrative and bureaucratic methods of management by economic ones. What is this leading to? First and foremost, the volume and structure of output will match the structure of social needs more closely. In the first place, the production of low-quality goods for which there is no demand and which have almost immediately to be repaired or dumped will cease and, secondly, the selection of goods will be widened and their quality improved so as to satisfy public demand more adequately, while the supply of equipment and inputs to enterprises will be simplified, thus enabling them to cut down on their accumulated stocks and speed up their financial turnover. Serious changes can also be expected in the shadow economy. At the moment it is extremely heterogeneous in the sense that some of its operations can be justified on the ground that, because market relations are artificially restricted, they serve a socially useful purpose in maintaining normal production. At the same time, other operations involve the theft of public property and the personal enrichment of a corrupt mafia. The development and legalization of market relations will allow sound linkages formed in the shadow economy to be incorporated in known transactions. Only illegal operations will be forced to remain in the shadow economy. This will help the fight against crime and sanitize the economy.

vii)   Relaxation of rules on individual and co-operative work

Up to the mid-1980s there was a paradox within our economy. Many sectors, regions and enterprises were suffering from manpower shortages but people who wanted to work more than 41 hours a week were not as a rule allowed to do so. Thus any possibility of taking a second job, i.e. of working in two different places (for example, in a factory and a research institute, at university and on a scientific journal, etc.) was strictly limited. As a result there was not enough labour to make efficient use of available equipment while available manpower was artificially 'frozen' rather than used. Underlying this policy was fear of an excessive growth in wages, a widening gap between supply and demand, and rising inflation. In fact, however, extra work would increase the supply of goods and services, thus contributing to a decrease rather than a growth in shortages. Individual and family forms of work were in a similar position. They aroused a certain suspicion as to their 'unsocialist' nature, suggested the idea of dishonest methods of enrichment, and were therefore not encouraged but restricted by all possible means.

The ideology of restructuring takes a completely different attitude both towards second jobs or overtime and to work done by individuals and small co-operatives. Former legal restrictions on extra work have been significantly reduced or eliminated altogether. A new pension law currently in preparation envisages strong incentives for people of pensionable age to continue working. Every additional year of work will increase the pension by several per cent. Different forms of paid work for students and schoolchildren are being actively developed – building-site teams, school teams on farms, and holiday work camps where children can earn money for themselves by combining leisure with work in gardens, greenhouses and vineyards.

There are various openings and directions for individual, family and small co-operative business activity. Families and individuals are engaged mostly in the production of agricultural produce, particularly early vegetables, fruit and flowers which are much in demand. People with the right training can make fashionable clothes and shoes, original jewelry and so on. In order to carry on a handicrafts business and sell its products, it is only necessary to obtain a licence and not employ other people.

Open-air markets selling paintings in Moscow parks and other towns have become very popular. Painters and craftsmen bypassing any sort of selection board meet up with potential buyers and obtain some idea of the sorts of things that are in demand. Visitors to the art markets can not only buy a painting or some other object but get a general impression of the work of contemporary artists.

The work of small co-operatives (usually consisting of five to 30 persons) is also being encouraged. People employed in the public sector work only part-time in the co-operative but some members work there full-time. Unlike individuals, co-operatives are legal entities, formally registered with the local councils and having certain legal rights. They can thus not only produce things for the public but can enter into contracts with state organizations and, say, supply spare parts in short supply for servicing their cars. They often obtain equipment from enterprises that has been written off as obsolete and then repair and improve it themselves. Co-operatives often make use of scrap containing parts which they need from factories or scientific research institutes. Today's engineers and even skilled workers have a wealth of ideas for technological innovation. Putting these ideas into practice is often difficult in large factories; in their own small workplace, however, it is much simpler and more interesting. As a result, some of the small co-operatives that I know manage to make valuable goods literally 'out of nothing'.

In Transcaucasia, the Baltic republics and later on in Moscow too it has become common for state-owned service establishments – coffee shops, cafés, small restaurants, hairdressers, beauty parlours, etc. – to be leased by co-operatives. The rent is agreed with the local authorities and is fixed for a period of five years. At the end of this term the contract is renewed and the rent may be raised.

I should like to make the point that small co-operatives and workshops unfailingly put their finger on unfulfilled needs. For example, in recent years there have been many complaints about the difficulty of making funeral arrangements. Grieving relatives have to undergo many ordeals since officials formally responsible for organizing this sad but necessary ceremony take advantage of the inevitability of the situation and the psychological condition of their clients and fleece them shamelessly. In these circumstances some young people in Moscow, including qualified doctors competent to issue a death certificate, lawyers, events organizers, musicians and manual workers, organized themselves into a co-operative which takes full responsibility for the organization of funerals. The relatives of the deceased deal with intelligent, tactful and decent people, everything is done without fuss, correctly, in an organized fashion, without any hold-ups. The fee for these services, although not cheap, works out at much less than what usually has to be paid to blackmailing officials. This could be said to be an isolated example. Nevertheless, it illustrates the general efforts made by co-operatives to seek out and fill the 'gaps' that exist in services to the public.

The development of small-scale forms of production increases labour participation rates, improves the quality of work, and makes better use of equipment, raw materials and other inputs, as well as people's creative potential. This in turn leads to an increase in the income and standard of living of individual, family or co-operative workers. Most important, however, is the fact that the needs of ordinary people for different goods and services are adequately met.

It seems clear to me that the transformation of economic relations in the Soviet Union makes it certain that two main aims will be achieved: a) greater efficiency in production and better satisfaction of public needs, and b) democratization and greater pluralism in economic affairs and a real possibility for everyone to achieve their own potential through work. Both represent considerable gains to society. However, in practice gains have their own costs. The most positive transformation of society always causes new problems. This also applies to the restructuring of economic relations. In the following section, therefore, I shall be discussing the social problems arising from restructuring.

THE SOCIAL CONSEQUENCES OF RESTRUCTURING

In view of the radical character of the present transformation of economic relations in the Soviet Union, its social consequences will be complex and diverse. It is hardly possible at the present time to foresee the whole spectrum, but it is fairly obvious that a whole number of social problems will emerge. I shall examine just a few typical examples of these problems.

i)   Reduction in the number of staff, together with changes in the content and increasing complexity of administrative work.

At the present time our economy is saturated with administrative personnel – they number about 18 million or 13 per cent of all employees. Such an inflated administration is one of the terrible social consequences of the lengthy period of stagnation and the bureaucratization of Soviet society. Clearly, with the change-over to economic methods of management, it will be possible and necessary to reduce the number of people employed in this sector by a half or a third. But this inevitably means retraining and finding new jobs for millions of people, and not simple operatives at that but people accustomed to giving orders to others and who enjoy both power and privilege. The problem is very complex indeed.

This is only one aspect of the problem under review, however. The other comprises fundamental changes in the content and increased complexity of all aspects of administrative work under the new conditions. This applies to all categories of administrative staff, from officials in central government departments dealing with different branches of the economy to enterprise managers.

In fact, officials working in central government departments, including the State Planning Commission, were accustomed to using strong-arm methods in their dealings with enterprises, exploiting the fact that they controlled all the resources essential for production. Before the reform, enterprises had virtually no rights at all. Collective and state farms, for example, could be set plans for harvests that were quite unthinkable for their areas. Planned incomes and financial transfers to the state were calculated on the basis of these inflated output plans. Workers were given bonuses only when plans were overfulfilled, which was out of the question. In addition, plans imposed from above were often not backed up with the necessary supplies of seed, mineral fertilizer, technology, etc. Farms, although they did argue with the planning authorities, finally submitted and placed themselves in an extremely disadvantageous position. They did not, of course, fulfil the plan and made losses rather than profits, whereupon the state would provide them with subsidies and ends were made to meet – at a great cost to society.

However, the situation is now changing. Administrative pressure, when applied to self-financing enterprises, proves to be clearly inappropriate. Enterprises use their extended powers to resist attempts to force them to produce goods that are unprofitable or for which resources have not been provided. The change-over from targeted to indicative planning and the increased role of enterprises in determining the most efficient directions for production require new management methods and, I would say, a new language of communication between different levels in the management pyramid. Thus the role of economic planning norms is growing enormously. These include the price of key products, the relationship between productivity growth rates and wages, the share of profits distributed between enterprise and state, the fixed amount of profits to be allocated to funds for expanding production and employee incentive schemes. Experience in elaborating and applying such set ratios has not yet been acquired: the old is no good here and the new hardly exists. Correct calculation of ratios requires the development of a special methodology and this in turn depends on an economic theory that is weak. The resulting situation is therefore far from easy. Those officials remaining in central economic departments will have a difficult time of it.

The same is true, for example, of bank staff. Over the last few decades banks have managed to turn themselves into institutions that are more administrative than financial and have completely lost their commercial functions. A banking reform is now being carried through. The Soviet State Bank is being split into several specialized banks for financing industry, construction, agriculture, etc. Under the new conditions bank employees will have a different job content: they will have to learn not only to count but to calculate, assess situations, take economic risks, etc.

The job of senior management is also becoming more complex, especially for directors of enterprises and groups: the extension of their powers will after all be accompanied by a corresponding extension of their responsibilities. Whereas formerly they mainly had to carry out orders, now they have to think about everything themselves – look for suppliers, reorganize production and introduce new technology, organize the workforce and improve the payment of wages, and co-operate with Workforce Councils, while all the time knowing that if they do not reach required standards of work, the workers will elect a new director.

The times make completely new demands on staff employed in economic management. They must be well educated in the fields of economics and law, find their bearings quickly in the changing network of economic relations, possess both organizational and entrepreneurial abilities, constantly update their information including that relating to foreign experience, and show skill in managing the workforce under them. To put it bluntly, the present generation of managers does not measure up to today's demands since they gained their experience in different conditions. Those who are already 50–60 years old will hardly be able to 'restructure themselves' fundamentally and adapt to the new circumstances. This

means that younger generations must be brought forward. But just to promote them is not enough. It is essential to create a programme for training the sort of administrative staff that is now needed. This requires radical changes in the work of the Academy for the National Economy, the Institute of Management and the departmental and regional centres for advanced professional training and retraining.
ii)   Raising skill requirements and the values of the creative component of work.

It is said that almost a quarter of all graduate engineers in the world work in our country. The army of agronomists, veterinary surgeons and livestock specialists serving agriculture is certainly no smaller. In any event, on an average farm in Siberia there are not less than 20–30 specialists. One would think that high rates of technological progress could be expected but in fact production is marking time. Several research studies have been carried out in the past few years in an attempt to discover reasons for the inefficiency of work done by graduate engineers. It was discovered that the overwhelming majority of them (more than 80 per cent) were not in fact employed in engineering at all but were filling in various slips of paper, making reports, answering enquiries, etc. Those who worked directly with technology and were responsible for making technical decisions were bound hand and foot by all manner of instructions restricting their work and could in fact do nothing. All this means no less than the devaluation of their social value and prestige. Not surprisingly, the level of their wages in the early 1980s was no different from that of unskilled workers, and in some cases was even less.

The change-over to economic viability will make workers directly interested in increasing efficiency, including by means of new engineering decisions. The self-financing system, i.e. the decentralization of investment will, moreover, enable these decisions to be put into operation. In these circumstances it will soon become apparent that there are engineers and engineers, and one specialist with talent can achieve a result that a hundred others could not reach. There will be competition among enterprises for the most highly skilled engineers: they will be won over from other enterprises by means of higher wages and better fringe benefits. The social prestige of highly skilled labour and the level of professional know-how will inevitably start to rise and specialists will begin to be valued not for their job grade or diploma but for their actual creative results. In general, the creative component of labour will gradually become more significant than the operative component measured by the number of hours spent at work.

Highly qualified staff who are also talented will be in particularly short supply but lower-grade workers will also be in demand. As for so-called specialists whose grasp of the job is not as good as that of many workers, they of all people must, like the 'pen-pushers', change the character of their work. For their services to enterprises are not really needed. We have here yet another complex social problem, and many more millions of people who fell victim to social retrogression and the re-Stalinization period. 'Tragedy' is too strong a word to use here, but 'drama' is quite appropriate.

Moreover, if the established system of higher education in engineering, agriculture and other technological fields continues in the same old way, the number of dramas can only increase because the calibre of specialist it produces does not meet the new requirements of production. A radical restructuring of vocational training is necessary; it must be made more intensive, must develop stronger links with practical work, and must introduce active forms of training to develop students' creative potential. It is essential that students do more probationary work in developed socialist and capitalist countries. Alongside this, the financial responsibility of colleges and universities for the quality of their graduates must be increased, and the economic relations between production and education adjusted.

iii) Increased vocational, industrial and regional mobility.

Almost the most typical feature of our life before the reform was the extreme stability of all relations which, alongside its negative aspects, did have some positive ones, including the reliability of social guarantees. Restructuring directed towards faster socio-economic growth destroys this stability and makes life more dynamic and complex. In particular, a relatively rapid change is to be expected in patterns of employment. I have just mentioned some of the factors operating in this direction. These are, firstly, workers' interest in doing a given volume of work with a smaller workforce in order to increase earnings; secondly, the extension of an enterprise's powers to regulate the size of its workforce without being obliged to find jobs for workers made redundant and consequently making it possible to get rid of 'ballast'; thirdly, an accelerated rate of technological progress and the reorganization of production related to a decrease in the number of unskilled workers; and, fourthly, the inevitable closure and liquidation of loss-making enterprises offset by the expansion of more efficient enterprises and the building of new ones.

For all these reasons the number of jobs disappearing from the economy will no doubt rise considerably. This means that the number of people losing jobs and requiring new ones will also rise. In this connection many correspondents in the West constantly ask how we can reconcile high rates of technological progress with retaining the constitutional right of all Soviet citizens to work, i.e.

the absence of unemployment. The question is not easy, but I shall try to answer it to the best of my understanding.

I should like to start by distinguishing between 'absolute' and 'structural' unemployment, i.e. on the one hand, the overall balance between jobs and workers and, on the other, the partial balance between them within sectors, professions and regions. I shall begin with the first part of the question. It is by no means a simple task obtaining a dynamic balance between the number of jobs in the economy as a whole and the size of the labour force. Given a well-thought-out and rational approach to management, however, it can be done. There are several factors working in its favour.

a)   Workers will not be made redundant from enterprises all at once, but gradually. In many enterprises the rise in labour productivity will not lead to an immediate cut in the workforce but to a gradual fall in the number of vacancies. That is, at first a shortage of manpower will predominate and only later will enterprises gradually begin to make workers redundant.

b)   At the present time, due to a shortage of labour, most machinery is operated for one shift only. This is extremely inefficient. Higher productivity will allow work to be organized into two and possibly even three shifts without increasing the stock of machinery.

c)   There is today an extremely uneven distribution of manpower between sectors and regions. Among sectors suffering the greatest manpower shortages are construction, agriculture, the steel industry, and light industry: among the regions, the East and the North. In time these sectors and regions will be able to absorb many of the workers released in other areas.

d)   The service industries, whose level of development in the Soviet Union falls far below world standards, represent a large potential employer. Here it is not just a case of insufficient investment in non-manufacturing construction but also a direct shortage of workers – shop assistants, waiters, nurses, hospital orderlies, hairdressers, librarians, etc. Further advances and development in the service sector in many regions and towns are held up by the shortage of manpower, which by its very nature plays a decisive role in the service industry. At the present time about 25 per cent of workers are employed in the provision of services to the public, much less than in other developed countries. This means that a cut in numbers employed in other sectors could be substantially offset by a more rapid development of the service sector.

e)   A section of redundant workers will be able to find employment in the expanding area of individual, family and co-operative business activity.

f)   Finally, a planned society can in principle redress the imbalance between workers and jobs by regulating the number of hours worked in a day, week and year. In future the average working hours of a Soviet citizen must gradually decrease and the reform being carried through today will make this task easier.

The problem of there being absolutely no possibility of providing a number of workers with a job in social production thus hardly exists in this country. The provision of jobs for redundant workers is, above all, a structural problem but nevertheless a complex one. Three of its main aspects can be identified: the vocational, the regional, and the social. I shall take a brief look at each in turn.

I have already touched upon the vocational aspect of redundancy and the subsequent provision of jobs when discussing administrative staff and certain specialists in the production sector. The number of such jobs will fall sharply and people will have to change radically the character of the work they do and learn new trades. Whereas the younger generation will be able to manage this (possibly with help from the state), for older people and in particular those coming up to retirement age problems will arise that will be difficult to overcome. This is why when staff cuts were made in several government departments early retirement was offered to redundant staff with only 2–3 years to work before qualifying for a pension.

Another no less complex aspect of the problem under discussion is the loss of jobs for unskilled, usually manual, labour owing to rapid technological progress. These make up approximately 30 per cent of jobs in construction, 40 per cent in industry, and no less than 60–65 per cent in agriculture. In this case the only solution is mass retraining, enabling workers to acquire skills which are in demand. However, unskilled manual work is often done by older people who were not even able to complete secondary education and who have anyway forgotten everything they were taught in school. The majority of them are women. Will they wish or, what is more important, will they be able to acquire new skills? More probably, most older people will prefer to be employed in individual or family concerns, for example, in agriculture.

I shall now turn to the regional aspect of the problem. Reforming the structure of the economy will obviously cause an increased proportion of jobs to be located in the eastern regions (as opposed to the centre and the west) and also in large towns (as opposed to small towns and villages). This means that workers losing their job in some regions and towns will only be able to find a new one in others, i.e. they will have to migrate. Clearly, such migration must be voluntary and this means that it must be possible to change one's place of residence without suffering a decline in living conditions. However, at the present time, there is a very sharp difference in living conditions and the quality of life in different regions. Life is much harder in the eastern regions than in the southern or central ones. For decades people have been moving not to Siberia and the far east but from those regions into the centre and to the south. In the mid-1970s, it is true, migration from and to these east netted out and subsequently there was a greater flow in the easterly direction. This was achieved by increasing what are known as regional weightings which raised the level of wages by between 15 per cent in south–west Siberia to 100 per cent in the far north and other regions where life is particularly difficult. Similar methods will obviously have to be used in the future to encourage migration to areas of labour shortage.

A similar situation exists between town and village. On the whole living conditions in these two types of habitation have now largely levelled out. The advantages of living in town still lie in a better level of services, a greater variety of media information, easier access to cultural facilities, and so on. The advantages of living in a village include the absence of overcrowding and the chance of living in a detached house with a small plot of land, cultivating a private smallholding and enjoying good, fresh food. As regards incomes and general family welfare, conditions are more or less equal. In many regions migrational flows from country to town and town to country also net out. In those instances where reform of the economic structure requires a further reduction in the rural and a growth in the urban populations, there will be no opposition to young people in rural areas migrating to the towns. However, the demographic capacity of most large towns is at the moment extremely limited: there is insufficient housing, creches and nursery schools, social amenities and so on. As a result, the practice of giving 'hidden permits' has arisen in large towns where permission to move in is given only to people who have been especially invited to work there by certain enterprises or institutions which are obliged to provide them and their family with accommodation. This state of affairs acts to a considerable extent as a check on the growth of the principal towns although it cannot, of course, prevent it altogether. The need to relocate significant numbers of people from rural areas to the towns will obviously break this system down and raise in an extremely acute form the question of the rapid growth of large towns – largely at the expense of the villages as well as small towns. As a result, the social balance between town and country that was achieved with such difficulty will once again be seriously disturbed.

Finally, I come to the social aspect of the problem. The greatest difficulties in finding new work will be experienced by those categories of people who in the eyes of management possess a sub-standard or low-quality work potential. These are women, particularly those with small children who often need to stop at home with them when they are ill; the elderly, sick, and physically weak; relatively uneducated and unqualified workers whom I have already mentioned; people with a drink problem, drug addicts, etc. Clearly, politicians and experts will have to think very deeply about how to provide work for each of the above groups. They will, of course, have to be approached in entirely different ways.

I will take as an example just one of the above groups – young women with children who, other things being equal, have a fairly high chance of becoming the victims of job cuts. When considering this problem, it has to be borne in mind that up to the present time the level of employment of women in social production has been one of the highest in the world. In many Republics, including Russia and the Ukraine, employment of women comes close to equalling that of men. Of the total number of employees, women comprise 51 per cent despite the fact that they retire on a pension five years earlier than men.

It would seem that the high level of employment of women in social production is socially unjustified. It has had a negative effect both on the birth rate and on the upbringing of children. In the towns, and now sometimes in the villages as well, the one-child family is becoming the prevalent model, which does not even ensure that the population reproduces itself and is damaging to the upbringing of children in a family. Social habits are being lost, together with the custom of sociable work done together and help given by older siblings to the younger ones, which are characteristic of families with several children.

What then is the cause of the very high level of employment of women which forces them to a certain extent to neglect their social and family functions? In the first instance, it is the low wages paid to men, most of whom cannot today maintain a family on their own, even for the few years that the children are growing up. It must be added that non-working women, even those with children, have a low status in the eyes of most people. A woman is regarded as a complete individual, not inferior in any way to a man, and therefore obliged to have a profession and to work. Of course, women themselves have developed the need to work and to have social contacts at work, and to belong to a particular group of workers. They study hard, acquire new knowledge, and improve their qualifications. Consequently, women make up 61 per cent of college and university graduates.

Of course, the problem of female employment is not a 'purely Soviet' phenomenon. It is characteristic of all developed countries and much positive experience has been acquired in dealing with it. It shows that women's personal and social interests are best combined when they have a choice between full-time employment in social production, part-time employment and devoting themselves fully to the family. Sociological research has shown that, given the choice, up to 40 per cent of women would give up full-time employment and would prefer to work part-time. To make this possible, however, men's wages must be raised. While rapid technological progress and rising productivity are the main factor in cutting the demand for labour, they also help to raise wages. The development of small-scale forms of production will create further opportunities for the part-time employment of women. It is possible that these processes will act as a sort of 'buffer' for workers made redundant not only because of the closure of enterprises but also through the introduction of new technology and improvements in the organization of production.

Mention can be made of a whole number of other social problems caused by restructuring. These include the inevitable differentiation of income and consumption between social groups, the possible growth of inflationary tendencies, a particular sort of competition between production in the public sector and production by individuals. Thus, even a not very detailed examination of the possible social consequences of reform points to the fact that Soviet society is entering an entirely new stage in its development. The inevitability of conflicts in new unknown situations and the urgent need to deal with old, long-pressing problems call for a thorough reappraisal of social policies pursued in the past. In the new conditions these policies must be directed towards the renewal of goals and must be based on a different hierarchy of values. It is essentially a matter of formulating a new social policy that corresponds to the present stage of restructuring social relations. I shall discuss the content of this policy in the next chapter.

A Social Policy and Its Problems 3

THE NEW SOCIAL POLICY

In today's Soviet press the policy reflecting the decision of the Soviet Communist Party to seek out new, more effective strategies for resolving urgent social problems is often called 'strong'. The attention of the Party, the state, and economic administrators and managers has been sharply drawn to the resolution of social problems and the satisfaction of people's needs, and this is a clear reflection of the increased importance of the role of social policy in the arsenal of strategies employed to manage the development of society in the present historical situation. Whereas previously social policy has been regarded primarily as an instrument for managing improvement in living standards, it is now beginning to act as a lever for the active transformation and restructuring of the system of social relations.

How, then, can restructuring possibly be carried through rapidly and efficiently without relying on the 'human factor'? Neither technology nor the natural environment will be of assistance here. It is only the people who can do this. It is they and they alone who are faced with restructuring the material and technological bases of the economy, as well as their own relationship with their environment and with their own consciousness, way of life, and the style and quality of their work. The guarantee of success is first and foremost the active position of the mass of ordinary people, their support and contribution towards restructuring. It is therefore absolutely imperative that increasingly broad sections of working people are won over to the side of restructuring, and turned from onlookers into active participants. It will not be possible to perform this complex task by purely economic means; the best that could be expected would be a high standard of work and a responsible attitude on the part of working people towards public property, but economic measures cannot make them convinced supporters of a new system of social relations. To do that stronger measures are needed, addressing the whole spectrum of people's needs and interests. I am convinced that people can be made active supporters of restructuring only if they are won over as individuals.

To do this it is above all necessary to know the interests and needs of every social stratum and group. Although an appreciable role is played in people's behavioural motivation by such factors as values, tradition, habits, features of national culture, etc., nevertheless, the 'engine', the 'motive power', determining the final direction of the activity of one or other social group, is first and foremost its interests.

The network of interests operating within a particular society is interconnected, heterogeneous and contradictory. Its structure is fairly complex and has many facets. Over a long period of time Soviet social science has emphasized the undoubted primacy of societal over group interests and group over personal interests. Such a one-sided interpretation has done much harm not only to the science itself but also in practice, since it was employed to justify the suppression of personal interests to the benefit of the collective and of collective interests to the societal. This took place at a time when the precise content of social interests was not strictly speaking known, since public opinion was not a matter for study. Political figures took it upon themselves to interpret these interests, and the interpretation inevitably bore the heavy imprint of their own interests and ideas. It is only necessary to recall the campaign conducted in the late 1950s and early 60s on the enforced collectivization of cattle privately owned by collective farmers. This campaign was carried on under the slogan of subordinating personal interests to social ones, but it did in effect deal the Soviet livestock industry one of the heaviest blows ever.

At the present time views on this question are more balanced and considered. The primacy of social interests over collective and personal ones is treated not as a possible (and appropriate) infringement upon 'lower' interests to the advantage of 'higher' ones, but as the most important condition and prerequisite for the fullest satisfaction of both group (collective) and personal interests. The justice of the contrary assertion is also acknowledged – that social interests can be satisfied only when group and personal interests have been realized.

However, the division of interests on the vertical, hierarchical principle is only one of several possibilities. Firstly, the interests of any subject (whether individual, collective, regional, demographic or other group) vary according to which period they relate to. Short, medium, or long-term interests may not only not coincide, they can come into direct conflict with one another. A classic example of this is the contradiction between the aim of maximizing current consumption and the desire to increase investment so as to provide additional income in the future. This contradiction is manifested on a national scale, at enterprise level, and even in a single family.

Secondly, every social subject has interests in different areas – the economy and politics, work and leisure, cultural pursuits and sport, the sphere of personal development and contact with the family, etc. In conflict with one another and ranked according to the value system of individuals and the external circumstances of their lives, all these different interests in the last analysis form a sort of resultant force which lies at the basis of actual group behaviour. Obviously, socio-political decisions, aimed at securing the successful progress of restructuring, will be genuinely effective only if they are based on sound knowledge of the positions, interests and behaviour patterns of all the social strata and groups affected by them.

The most important characteristic of socialist society, and one that is emblazoned on its banner, is the aspiration for social justice. Everybody living in this country grew up to the accompaniment of assertions that Soviet society was the most just in the world, that nowhere could a man breathe more easily and freely, that the custom of addressing a stranger as 'comrade' of itself ensured a friendly, almost family relationship between people. As long as social practice did not diverge too diametrically from these assertions, belief in the progressive and just nature of the socio-political regime secured most people's personal identification with society's aims and values. This could well have been the main secret of the strength of Soviet society in the 1920s and even the 1930s, not to mention the period of the Second World War.

However, the other side of that same dependence on a belief in the justice of the regime and the correctness of political government as a determinant of people's behaviour was equally powerful and significant. In particular, the last few decades which have been notable for their proliferating and deepening social, economic, political and legal injustices led to the alienation of working people from official ideology and frequently from socially useful activity altogether. Lack of belief in the slogans put forward by the Party and the state, in the possibility of life changing for the better, in the feasibility of a successful struggle against evil, an all-pervading scepticism and often cynicism on the part of young and middle-aged people – this is the price that our society has to pay for mistakes tolerated in the past.

I say frankly: it is not an easy burden to bear. The vital resource for restructuring is in short supply, namely, the enthusiasm and energy of young people who are, I believe, capable of restructuring, not just an obsolete socio-political system, but the whole world. Any hope of restructuring without this resource is like launching a rocket without fuel. There is only one conclusion: we must create this social energy resource in the course of restructuring, developing it at the same time as we change the system of social relationships.

For this, a strong, honest and just social policy is necessary, capable of convincing the most hardened sceptics that this time the Party's word does not diverge from its deed, that the course of society's strategic development is being recharted and does now lead in the direction of socialism.

Our literature on the subject does not at the moment make the distinction between the broad and the narrow concept of the term 'social policy'. These concepts should, however, be distinguished by calling them, say, societal and social policies.

Social policy in the narrow sense is the programme of state measures to support those groups and social strata that find themselves for a number of reasons in the greatest difficulties, that suffer from specific circumstances and cannot improve their situation by their own efforts. Such groups include, for example, pensioners, orphans, students, working mothers, low-paid workers, inhabitants of small villages or particularly remote regions, the disabled, and inadequately housed families.

The chief aims of social policy at the present stage can be stated as follows: firstly, creating conditions for the fullest satisfaction of the material and spiritual needs of all social groups and, secondly, strengthening justice in all social relationships – economic, political, legal and moral. To put it crudely, the first aim consists in increasing the size of the 'cake' intended for public consumption and the second in dividing it up in accordance with the public sense of justice. It has to be said that such a down-to-earth concept of justice can diverge very widely from the scientific concept. In such a case public opinion must be gradually changed and made more competent. It is important, however, that social policy is perceived by the public as being just, here and now, and not just in the future.

Societal policy is broader in content than social policy. It is aimed at achieving a more complex and important goal – the thoroughgoing modification of social structures and institutions in order to achieve more genuinely socialist relations. In other words, to transform the historically created administrative and bureaucratic system into a complex, multifarious and at the same time classless socialist structure, ensuring efficient economic development and raising people's social quality as citizens and individuals.

In accordance with these aims, societal policy has a distinct social and class orientation, i.e. it is directed consistently and unequivocally in support of forces that will regenerate and cleanse society and towards patiently winning the trust and support of that section of working people that does not yet have a clear enough understanding of where its interests lie, while consistently restraining and eliminating forces that oppose the movement towards socialism. The breadth and scale of these aims underlie the richness and diversity of the means at the disposal of societal policy. As well as social policy measures (in the narrow sense of the word), these strategies include improvement of the economic mechanism, a personnel management policy, the regeneration of political and legal institutions, and the development of openness.

The economic mechanism and social policy represent different but associated elements of societal policy. Their relative independence of each other is due to differences in the functions they perform and the strategies they employ. The economic mechanism chiefly regulates the current economic interests of individual workers and entire workforces. It acts as a stimulus to the various modes of economic behaviour that secure sufficiently rapid and efficient economic growth. Social policy, on the other hand, is aimed at creating good living conditions and making it possible for all groups and strata to develop socially. It regulates people's values, needs, interests and motivation, and brings about their personal identification with the social aims and ideas of restructuring.

However, the economic mechanism and social policy are interconnected. Any economic mechanism is bound to place certain groups in a less advantaged position than others and, within its own terms of reference, it is not possible to correct this injustice. As a result, a social policy is needed that is capable of redressing the balance and alleviating the hardship of certain groups. On the other hand, social policy measures may have a rather adverse effect on people's economic behaviour. Thus, the present system of retirement pension provision discourages pensioners who still retain vital energy from continuing to work. Taking another example: in some large families, uneducated parents who may draw a significant sum in the form of child allowances refuse to take a job and are, in effect, parasites upon their own children, depriving them of essentials. The economic mechanism and social policy must not therefore be formulated in isolation but on the basis of common ideas and in pursuit of common goals.

As a result, in addition to its own functions, social policy inevitably acts as an auxiliary to efficient economic development. A certain inversion comes into play here. While from the theoretical point of view, economic development is the means, whereas social development is the aim of socialism, in practice the resolution of social problems often has to take second place to economic interests, i.e. economic development is regarded as the aim, and an improvement in living standards simply as the means of achieving it. This contradiction completely permeates our whole existence today. To a certain extent, however, it is conditioned by the stage of development that society has reached. The resolution of any social problem requires material resources, and any significant advance in the social area is impossible without rapid economic growth. The state must therefore manoeuvre between economic and social aims, achieving a balance between them as best it can.

By and large measures aimed at raising economic efficiency and increasing social justice coincide. Thus, distributing personal incomes and other benefits in accordance with the amount and quality of work done by different social groups simultaneously performs both tasks. This, however, is more of a general tendency. In practice, every so often the economic and the social criteria for tackling certain matters come into conflict so that preference has to be given either to one or the other.

Take, for example, the notorious practice that occurs in the construction of industrial projects in undeveloped regions, where factories must be built at the same time as blocks of flats, nurseries, schools, shops, and hospitals, not to mention road or rail links and power supply lines, etc. As a rule, even at the planning stage, designers cannot work within the prescribed financial limitations and begin to think of how to cut building costs. Everybody knows that this cannot be done without using expensive modern technology. Economies are made by cutting down on the construction of public facilities and amenities, which are indefinitely postponed. The following type of reasoning is used: 'Let people live in barracks and other types of temporary accommodation for the time being. They'll suffer a bit, but when the factory is built, we'll soon catch up with the backlog in social construction.' Nothing is said about the fact that this 'soon' can amount to a 10–15 years' delay. Unfortunately, such a model for the development of new regions has been the rule for decades, and it is not an easy matter to overcome this stereotype. It can be seen in many dozens of ugly towns with a poor infrastructure, difficult living conditions and a resultant very mobile 'floating' population with a far from satisfactory work record. Correcting and eliminating this type of mistake, achieving a balance between the economic and social development of towns and regions is one of the important tasks of the strong social policy currently being put forward.

I have already mentioned the fact that by the early 1980s a large number of acute social problems had accumulated. In the 'stagnation' period these problems were not only not being tackled, but were not even the subject of public debate. They were hushed up, pushed into the background, creating a pre-crisis, if not a crisis, situation.

The first of these problems was the increasingly acute scarcity of essential foodstuffs, a deterioration in their quality, and the concealed, but obvious and appreciable, rise in retail prices which the growth in money incomes had difficulty in keeping up with.

In common with most other Soviet specialists, I have no faith in the optimistic statistics concerning the trend in living standards that have been published by the Central Statistical Office over the past decades. Even so, they indicate that the pace of improvement decreased with each five-year period. According to public opinion, however, standards of living fell rather than rose in the 'stagnation' period, in any event for the largest groups in the population. It was particularly difficult for people on fixed incomes – pensioners, for example. As a result of the increased cost of goods and services, their real incomes decreased and life became increasingly difficult. That is why (although it is not the only reason) pension reform is now so urgent.

A no less pressing set of problems relates to the provision of accommodation. In spite of the fact that in the course of the sixth to eleventh Five Year Plans more than 65 million flats were built, with an average floor space of more than 3,000 million square metres, and 236 million people acquired new homes, housing provision is still inadequate and is far from satisfying demand. Waiting lists are growing longer rather than shorter and not everybody who wants to live in a larger flat even qualifies to be taken on. In Novosibirsk, for example, only households in which each member has no more than eight square metres of living space qualify for the waiting list, and in some other towns this criterion is even narrower. A rapid rise in the wages of building workers without a corresponding rise in productivity and the increased cost of building materials have led to a 20–25 per cent rise in the cost of building flats in each five-year plan period. There was a sharp rise in the prices of co-operative flats which only the prosperous minority was able to afford. There has been a sharp deterioration in the quality of construction. Most families, on acquiring a new flat, have first of all to bring it up to an acceptable standard. Finally, the growing shortage of flats has made their allocation more difficult and fraught with problems. The unequal distribution of house-building between town and country, republics and regions, and different social groups has become more extreme than ever.

Public services have equally complex problems, particularly in the fields of education, health and culture. The social value attached to health is increasing the world over. This tendency can be seen in the Soviet Union also: with each passing decade an increasing proportion of people cite health as the most important factor in their lives. In fact, however, the Soviet health service is in a critical condition. As far as the number of doctors per ten thousand people is concerned, we are, it is true, almost the best in the world. But what is the standard of their qualifications and conditions of work? There are not enough hospitals, clinics, out-patients' departments, or adequate in-patient accommodation. There are constant queues in the doctors' surgeries and a ridiculously short time is allotted to seeing each patient so that the patient cannot count on receiving careful attention. In rural areas medical treatment is particularly difficult to obtain as there is virtually no home visiting and sick people usually have to go to the doctor's surgery some ten or more kilometres away. To this must be added an acute shortage, and sometimes a complete absence, of modern medical equipment, diagnostic aids, physiotherapy and effective medicines.

Having analysed the situation, the Party leadership and the government have come to the conclusion that radical reform of the national health service is imperative. But similar reforms are needed in nearly all the other service sectors – education, cultural facilities, retail trade, personal services, public catering, and passenger transport. All those sectors that are meant to ensure adequate living conditions have fallen behind to an intolerable extent and are in need of rapid development.

As can be seen, many acute social problems have been inherited from the past and the present restructuring of economic relations described in the previous chapter is giving rise to a host of new problems. All this creates a certain degree of social tension. People are gaining a clearer understanding of how neglected this area is, how complex and far-reaching the measures that have to be taken, and how much stronger and more effective social policy must become.

What qualities must social policy possess in order to be described as 'strong'? In my opinion, it should differ from previous policies in the following ways:

i) It should completely abandon the 'remainder' principle of investment, according to which only those resources that remain after the needs of production have been met are allocated for tackling social problems. It is essential that the growth rate of social expenditure should outstrip the growth rate of gross national income.

ii) It should resolve basic social problems instead of following the usual practice of making 'stop-gap' statements about grand strategic goals. It should concentrate attention and resources on dealing with a limited number of questions that represent the 'most painful' issues for society.

iii) It should cease to apply identical social solutions on a country-wide scale and adopt a differentiated approach to the social problems of town and country, different national republics and regions, small and large towns, and different demographic and professional groups.

iv) It should change the emphasis in political aims. Unlike the previous aim of 'establishing complete social uniformity', greater importance should now be attached to such tasks as raising living standards and achieving more just redistribution. In addition, social policy is consistently directed towards activating economic behaviour and encouraging useful economic initiatives.

At first glance, the two chief aims of current social policy – raising people's standard of living and achieving a more just distribution – seem unrelated. In principle, a small cake can be shared out fairly, and a large one unfairly. In real life, however, these problems are interconnected since historical ratios between distribution and consumption are extremely stable and unresponsive to change. It is very difficult to take away from any social stratum or group what they have had for decades and which has become an integral part of their way of life. Except in the case of wealth deliberately stolen from the people, such redistribution is not after all very fair. That is why social policy regulates redistribution of the annual increase in wealth rather than the total amount.

A large increase in national income and consumption would make it possible to raise the earnings of those categories of workers whose wages have fallen behind; to provide more new flats for people living in overcrowded conditions or in basements or semi-basements, for large families, etc., etc. In a word, the more rapid the rise in people's living standards, the easier it is to improve distribution ratios. However, when living standards are stagnating and consumption is hardly growing at all, it is more difficult to deal with social problems, and social development takes on a haphazard character. At the same time, the general increase in 'social entropy' leads to the growth of injustice and a chance element in distribution. Group egotism increases, and it is not the most worthy and industrious who flourish but the smartest and most cunning.

As a result, the two aims of social policy actually merge in practice. In order to achieve social justice, consumption must be increased much more rapidly than hitherto. To do this, however, without any intention of increasing social justice means losing the basic point of reference.

These days the concept of social justice is used more often than before in the press and in the works of sociologists. Experts argue about the exact meaning of the concept, while journalists cite instances of officials in various departments trampling on the ideas of justice.

Millions of ordinary people write to the newspapers or the authorities in an attempt to obtain justice for themselves or their families. I believe most Soviet people today would be genuinely surprised if they realized that only a few years ago the term 'social justice' was regarded by Soviet social scientists as something alien to socialism, smacking of 'bourgeois liberalism'. A small collection of articles, which used the term 'social justice' in its title, was published by the Institute of Sociological Research of the USSR Academy of Sciences in 1983, and, in fact, it was not easy to get it into print.[1]

Dozens of books and more than a hundred articles have now been written on these questions. It is more or less generally accepted that the actual content of the concept 'social justice' must depend on the type of society and the relations inherent in it. In a socialist society it is understood in one sense, in a capitalist society in another, and in a feudal or slave-owning society in yet another. We talk more often, therefore, not about social justice in general, but about 'socialist justice', understanding by that social justice in the socialist sense.

Socialist justice has many aspects: social, economic, political, legal and moral, each of which is very important. I myself, as an economist and sociologist, am concerned primarily with the socio-economic aspect of the concept, the substance of which is expressed in the principle: 'From each according to his abilities, and to each according to his work'.

Some specialists, not to mention most ordinary working people, are inclined to the opinion that social justice under socialism, as in other types of society, is expressed by a degree of equality between all social classes, strata and groups, i.e. it is achieved only on the basis of social uniformity. At first glance, this idea has its attractions, but its weakness is its lack of historicity and the absence of any relation to the concrete conditions of time and place. At the present stage of the Soviet Union's development, the slogan of universal social equality, irrespective of a person's contribution through work towards the development of society, is in my view reactionary and harmful. We understand socialist justice in the sense that all members of our society, in whatever part of the country and into whichever family they were born, should be able to develop their natural abilities, receive comprehensive and vocational education, be trained for efficient and qualified work, and be given the opportunity of utilizing their knowledge and skill in the economy. However, the share of social wealth received by different groups of workers must directly depend on their work.

The above criteria may be applied only to the healthy and able-bodied section of the population, however. There are socio-demographic groups of people who cannot and should not work, such as children, the disabled, and old-age pensioners, some of whom, moreover, do not have any family. The principle of socialist justice must include social guarantees for these groups also.

Apart from this, distribution according to work done usually takes place in respect of that part of income spent on personal consumption, i.e. food, clothing, footwear, household furnishing, holiday trips, etc. One of the advantages of socialism, however, is the broad development of public forms of consumption and use – education services, specialist training, health care institutions, sanatoria and rest homes, sports centres, etc. The availability of these services for different groups depends on the location of amenities and facilities and the development of public services. The location of a social infrastructure in different regions and residential centres (from large town to small village) is a specific element in relations of distribution that are closely bound up with the problem of social justice.

The following sections of this chapter develop what has been said so far. They examine problems connected with ensuring people's right to develop and make use of their abilities, the principles guiding the payment of wages, the regulation of the consumer market, and the system of socio-economic guarantees available to the public.

DEVELOPMENT AND REALIZATION OF ABILITIES

The essence of socialist social relations is briefly expressed in the principle 'from each according to his abilities, to each according to his work'. In the Soviet Union children learn this principle, if not in the nursery, then in the first classes at school, and hear it so often that when they grow up it often becomes hackneyed and trivialized and 'goes in one ear and out the other'. When, however, one directs attention to this principle by asking what it does in fact mean, the overwhelming response will be: the necessity to distribute personal incomes according to the quantity and quality of work done. In other words, public perception of the second part of the principle of socialism has imperceptibly begun to predominate over the first. However, the creation of conditions when all members of society are able to develop their abilities and utilize them effectively has scarcely less significance in the formation of socialism than the distribution of incomes according to work. For it is just that which represents a stage in the progress of our society towards its highest goal – the many-sided and harmonious development of the human personality, and the level of self-realization of that personality in creative work. It would seem that as society progresses and, in particular, people's material needs are met, so will the consistent application of the principle 'from each according to his abilities' grow in significance as one of the aims of socialism.

But what in concrete terms does this formula mean, i.e. under what conditions can it be said that a person's contribution towards social development really corresponds to their abilities? I would name three such conditions. The first consists in giving all children, teenagers and young adults the opportunity of developing the broad spectrum of their abilities before they start work. It consists in creating the necessary conditions so that by the time they leave school most young people have acquired the vocational and practical, social and moral qualities that will allow them to make reasonably full use of their abilities in creative work.

The second condition consists in providing every worker with the kind of job or the opportunity to pursue an occupation that not only ensures that their existing abilities are utilized but that they are developed as well.

The third condition is giving people employed in social, co-operative or individual production the practical opportunity to work to their full ability and in this way achieve a greater level of professionalism and optimal results as well as realize their own potential in amateur entertainments, sport, art, and voluntary social and political activity.

Each of the above conditions has an inner structure, i.e. contains a number of more concrete requirements. Let us examine, for example, the problem of developing intellectual and physical abilities, beginning in childhood and finishing when working life begins. At least two aspects associated with the formation of professional and moral qualities can be distinguished here. The first presupposes favourable conditions (these should not be too differentiated for different social groups) for obtaining primary, secondary, vocational and university education, i.e. knowledge including qualifications that gives access to particular kinds of work. The second aspect entails providing suitable conditions for the effective socialization of the young and the handing down of moral principles from the older generations to the younger ones. Experience has shown that the extent of a person's knowledge and their moral qualities do not necessarily go hand in hand, just as a high level of professionalism does not of itself make a person an outstanding worker. More than that, a range of vocational skills combined with a moral vacuum and cynicism represent a considerable danger to society, inasmuch as people with these qualities become 'fixers' in the shadow economy, embezzlers, extortionists, and bribe-takers.

Tsarist Russia was a country with very extensive illiteracy while the Soviet Union has become a country with a highly-developed educational system and an educated and cultured people. At the present time the complete secondary (10-year) education of young people is compulsory and is provided free of charge. In 1939 out of every thousand workers employed in the economy, only 110 had received secondary and 13 higher education. In 1987, however, the respective figures were 764 and 125. In four decades the relative number of people with secondary school education had increased nearly seven times, and those with higher education nearly ten times.

The network of creches and day nurseries has been widely extended. Since 1960 they have doubled in number and the number of children attending them has quadrupled. Whereas in 1960 only 13 per cent of children attended these places (24 per cent in towns and 4 per cent in the country), now it is 57 per cent (70 per cent in towns and 37 per cent in the country). More than 50 million children attend such after-school centres as youth clubs, music, art and ballet schools, workshops for young technicians and naturalists, children's libraries, sports clubs, etc. The state attaches great importance to the fact that schooling is universal, provides all school-leavers with a full secondary education, and affords them equal opportunities in society. At the same time, however, it tries to maintain a variety in types of school, increase flexibility in syllabuses and courses, and pay greater attention to the development of individual abilities. To this end, children are increasingly being educated in accordance with their individual requirements and talents. A network of special schools and classes is being developed where some subjects are studied in greater depth and where a number of the courses are taught in a foreign language.

After leaving school, most young people can continue their education at technical college or university. Whereas in 1968, 45 per cent of school-leavers received further education, in 1986 it was more than 60 per cent. All in all the figures are fairly impressive. In this area, however, there are more unresolved than resolved problems, and the public is deeply concerned about the state of our educational system.

In February 1988 a Plenary Session of the Party Central Committee examined questions relating to the radical restructuring of secondary and higher education. It looked at the practical task of creating a system of continuous education to cover all levels – pre-school nurseries and after-school centres, comprehensive secondary schools and vocational and technical colleges, and specialist colleges of further education and universities as well as in-service and retraining centres. The bureaucratic management of education was severely criticized: an alternative would be to introduce self-management into schools and colleges and make them independent in their search for the best forms and methods of teaching young people. The meeting emphasized the need to expand the material and technological basis of education, significantly increase resources allocated to the building and provisioning of creches and day nurseries, transfer most schools to the single-shift system, create suitable material, social and other day-to-day conditions enabling teachers to work creatively, and produce many more modern teaching aids including books, audio-visual aids, laboratory equipment, toys, etc,.

Social problems relating to the organization of education also need resolving, in particular the great differences between schools as regards teaching content and the level to which pupils' abilities are developed. This problem has aspects that are regional, national or ethnic, or purely social in character. Thus, a rural school still lags far behind an urban school as far as teaching standards are concerned, as does the average urban school behind a school in the capital city. A difference is also apparent in the standard of teacher training, the quality of school buildings, their provision with laboratories, modern teaching equipment, libraries, etc. Pupils from rural schools, therefore, have significantly less chance of continuing their studies in 'centres of excellence' than their peers living in the towns. Thus, in the 1986/7 academic year 50 per cent of college or university students had parents who were office workers, 41 per cent were the children of industrial workers, and 9 per cent came from peasant families. In less prestigious further education colleges, students whose parents were office workers constituted only 27 per cent, the children of industrial workers accounted for 58 per cent, while those from peasant families were 15 per cent of the total enrolment. These figures show that there are still appreciable differences in the quality of education received by different social groups and, consequently, in their opportunities in life.

Another inequality that is difficult to eradicate exists between pupils who have Russian as their native language and those who do not. Russian schoolchildren have access to the riches of their own and most other national cultures since the best literature of the Union republics is usually translated into Russian. Other nationals are often faced with the question of which school they should send their child to – to a Russian-language or a national-language school (e.g. Armenian, Estonian, Uzbek, etc). On leaving a Russian school, a young person has a fair knowledge of the Russian language, which facilitates admission to the better colleges and universities. However, teaching in Russian schools in all the Union republics follows a uniform syllabus. Pupils of these schools, therefore, obtain minimal knowledge of their own national culture, and many parents prefer to send their children to schools that devote more attention to the history, culture and art of their own people. In most of these schools, however, the children have a poor grasp of Russian and this limits their chances of receiving a first-class further education. It should be possible to run additional classes related to the study of other national cultures in Russian schools in the Russian Republic and to improve the teaching of Russian in national schools. In principle this is quite possible but in practice it is not yet being done, and the problem remains acute.

Considerable inequality also still exists in teaching children from different social strata. The situation is least satisfactory for children of collective farmers and rural workers, somewhat better for the children of urban industrial and office workers, but best of all for children of the intelligentsia and particularly top officials. In almost every large town there are some 'model' schools with well-qualified and able teachers, smaller classes, modern computer technology, language laboratories, sports halls, swimming pools, first-class workshops and so on. Most of these schools specialize in teaching physics, mathematics, chemistry, biology and other subjects to a high level, and some students leave with translation diplomas. Some children of industrial and office workers attend these schools but as a rule the majority are children of the upper intelligentsia. Moreover, parents with a high social status can, if necessary, hire home tutors, etc. As a result, a less gifted child from a 'good family' can finish school with better results and enter a more interesting profession than a more able fellow-pupil who does not have such advantages.

Social passions usually run high when the time comes for school-leavers to go to a polytechnic or, particularly, a college. In principle this is done on a competitive basis by means of selective entrance examinations. There are several applicants for every place at most colleges and universities, sometimes even more than ten, and those who achieve the highest marks gain admission. This would seem quite fair since the level of knowledge shown reflects both natural ability and the applicants' desire to study and their ability to work hard and conscientiously. In some colleges, however, the competitive system of admission is being breached: corruption, extortion and bribery are springing up. Admission may depend not on ability but on payment of a sum of money. Grades for examination passes are even given in exchange for money. Naturally, under these circumstances, the teachers (if they can be called that) lose the moral right to ask anything of their students, including expecting them to attend lectures and seminars. As a result the very idea of higher education is devalued and the acquisition of knowledge is replaced by an unmerited diploma given out at the end of the course.

What such a system leads to can be judged from the following extract from the newspaper *Sotsialisticheskaya industriya* (3 February 1988):

A special commission of the Soviet Ministry of Higher Education carried out an inspection at the Bryansk Technological Institute. Out of 98 first-year students in three faculties, 81 could not justify the marks they were given in the entrance examinations in mathematics. In physics not a single student passed the test, and out of 240 extremely simple problems, the number solved was . . . ten! In the third-year course maths tests were held. Only three students displayed enough knowledge to earn a satisfactory mark. The others did not even understand what the questions were about.

This is an extreme example. But the fact that it can happen at all indicates that acute social problems exist in the field of education. Restructuring social relations will create the conditions for creating a healthier situation but the process is not easy and will take time.

Problems no less, and perhaps even more, complex are associated with the moral education of young people. The dreadful bureaucratization of the education system which began in the Stalinist period and grew worse in the stagnation period has inflicted irreparable damage on several generations. Instead of developing children's honesty, openness, fairness, spirit of enquiry, and independence of thought, the bureaucratic soul-less school became a kingdom of hypocrisy revealing a divergence between thought, word and deed. It created and in many ways continues even now to create double moral standards, deceitfulness, conformism, moral nihilism, and alienation from social values. Our society is now paying the price for long-standing conformism to the phenomena of stagnation in the 'inexplicable' attitudes adopted by children, the extreme anti-humanism and cruelty displayed by teenagers, and the irresponsible behaviour of adults.

The following was written by Academician V. Trefilov, the Vice-President of the Ukrainian Academy of Sciences:[2]

It gives me no peace of mind to know that the Chernobyl Nuclear Power Station was brought to catastrophe by people with engineering diplomas in their pockets. Where were their knowledge and civil conscience that fateful night when, contrary to the strictest orders, they broke the whole sequence of the security system . . .? How can one understand the people who stood on the bridge of the ships that collided on the Black Sea? In our times, whether flying an aeroplane, operating a reactor, constructing an electronic microscope or managing scientific and technological progress, success depends in equal measure on professionalism, competence and high standards of discipline and civic responsibility. The 20th century is the century of specialists. But it is also a century that makes very high moral demands on them.

Trefilov proposes 'a thorough and thoughtful review of our system of retraining and advanced training in technological progress in all our universities, courses and schools of advanced studies. Subject teaching must of necessity be combined with moral and political education'. Clearly, a high standard of personal and social morality is no less important than professional knowledge for the development and utilization of the abilities of working people.

Since neither school nor the Communist Youth League has yet come to grips with these tasks, the main hope for instilling moral values in children must be placed in the family. It is in fact difficult to overestimate the influence of parents in their children's upbringing and socialization. There is much truth in the old saying 'like father, like son'. The pity is that the modern family is itself undergoing a serious crisis. The number of divorces per thousand marriages is increasing, the average length of time that couples remain together is getting shorter, and there is a growing number of one-parent families, usually consisting of children being brought up by their mother who usually goes out to work. Moreover, the increasingly common one-child family rules out any help being given by the older children in bringing up the young ones. The growing number of small families and their 'nuclearization' is weakening the role of grandparents. As a result, the social and moral qualities of some young people are deteriorating, which often detracts from the effect of increased education.

Thus, it is early days to talk about creating conditions for the harmonious development of the abilities and work potential of all members of our society. This requires a social policy directed towards a comprehensive reform of the educational system which would bring its particularly backward areas up to standard and take measures to strengthen society's moral principles.

I shall now turn to an examination of the second condition for making efficient use of people's abilities, namely, the possibility of giving all workers jobs or functions that correspond to their personal inclinations, talents and education. This depends on several factors, firstly the existence of a general balance between the structure of employment, on the one hand, and workers' social need for employment of a certain quality, on the other. I mentioned above that there is no unemployment in our country, nor is it envisaged. The initial stage of the required balance has therefore been achieved: everyone who wants to work can easily find a job. But is this the job the person would want in order to make full use of his or her abilities? More than two thirds of the jobs in agriculture, more than half those in construction and more than a third in industry require unskilled, manual labour. The Central Statistical Office estimates that the number of workers whose jobs need to be mechanized as a matter of priority amounts to 15 million. However these jobs are distributed among different social groups, it is still not possible to satisfy people's need for interesting and demanding work.

In this connection, mention must be made of the comprehensive and specific plan for doing away with unskilled manual labour that was initiated in the late 1970s and early 1980s. It was assumed that this would take 15–20 years. However, the programme was not accepted at government level. Either the underlying rationale was not sufficiently convincing or its sponsors did not have enough 'clout'. In any event, the question was dropped. In practice, the gap between the rising level of vocational training and the structure of employment was widening. A pressing task for current policy therefore is the social re-orientation of scientific and technological progress in such a way as to ensure not only rising economic indicators but also better satisfaction of workers' need for skilled and interesting work.

The availability of jobs that correspond to the experience and abilities of different groups of workers also depends on where those jobs are to be found and on people's freedom of movement between regions and towns. For example, in a rural area job choice is very much narrower than in the towns. In rural areas most women work with livestock or grow vegetables, while men usually work as machine-operators or drivers. In small and medium-sized towns the choice of occupations is significantly wider due to the presence of a number of factories and service establishments. The widest choice, however, exists in large towns with a population of more than 500,000.

This situation exists throughout the modern world and is unlikely to change in the foreseeable future. And in itself it is not a source of social injustice. What is important is that people who want to do more complex and skilled work should be free to change their place of residence and to move from country to town and from a small to a large town. In the Soviet Union, however, there is a low level of regional mobility: only 5 per cent of the population change their permanent place of residence each year, and most of them are young people going away to study or returning home afterwards.

People are prevented from increasing their mobility by a whole number of circumstances: the existence of language barriers due to the Soviet Union's multi-national character; the extreme difficulty in obtaining a permit to live in many towns; the housing system whereby a family cannot give up their flat in one town and be offered a similar one in another. Almost the only way of moving from one place to another without an offer of work from an organization which is obliged to provide accommodation is by exchanging flats. But this too is hedged about with many restrictions caused by the suspicion that if an unequal exchange takes place the party losing out could receive a sum of money by way of compensation and thus make a profit from the transfer of state housing. Also, when flats situated in different towns or regions are valued, personal circumstances play an important part, as do the value systems of the people concerned. One person, let us say, is prepared to squeeze into a tiny flat in a large town, while another is prepared to move into the countryside if only to have more room to live in. It is difficult for them to effect an exchange, however. People become tied to particular places and consequently regional variations in the structure of employment take on a social character.

Job availability also depends on personnel policies adopted by the authorities and senior management in industry. The question is, who is promoted to prestigious, creative and highly-paid positions: people who are more capable and better trained or those who show more devotion to their superiors, are more 'obedient' and ready to carry out any order without questioning its validity?

Unfortunately, the Leninist principles of personnel policy – openness and democracy in promotion decisions, accountability, allround consideration of practical and political qualities – all these were forgotten in many republics and regions in the stagnation period. Let us take just one example. In January 1988 a Plenary Session of the Central Committee of the Kazakhstan Communist Party examined questions relating to personnel policy. Reporting the session G. Dildyaev and T. Esilbaev write as follows:[3]

> Decades of protectionism, nepotism, and the power of the old-boys' network have given jobs to a lot of unworthy people. Not all the weeds have yet been rooted out. Early last year [i.e. soon after the disturbances in Alma-Ata in December 1986], while attempting to improve the moral and psychological climate and maintain respect for top officials, the Central Committee was in no hurry to re-shuffle the leadership. And yet some of them had been promoted by their protectors and, despite this, were continuing to hold posts they did not deserve. Today the Plenary Session conceded that this was a mistake. Not because these people were consciously obstructing the restructuring process, although such things have happened. No, most of them just could not fall into step with the demands of the time, they were prevented by the weight of old stereotypes and obligations to those who had quite unjustly given them the boss's chair.

It should be added that in some regions positions holding out the promise of great financial gain (in management, sale of goods and equipment to industry, retail trade, public catering, etc.) were not only given to the bosses' favourites but were even sold at a high price. We can imagine the position of people who were well-trained, had a clear-cut programme for increasing efficiency, possessed the practical and moral qualities needed for leadership, but did not have the necessary family connections or a lot of money. Did they have the chance of working according to their abilities? This applies not only to top appointments but in ordinary cases of promotion according to skill. The democratization of personnel policy, the regeneration of its principles, is both an aim and a condition of the success of restructuring and part of the new social policy.

Finally, we turn to the third condition for the practical implementation of the principle 'from each according to his abilities' – by giving everyone the opportunity to work to the full extent of their physical and intellectual abilities.

During the stagnation period heavy restrictions were placed on the freedom of nearly all categories of employees, 'tying them down' with hundreds of often contradictory instructions. In fact, it was not just a matter of instructions. I mentioned above that 80 per cent of agricultural workers considered they were not working at full capacity and could work more efficiently. What is stopping them now? The great majority of workers point to the poor organization of production, shortages of essential materials, fuel, seed, animal feed, constant breakdowns of equipment, a lack of spare parts and the resultant lengthy delays for reasons beyond their control. To this they add a poor structure of wages, a conflict of interests between different sections of workers, and a system of incentives that encourages good interim results rather than a good final outcome. In their opinion, if these weaknesses were overcome, they could raise productivity by 30–50 per cent. This is what it was planned to achieve over a period of nearly two five-year plans at the cost of huge capital investment.

In the preceding chapter I discussed the constraint on top managers, who until recently could not (and frequently still cannot) take independent decisions. Now I should like to look at the position of writers, artists, architects, scientists, musicians, and so on. To work effectively they must have freedom from censorship, be able to present their work to those for whom it is intended, and receive objective and interested criticism. However, management of the cultural arena including professional associations of writers, artists, journalists, actors and producers was until recently just as bureaucratic as management of the economy. Powerful publishing firms saw it as their main aim in life to edit out everything that was lively, vivid or unusual. Free and unfettered thought aroused editors' indignation and was considered by them as 'ideological scrap'. The result was, on the one hand, the prevalence of insipid books, plays, and films and, on the other, the screening-off of readers and audiences from great works of art. The publication in many of our literary journals of works written five, ten, fifteen years ago, which evoked enormous interest at the time but were prevented from finding a readership, is one of the best outcomes of restructuring in the cultural field. Such, for example, were the novels *Children of the Arbat* by Rybakov, *White Clothes* by Dudintsev, *Doctor Zhivago* by Pasternak, the play *And On . . . and On . . . and On* by Shatrov, Bulgakov's writings, etc.

The following is an extract from a statement by Elem Klimov, the new chairperson of the Union of Film Workers, on the destructive effect of the stagnation period (re-Stalinization) on the creative personality:[4]

> At that time many people had the feeling that it was impossible to produce anything serious in the cinema. And this was terrible because it was as if either you had no future or you had to adapt yourself, change your principles and aspirations. Some people did indeed do this – betrayed themselves . . . Who will return to these many talented people the long years spent in meaningless, stupifying struggle?

Klimov is echoed by Chingiz Aitmatov:[5]

> Our greatest fault in the stagnation period was that by leaving things to others we allowed society's potential for transformation – in work, the economy, scientific and humanitarian knowledge – to become deadened. We ourselves put the shackles of dogmatic and conventional thinking on the freedom-loving flight of discovery and daring. We refused to seek out socialism's inner alternatives or its contradictions. We preferred not to think about the fact that statements often diverge from practice.

By 'we', Aitmatov means the Soviet people as a whole, responsible for its own history. But a more concrete analysis makes clear that in the period of re-Stalinization 'we' conducted ourselves in very different ways. Some people, like Aitmatov himself, did everything in their power to resist the pernicious spirit of stagnation and give people the truth through culture, art, and science, while others devoted their energies to 'pulling, not pushing'.

Aitmatov continues:

> Restructuring and openness now carry within them the recovery of our sight and self-release from the heavy burden of the past in all spheres of life. And this road to a cleansing and to freedom seems to me in present-day circumstances the most fruitful, wise, and humane, and in accord with the enlightened manner of the times.

It is difficult not to agree with this. But it must be clearly understood that the road is difficult and demands much effort and time.

The general conclusion to be drawn from what has been said in this section is that, despite considerable social victories and advances, the principle 'from each according to his abilities' has not been put into practice adequately. Its more consistent implementation will require a multiple effort from society and its effectiveness will depend above all on how consistently and thoughtfully any necessary measures are reflected in the social policy of the Communist Party and the Soviet state.

INCOME DISTRIBUTION POLICY

The most general formulation of the principle of distribution according to work, put forward by Marx in *Critique of the Gotha Programme*, states that after any necessary deductions for satisfying social needs every worker in socialist production receives from society the same quantity of labour as he himself gave to society in another form. In other words, relations between society and workers operate on the basis of equivalence. Workers receive the larger part of the payment due to them in the form of money, they spend it as individuals, and they take their share of the remaining part of expenditure together with other members of society. Understood in this way, the principle of distribution presupposes the combination of two types of evaluation: firstly, the quantity and quality of the labour given to society by different groups of workers and, secondly, the various types of consumer goods received by them in exchange. The first type of evaluation is obtained by variously determined rates of pay (salaries, piece-rates, bonuses, etc.). The second type is obtained through retail prices for consumer goods or services. This means that a condition of effecting distribution according to work is that not only should the wages of different categories of worker correspond to the quantity and quality of their labour but the prices of consumer goods should correspond to their social market value. The first part of the problem involves the comparative measurement of qualitatively different types of labour, and the second, of different types of goods.

The Marxist classics did not reveal the exact content of those particular features of labour which can and must be used in making comparative measurements of its various forms for the purpose of distributing income. Moreover, as has been shown in practice, there are different approaches to this task. The most fundamental difference is the social evaluation of labour, a) according to its volume and

b) according to its final outcome. It is hardly necessary to explain the difference between the quantity of labour expended and its outcome, i.e. the value of output where economic efficiency is a basic determinant. There are also different approaches to the comparison of the final outcome of labour. Whereas the quantitative side of such a comparison presents no particular difficulty, the qualitative side is extraordinarily complex. Let us take, for example, the work of scientists or writers. The quantitative outcome of their labour can be evaluated according to the number of pages written. It is obviously much more difficult, however, to make a qualitative evaluation of the text and its artistic, scientific, philosophical and moral qualities.

In different periods of Soviet power and in different sectors of the economy a great many different principles for the evaluation and measurement of labour for the purpose of income distribution have been tried out. They can be divided into two types – the administrative and the economic. In the previous chapter I analysed different methods of regulating wages as a specific component of the economic mechanism. I shall now examine the same problem from another angle, namely, from the point of view of social justice and, accordingly, of social policy.

I would remind the reader that essentially the administrative regulation of wages meant that enterprises and organizations were instructed 'from above' regarding the size of their wage bills and the exact terms on which they paid each group of workers. The positive aspect of this system, which explains why it was used, is a) the fairly rigid regulation of the money supply, i.e. the weakening of inflationary tendencies, and b) the planned regulation of wage payments by industry, category of employment, and region, i.e. broken down according to government department, category of worker, and geographic region. Its main drawback is the rigid 'ceiling' on pay for any type of work irrespective of result, which restricts initiative, enterprise and creativity.

The economic method of wage regulation has a different social content. Here calculation will be based on sales revenue. Central and local taxes are paid at a fixed rate and the cost of inputs is covered, and then the rest (the enterprise's gross income) is divided up between wages, the financing of expansion, and social welfare schemes. The advantage of this method of income distribution is that earnings are directly related to output and productivity. Judging by the experience of a number of socialist countries, its main drawback is that the gap between incomes (purchasing power), on the one hand, and the availability of goods, on the other, may widen which brings the threat of inflation. The macroeconomic regulation of wages also becomes more complex, once wage fixing is decentralized and becomes less amenable to control.

The long-standing predominance of administrative wage regulation has had two specific results that are not easy to explain to a Western reader – the 'levelling off' and the 'topping up' of wages. 'Levelling off' occurs when highly-skilled work is paid at almost the same rate as (sometimes less than) unskilled, when physically hard work is paid only slightly more than light work, and highly responsible work almost the same as that entailing no responsibility. Pay differentials for qualitatively different types of work do, of course, exist but bear little relation to differences in labour input. 'Topping up' is akin to 'levelling off'. This is the term given to the system which destroys the most natural logic of economic relations. Instead of wages being calculated on the basis of output, output indicators are set artificially at a level justifying a fixed level of wages. For example, skilled building workers will not work for less than 350 roubles a month. Suppose that due to irregular delivery of cement they have to waste a lot of time and earn only 250 roubles. If that was all they were offered, they would get angry with the managers for not organizing the work properly and, since there is a general shortage of labour, go to another building site. To avoid this happening, the works superintendent quite arbitrarily pays them more than they have earned and in this way 'tops up' their wages to the required level.

'Topping up' is a particular kind of response to the inadequacies of centralized wage regulation which is often done without any idea of actual local conditions. Most frequently it is employed to overcome the patent absurdities of wage levels fixed from 'above', i.e. in order to make the evaluation of different types of work seem fairer to the employees. After all, those building workers do not in any way hold themselves responsible for the non-delivery of cement. 'Topping up' and 'levelling off' in fact completely cancel out the advantages of centralized wage distribution. On-the-spot regulation tends to become anarchic and this leads to distortions in wage relativities at the macro-level.

Economic books and journals abound in examples of this type. Thus, identical jobs are often paid very different rates according to whether they are done in well-managed or badly-run factories or in 'rich' or 'poor' government departments. For example, loaders and scaffolders in heavy industry earn up to 500 roubles a month but in the food industry, particularly in meat-processing plants, they earn not more than 200 roubles, as if it were already taken for granted that they would make up the difference 'in kind', i.e. in stolen meat. Apparently, this is taken for granted not only by the workers themselves who are quite satisfied with their wages and form a stable workforce but also by the management and the state authorities who have accepted an extraordinarily high level of loss in meat processing

— as much as 7 per cent. In fact, research has shown that not more than one per cent of dead weight is lost in processing. The remaining 6 per cent goes towards compensating for the 'social injustice' of an unjustifiably low level of wages. In this case, however, the method of establishing 'justice' is socially the most harmful.

The salaries paid to skilled personnel were depressed in comparison with those of ordinary workers. For example, in 1986 the average wage of graduate engineers and skilled operatives in industry was 239 roubles and of workers, 216 roubles. In construction, manual workers earned 253 roubles on average and skilled operatives 247 roubles, i.e. slightly less. A particularly low wage is earned by specialists in non-productive sectors who have to be highly trained and dedicated to their work in view of the fact that they work with people. In the same year the average wage in the cultural field was 118 roubles, in the health sector 135, in education 156, in the arts 148, and in science 208 roubles. Doctors, teachers, artists of stage and screen, painters and scientists were paid on average less than industrial, construction and collective-farm workers. This raises the question whether under such circumstances rapid scientific and technological economic advance can be expected.

From the point of view of the social justice of relative wages, it is very important that regional differences in the cost of living are eliminated. In the Eastern and Northern regions of the Soviet Union in order to remain healthy and capable of work people need food of a greater calorific value, warmer clothing, more fuel, etc. In addition, due to high transport costs in distant regions, the price of consumer goods is higher than in central regions, while the choice of goods is narrower. A significant quantity of food is tinned, which means that it is less appetizing and nutritious and also costs more. Regional pay weightings are fixed in order to offset differences in the cost of living. In the south of Western Siberia wages are 15 per cent higher than in the central regions, in Eastern Siberia they are 25 per cent higher and in the regions of the Far North they are double.

Centrally-fixed weightings based on an accurate comparison of the cost of living in different regions is one of the advantages of the current method of wage regulation. In practice, however, even here we do not find what might have been expected. Firstly, regional weightings do not in most cases fully offset the higher cost of living. In the North and East, therefore, life is still more difficult than in the Centre. Secondly, government departments enjoying a high status fix higher weightings for their workers than the local average. For example, in most districts of the Baikal-Amur Railway area, the average weighting is 50 per cent and for railway construction workers 70 per cent. As a result, workers earn different rates for the same job. However, as soon as the railway is built and workers transfer to the construction of housing and public buildings, their wages fall without justification. All this indicates that the advantages of regulating wages centrally for the whole country are often illusory because in principle it cannot be done on the basis of overall productivity but is always calculated from previous levels. In the face of life's complexity, wage regulation is not feasible and actual wage trends become semi-random.

The new economic strategy is designed to replace administrative methods of wage regulation with economic methods, or those linked to market mechanisms. In fact these methods had already begun to break new ground in the late 1950s and early 1960s. It was at that time, for example, that the Pervitsky team of machine operators who were known throughout the country worked in accordance with the principle of a workforce contract, as we would call it today. At that time, too, Ivan Khudenko – an uncomprising and tireless champion of socialist efficiency, who was slandered by the authorities then in power in Kazakhstan and who died in 1974 in an Alma-Ata prison on trumped-up criminal charges – began his extremely interesting, difficult and invariably successful experiments in agriculture. Khudenko's basic idea was very simple. His workforce undertook to deliver a planned quantity of output at half the going price on one condition: that it could take its own decisions about how best to allocate the income it received between wages and investment. Khudenko engaged his workers himself and constantly cut the number employed on a particular job. He tested his methods on several collective farms in succession. On one arable farm, instead of the 830 previously employed, he kept on 619 workers, and used only 69 tractors out of the 219 available and even so began to achieve better harvests than ever before. He increased productivity three, five and even ten times. Articles were written about him, films were made, he was both a living legend and the subject of fierce arguments. His workforce not only worked well, they earned a lot, built beautiful houses and laid down gardens. In other words, they rapidly improved their lives. That is why, evidently, the rumour spread that Khudenko's experiments were anti-socialist ('kulak') in character and were carried on for personal gain. When the bailiffs arrived, however, to confiscate his property in accordance with the court sentence, apart from documents, manuscripts and a minimum of basic necessities, they found nothing. Ivan Khudenko did not have a second home in the country, nor his own car, nor any money put away. I knew Khudenko personally and admired his selfless activity. It is a bitter thing that he did not live to see the day which could be called his own and which, although posthumously, honours his name.

But Khudenko's experiments were far from an isolated case. The builder Serkov and the agronomist Zhulin worked on different variants of what was essentially the same idea. Later the Sumy, Kaluga and some other teams of workers began to experiment along the same lines. The principle of contractual payment operated for decades in the gold mining artels of Magadan. The state enterprises allocated to these artels sections of the mine where it was impossible to use heavy machinery, agreed to provide them with everything they needed to live and work efficiently, set them a production plan, and negotiated a price for the gold. From then on relations were conducted on market terms: the miners were paid according to the amount of gold that was mined and handed over to the state mining company, and deductions were made from their income for the vehicles, bulldozers, tents, and food they were given. The amount of gold per worker invariably turned out to be several times greater. An efficient form of pay, the artel's direct interest in extracting the maximum amount of gold, and maximum economy in the use of resources all had their effect.

A similar situation has developed in hundreds of rural building teams which come every year to the Urals, Siberia and the Far East from the republics of the North Caucasus and Transcaucasia, West Ukraine and Moldavia. In early spring these workteams conclude contracts with collective and state farms to erect work premises, housing, hospitals, schools, etc. The farms provide them with food and temporary accommodation, building materials and equipment. Agreements are made regarding the overall value of the work and approximate deadlines. The overwhelming majority of these seasonal workteams work from dawn till dusk, their work is of a high quality, reliable, and attractive, for they spare no efforts or skill. As a result, their earnings are high – an average of 1000 roubles a month, fair pay for good work. Their productivity is several times higher than for ordinary building workers. If they were to earn only 300–400 roubles a month, could they possibly leave their families for seven-eight months at a time, and take on such strenuous work? Of course not.

I say all this so that the reader should not be under the impression that up to the 1980s the administrative wages system, which took no account of the final outcome of work done, was the only one in the Soviet Union. Of course, it did predominate but over many decades, like grass growing through asphalt, new forms of work evaluation and payment forced their way through, clearly demonstrating their efficiency: average earnings rose considerably, but at a slower pace than productivity. The social evaluation of work in terms of output invariably proved its advantages both for the workforce and for society as a whole. On the whole, however, the new forms of wage payment remained on the periphery of the economy, usually where it would have been impossible to get anything done without them. They were not tolerated in the main sectors of the economy, however, being called 'unsocialist', 'petty-bourgeois', 'kulak', 'money-grubbing', etc.

At the April 1985 Plenary Session of the Party Central Committee and at the 27th Party Congress the task of making wages dependent on output was placed at the top of the agenda. Academics and practitioners proposed and supported various methods of doing this in a way that would be appropriate to conditions in different regions, sectors and types of enterprise. The most popular, however, was the workforce contract which was similar to Khudenko's experiments, except that the collective farm under his management had a contract with the Kazakh Ministry of Agriculture, while now most contract workforces in agriculture and industry conclude contracts with the management of the enterprises where they work. These contracts stipulate the terms on which inputs and equipment are supplied as well as the unit price of output. The workforce contract is by no means a universal panacea, especially if it is concluded as a formality, as often happens. When it is taken seriously and democratically, however, it usually gives good results. The same can be said of output-related pay.

As a rule, new forms of work evaluation and pay appreciably increase income differentials. Workers who show initiative and enterprise, have good qualifications and a knowledge of market forces as well as physical strength, and possess a number of different skills can greatly increase their earnings. Relatively unskilled workers, however, quickly lose out, since 'levelling off' and 'topping up' are coming to an end. Many people who have grown accustomed to the 'conveniences' of the old system consider the new system unfair although, now that it has received official backing, they rarely venture to call it 'unsocialist', let alone 'bourgeois'.

The element of 'market forces' contained in workforce contracts can be seen in the agreement on prices between producers (sellers) and customers (buyers) and in the fact that the sale of output plays a central role. But this is still not a genuine market, since unit prices are derived from enterprise or departmental administrative costs and not based on socially necessary expenditure on a country-wide scale. The prices remain stable for a long time and are hardly affected by fluctuations in supply and demand. Naturally, supplies of inputs and equipment are determined by the purchaser. Thus contract forms of payment represent an intermediate stage between centralized wage regulation and a free buyers and sellers market.

Market relations in the generation of personal income have 'flooded in' through the gates of individual, family and small co-operative production activity. These were developed in the Soviet

Union up to the late 1920s and were then rapidly reduced to a minimum. For decades almost the only surviving vestiges were to be found in the individual holdings run by collective farmers and state-farm workers. In the 1970s the cultivation of tiny orchards and allotments (no more than 0.03–0.04 hectares per family) was also allowed. Following decisions taken in the past few years, however, individual work and new co-operatives have developed rapidly. After the new Law on Co-operatives came into force in January 1988 more than 700 co-operatives had been organized in Moscow and hundreds of new ones were in the process of being set up. More than 300,000 people throughout the country acquired licences to work on an individual basis. There is a particularly wide range of small-scale forms of production in the Transcaucasian and Baltic Republics.

In the case of individual or group enterprise, personal incomes are formed on the basis of market principles. Wages come from sales revenue after production costs and taxes have been paid. Because these entrepreneurs are directly interested in achieving a high level of output, they not only work harder but mobilize their intellectual abilities and social contacts and look for profitable areas of work and good markets. As a result, successful co-operators and the self-employed earn far more than the average wage in the state sector. As regards the unsuccessful ones, they usually go bust, give up the game and take ordinary jobs in social production.

As I see it, the high incomes earned by very successful small producers are in no way contrary to socialist justice. The fact is that the state economy, almost exclusively comprising large enterprises and groups, has fairly convincingly demonstrated its inflexibility and inability to fill in many of the 'nooks and crannies' with goods that people need. This not only applies to technologically sophisticated personal computers or videos but to the simplest of articles such as woolly hats, bedroom slippers, and faded jeans, not to mention fresh butter, milk, vegetables and fruit. It goes without saying that small producers gravitate towards areas of high demand. This benefits not only them but society as well since it enables people's needs to be satisfied.

A number of circumstances have to be taken into consideration in assessing the level of income earned by small-scale producers. Firstly, a significant number of self-employed people and a fifth of all co-operators are also employed in the state sector so that this part of their work is additional as far as society is concerned. Secondly, the whole of their output is produced by their own work since they are absolutely forbidden to employ paid labour. Thirdly, they themselves do all the work in obtaining technology, equipment, raw materials, energy, premises, etc. This is done not simply by purchasing them, which would be much easier, but by getting hold of them when most of them are in short supply. Fourthly, they risk going bust and losing their investments. Fifthly, they do not qualify for pensions or sickness benefits, and they cannot count on getting a flat or a nursery place through their place of work. Taking all these circumstances into account, the fact that many individuals have incomes that are three, four, or even five times higher than wages in the state sector seems to me to be economically and socially justified and does not provide any basis for considering these incomes to be 'exploitatory'. At the moment the prices charged by these small producers are high. But people pay them willingly – it is simply a way of satisfying needs, which cannot be done in any other way. As the volume of co-operative and individual production grows, competition will develop between producers, and the market mechanism will bring down the high prices.

I have discussed these obvious things in such detail mainly because in specialist articles and the press and most of all in the opinion of a section of the public, small co-operatives and individual operators are often presented in a poor light. Much is made of their secret use of paid labour and stolen materials, the tendency to charge inflated prices for their products in order to maximize their profits, the low level of professionalism, and the poor quality of their output. Examples are quoted of people who buy a licence for only 100–150 roubles and take out huge loans from the bank ostensibly for their business and then use them for other purposes, thereby cheating the state.[6] Such things do in fact exist, but surely not more than the much greater rackets and shady deals that take place in the state sector? Development of small-scale entrepreneurial activity puts the Party's economic strategy into practice. Its socio-economic substance does not in any way contradict socialist justice, although the actions of individuals and co-operatives can in some instances contain contradictory elements and require social control.

I should like, however, to mention another, more important, side to this question: because the development of co-operative and individual production reflects a fundamental direction for restructuring it comes up against fierce resistance from many of those who work in the administration. These people understand better than most the danger that the development of small-scale enterprise presents to themselves and their organizations. The individual and co-operative sector, despite the fact that it is tiny (apparently, tenths of one per cent of gross national output), is already beginning to make itself felt as a capable and successful competitor to state enterprises, especially in light industry and the service sector.

Let us take public catering as just one example. Eating out in many state-owned restaurants including heavily subsidized ones is sheer hell: it takes ages, it is expensive, and the food is poor. A meal in a co-operative café as a rule costs twice as much and one often has to queue, but the service is first-class and the pleasure given by the appetizing food remains in the memory for a long time. The number of co-operative and private cafés and restaurants is gradually growing, and they are beginning to present real and perceptible competition to state enterprises. A little more, and the state network will have to be closed down. It is extremely profitable to work in such a place for it is a typical example of the sellers' market, dictating its own terms. This is taken to mean that competition should not be allowed, and by fair means or foul the issue of new licences should be forbidden or at least made very much more difficult to obtain.

An opinion poll conducted by the Institute of Sociological Research of the Soviet Academy of Sciences in collaboration with the newspaper *Izvestiya* among officials employed by local Soviets produced typical results. Only 26 per cent expressed the opinion that the co-operative and individual sector would develop further, while 41 per cent of these same officials and 60 per cent of health service workers thought that stricter control over the activity of co-operatives was necessary. As regards co-operators, 35 per cent of them had great difficulties as early as the organizational stage. Ten per cent of all co-operatives were initially refused registration and only after appealing to higher authorities were they able to start work. One in three of the co-operators considered the main obstacle to the development of co-operatives to be mistrust and extreme officiousness on the part of the local authorities. Thirty-seven per cent observed that uncertainty about receiving local authority support was the main reason why millions of people were reluctant to put their individual operations on a legal footing by buying the right licences. After analysing the returns, the pollsters came to the conclusion that state organizations entrusted with providing assistance to the co-operative movement often in practice opposed its development.

This conclusion is borne out by a large number of facts. For example, in Evpatoriya (a tourist resort in the Crimea) the local authorities closed down a co-operative making jewellery solely because they considered its members were earning too much. An opinion poll on this issue showed that 30 per cent of the public thought the action of the authorities to be correct, 14 per cent thought it too hasty and not in the new spirit of openness, while 56 per cent considered it to be wrong. It is odd that a number of respondents, who approved the action of the authorities, backed up their opinion by arguing that the co-operative made jewellery, adding that if its products had been 'more useful' perhaps it should not have been closed. Be that as it may, the majority came out fairly categorically in favour of the development of co-operative forms of production. Thus, V. Kulichkov, from Chelyabinsk, in the Urals, writes in the magazine *Ogonek* as follows:[7]

A firm stand has to be made in assessing the actions of bureaucrats who sabotage the activity of co-operatives – the only producer and trading associations in our country which work according to a flexible and viable system.

S. Zhukovskaya, from Riga, echoes him:

We should not be afraid of the high incomes earned by co-operators. We must learn to regulate these incomes by using economic levers. To close an enterprise because of its high earnings is barbarism and ignorance.

It would be difficult not to agree with this.

However, the problems that co-operators face in their struggle with the bureaucracy fade in comparison with the difficulties experienced by the self-employed if only because it is harder to struggle on one's own. The story of Nikolai Sivkov went round the whole country after it had been reported in *Izvestiya* and in a television programme about 'The rich peasant of Archangel'. The hero of this tale who lived in a village with his wife and grown-up son reared and sold to the state about twenty bullocks, i.e. as much meat as could be delivered by a small team of farmworkers. Of course, the family had an unusually high income. Annoyed by this, the local authorities prohibited Nikolai Sivkov from engaging in such activity in the future, in spite of the fact that there is a shortage of meat throughout the country. *Izvestiya* printed several items giving further developments in the story which, thanks to the intervention of the press, had a happy ending. Now the 'rich peasant of Archangel' is chairperson of the 'Red Hill' co-operative, named after his village. Apart from him and his son, there are three others in the co-operative. Two hundred hectares of pasture land have been transferred free of charge for the use of the co-operative, including islands in the floodlands of the North Dvina river where cattle can graze virtually without supervision. The Bank for Agriculture and Industry gave the new co-operative long-term credit for starting up the farm at 0.75 per cent per annum. The interest on extended loans is 3 per cent, so that economic levers of management are coming into operation at last.

Matters are not always settled in such a way everywhere, however. In some regions individual producers continue to be regarded almost as enemies of socialism. This is what journalist Andrei Nuikin writes about the matter:[8]

> I cannot get the facts quoted in I. Gamayunov's article 'The Criminal Tomato' out of my mind. For years, the zealous administrators of the Primorsky and Dubovsky districts of the Volgograd province have been bullying the inhabitants of the areas entrusted to them, particularly elderly people, pensioners, the industrially disabled, and war veterans. The aim is an 'affair of state': to stifle all private and property-owning interests and develop in young people a proper devotion to public forms of employment. The methods are criminal. The whole of local 'society' – the Soviet and Party authorities, the police, the procurator's office, the press, 'week-ending' hooligans, and schoolchildren – have been spending their free time, released from work and study in this lofty cause, have put their hearts into harassing, day after day, those who shed their blood on the banks of the Volga, who brought up today's citizens without husbands to help them, and raised the country from the ruins. They burst into their houses and allotments, count the tomato plants, crawl along greenhouses with tape-measures, mobilize a whole army of informers to find out which of the old people (what a secret!) heat up stoves in their greenhouses at night against the orders of the city bosses . . . How we miss from our tables those beautiful Lower Volga tomatoes! How sick we are of those tasteless unripe things brought from goodness knows where! But there they are pulling them up by the roots, leaving them in the sun without water, destroying the green-houses with bulldozers, fining the owners, forming cordons of zealous policemen to prevent the tomatoes being taken to market (they are not even accepted at the co-op depot), closing the docks, and falsifying documents.
>
> How can these 'servants of the people' who find themselves – and not by chance either – on the same side of the barricades as hooligans who have been identified as such in the courts, be let off with a few reprimands? Is that how they will represent Soviet power and the Communist Party on the Russian plains? . . . In the face of facts such as these we must either sentence the guilty ones and remove their protectors (the provincial authorities) from office as soon as we learn about them or stop pontificating about our revolutionary and communist spirit.

Social policy with regard to co-operative and individual production needs to be precise and clear. Their development has been welcomed and encouraged by the state which not only registers co-operatives and issues licences to individual producers, but also provides help in renting premises, acquiring depreciated heavy equipment and valuable factory scrap, etc. Small producers and individuals are allowed to undertake all kinds of production activity, apart from those that have been specifically listed as forbidden. In cases where a particular kind of activity is not specified by law, the matter is to be decided in the producer's favour. Financial and control bodies are to keep an eye on co-operatives and individuals to see that they do not overstep the law. As these forms of activity develop and more profitable enterprises come into existence, it will be necessary to devise a progressive taxation system and eliminate successful tax avoidance strategies. It is becoming a matter of urgency to study the legal aspects of production more closely, in particular relations between co-operative and individual producers and state enterprises, procedures and conditions of sale, etc. The work and trading activity of small producers should be regulated mainly by economic methods, resorting to administrative methods only in exceptional circumstances.

Everything would seem to be clear. As the dramatist Alexander Gelman aptly put it: 'Justice consists in everybody receiving not the same amount but a different amount justly.'[9] 'Justly' means in accordance with the amount, quantity, and quality of work and, most importantly, its final product. At the moment, however, not everybody agrees with this point of view. The view is still stubbornly upheld in readers' letters to newspapers and magazines and in articles by some specialists and journalists that the state should exercise firm control over the income and expenditure of every citizen and confiscate from their personal property 'everything that has been gained and constructed over and above what is laid down by law.' It is also proposed that children should lose the right to inherit property from their parents because they have not earned these goods by their own labour. Most frequently no distinction is made here between sums of money acquired by illegal means (for example, by theft of public property) and those earned by exceptionally talented people, whose work is particularly valued.

Andrei Nuikin recently took a stand against such points of view. In the article already quoted he writes:

It is significant that . . . nearly all those who support the expropriation of excessive amounts of property and money are up in arms against iniquitous incomes in general terms but when it comes down to it for some reason with a rare unanimity they demand the 'dispossession of the kulaks' only in the case of those who are 'making immense fortunes' out of their small plots of land, handiwork or talent . . . Not a word is said about illegal incomes but only that the law should set quantitative limits to property. As to the means by which property has been acquired — not a word!

The inventor who has saved the country millions of roubles, the builder who has worked for years on end in the Polar regions, the poet whose works, in editions of 100,000, are snapped up by readers in a matter of hours – all these have the same rights and status as the bribe-taker, embezzler, or the literary hack foisting his untalented, illiterate, and very long novels on publishers and journals that depend on him. In whose interests, it may be asked, has the line between those who have earned a lot and those who have stolen a lot been erased? The rails along which our future life is to run tend to turn again and again with curious obstinacy to where cheats always win and workers lose out badly. And the finger is moreover pointed at them as if they were the cheats. This is the kind of 'proletarian ideology' that some people have come to.

It is difficult not to agree with this. In fact, socialist justice in income distribution is essentially based on the fact that people who make an outstanding contribution to social development are rewarded, while an uncompromising battle is carried on against all attempts at enrichment by dishonest means – the use of one's position at work for personal ends, the taking of bribes from one's subordinates, financial fiddles, organized crime, etc. The long years of 'levelling off', however, were bound to have an effect on public awareness. It lags behind the demands of our day and age and has become an additional brake on economic development. That is why today one of the most important conditions for strengthening socialist justice is to explain to the general public the elementary fact that, if earnings correspond to a worker's real contribution to the social economy, it is not shameful to earn well; that the old saying, 'You don't earn a fine mansion through honest work' does not hold true today, and many owners of 'fine mansions' earned them through their own hard work and talent; that the principle of distribution of income according to one's work never did mean simply according to the amount of time spent at work; that different rates of pay for efficient or unprofitable work are socially just, while equal pay is deeply unjust.

It should be mentioned in this connection that beyond the particular features of the administrative and economic systems of work evaluation a deeper and more general problem can be seen relating to the question of social reward for the creative component of work. The principal engine of scientific and technological progress, and indeed the whole development of the economy, is scientific, engineering, technological, organizational and economic creativity. The biggest curse of our society is when workers carry out their duties without any element of creativity, which essentially comes down to

simply filling in one's time at work. The small number of rationaliz-
ers and inventors, the deskilling of many engineers, the lowering of
degree standards, the rarity of socio-economic experimentation on
the basis of 'grass-roots' initiatives, and lack of enterprise on the
part of managers – all these are the result of a complete disregard
by the administration of the need to pay for the creative component
of work. In our social psyche there is very little cognition that a new
scientific or organizational idea may be a valuable asset which should
not be given away free and still less imposed by force, but should
be sold at a good price to consumers in a competitive market. It is
not surprising that we have so few research consultancies based on
business principles and do not observe authors' copyright practices
that operate in advanced countries throughout the world.

Analysis of relative wage rates shows that existing differentials
tend to be based on such characteristics as the heaviness, intensity (rhythm), monotony and technological complexity of work,
but that in principle they underestimate the creative nature of
certain types of work and the relative significance of creative
components of jobs under comparison. This means, in fact, the
tacit (or almost unconscious) exploitation of creative categories
of workers by non-creative ones and, within specific categories
of work, the exploitation of creative personalities by non-creative
ones. Incidentally, in co-operative and individual production there
is no such exploitation, which is one of the main reasons for its
efficiency and earning capacity. This also applies to the forms of
wage payment in the state sector which are based on an evaluation
of output.

To sum up: the basic principles of a socially just policy of personal
income distribution are clear enough. They are: relating wages in the
state sector to final output with regard to quantity, quality, scarcity
and productivity; rational economic regulation of the incomes of
co-operative and self-employed workers; recognition that the trend
towards growing income differentials is a natural phenomenon and
one that is useful to society. A distinction in principle must be drawn
between high incomes made by honest or dishonest means – in
other words, as a result of talent and industry as against bribery
and corruption. A constant and uncompromising battle must be
waged against economic crime, and for the cleansing of society of
the dirt that has accumulated here over many long years. The further
development of openness in income distribution and, in particular,
the publication of wage rates, the terms and amounts of bonus payments, and actual levels of pay must form part of this. Finally, these
principles include the root-and-branch democratization of the whole
process of work evaluation, taking it out of the manager's office into
meetings of the workforce who know better than anybody what sort

of work is worth what. I believe that if we move in this direction we shall be able to bring about a much greater degree of justice in regard to income distribution.

REGULATION OF THE CONSUMER MARKET

In the previous section we considered living standards associated with the receipt of money incomes. We shall now deal with the second stage of that process – the conversion of money incomes into essential consumer goods which in the Soviet situation is no less important. From the societal point of view social relations should preferably be organized in such a way that there is a single consumer market throughout the country which is not fragmented into a complex network of elements including a 'shadow' economy.

I use the term 'single consumer market' to mean the system of social relations in which retail prices are determined by their market value, i.e. which take into account, firstly, average socially necessary production costs, secondly, average transport costs, and, thirdly, supply-demand relationships in the local market. A single consumer market does not mean that prices of identical goods are the same in all parts of the country. For example, it is economically justified that tomatoes costing 20–30 kopeks a kilo in the Lower Volga region can be sold at much higher prices in the Polar regions. Uniformity of the consumer market does not mean price uniformity but rather that the same principles are used in setting prices and that goods on the market are available to all buyers. Thus, by travelling south someone living in the Polar region who rarely sees fresh tomatoes at home can buy them at the same price as the local inhabitants.

There are at least three social advantages in having a single consumer market rather than one that is fragmented and segmented. Firstly, there is the democratic organization of trade, giving everyone equal access to shops, cafés, restaurants, hairdressers, shoe repairers, etc. Secondly, there is the guarantee of access to goods depending on income alone without any administrative restrictions. Thirdly, there is equality of purchasing power, no hidden redistribution of incomes in the form of goods or services, and no possibility of exploiting shortages of goods or practising various kinds of extortion and swindling. A single consumer market is socially healthy and for that reason its creation is one of the components of today's social policy.

At the moment, the market in goods and services cannot be called a single market. It is divided into several different channels for obtaining consumer goods and services which differ considerably as regards variety, quality, price and availability (including whether or not there are queues, whether advance orders can be placed, and so on). As many as ten different parallel circuits exist for acquiring goods. They include:

i) State trading in food and manufactured consumer goods concentrated mainly in the towns and almost absent from rural areas. The doors of state shops are open to everyone, whether local inhabitants or visitors. This is the most democratic trade channel and is marked by stable, comparatively low prices, particularly for food. The shortcomings of this type of trade are, firstly, constant shortages particularly of essential goods and, secondly, the fact that supply depends to an extraordinary extent on the character of the buying public. In capital cities such as Moscow, Leningrad, Kiev, and Minsk, one can usually buy almost everything that one needs in the state shops. There is a comparatively wide choice of meat and dairy products, vegetables and fruit. Manufactured goods include a quantity of fashionable and attractive clothing and footwear. In other towns there is much less choice and some goods appear in the shops only at irregular intervals. The availability of goods in small towns is very poor indeed. For decades people living within travelling distance of large towns have been going on shopping trips to, for example, Moscow or Leningrad to buy meat, sausages, fruit and other things in large quantities. Every day hundreds of local and long-distance trains leave the Moscow stations crammed with suitcases, rucksacks and holdalls full of food.

ii) Another channel for goods is the urban network of co-operative shops, selling food in particular, which has developed a lot over the last five-seven years and which is run by the Central Union of Consumer Co-operative Societies. For many years the Central Union was primarily responsible for purchasing live cattle and poultry, milk, eggs, potatoes, and vegetables from individual smallholdings and supplying the rural population with basic necessities. It was then given the right to sell agricultural produce in its own urban shops at prices considerably higher than the state prices. For example, one kg of meat costs about 2 roubles in state shops while in co-operative shops it costs between 3 roubles 50 kopeks and 5 roubles. There are now co-operative shops in every town where one can buy two or three kinds of meat, several sorts of sausage, butter and other produce not available in state shops.

iii) Then there is co-operative trading in manufactured goods in villages, which is also organized by the Central Union. In the overwhelming majority of rural areas this is the only form of organized trade in foodstuffs and consumer goods. Prices in rural co-operative shops are the same as or slightly higher than in the state retail network. A consumer co-operative society is paid a small fee for the use of its services and carries out the functions of self-management and administrative control. The Central Union is responsible for selling 20–25 per cent of all goods in rural areas. While it is true that 35 per cent of the total population at present live in the country, nevertheless rural inhabitants receive an appreciable proportion of their incomes in kind so that their demand for purchased goods and services is somewhat lower than that of town-dwellers. Apart from this, most country-dwellers prefer to make their most important and expensive purchases in urban shops.

iv) There is also the sale of second-hand goods on commission where goods are accepted from the public for sale in return for a percentage of the receipts. The prices in these shops vary in accordance with demand for the goods on offer. These commission shops exist in every town but they do not always compete successfully with second-hand markets where transactions take place without any middle-man between buyer and seller and without any commission.

v) There are second-hand and street markets where any member of the public can sell things at uncontrolled prices. People need these markets, both to get rid of things they do not require and which are still in good condition, and to buy necessities that are not available in the state sector. There is almost no such thing as shortage on the street market: everything is here, from foreign videos to cosmetics or nails. Prices are fixed by supply and demand, which means that scarce goods cost more. Along with honest people, speculators are often active in these markets, selling stolen or contraband goods. For this reason, the local authorities usually disapprove of them. There was a period when the markets began to be closed down one after the other, but this hit the general public hard and provoked a flood of protest letters and requests that the markets be reinstated. In the last few years, as a result of the growth in individual businesses, the street markets have come into their own again and are now the main channel for the sale of goods made by small-scale producers.

vi) Agricultural produce is sold in urban collective-farm markets, which are notable for the wide variety, excellent quality and very high prices of the goods on offer. The market traders either come on behalf of collective or state farms and have their own stalls or are people selling their own produce or commercial traders who buy produce in the countryside and sell it in the towns. Although such activity is not encouraged and is even penalized by the state, it is carried on on a fairly large scale. At a good collective-farm market it is possible to buy anything one needs, but it will not be cheap.

vii) Food and manufactured goods are sometimes sold in factories or offices either at special shops or 'counters' or through the distribution of 'coupons' entitling the bearer to buy a certain amount of meat, butter, sausage, etc.

viii) The distribution of foodstuffs in short supply is organized geographically by town or region. This can be done via 'counters', coupons, etc. This particular form of trading differs from the others because it covers everyone, irrespective of employment. For example, everyone who lives in Akademgorodok in Novosibirsk, whether or not they are employed in social production and whether they are pensioners or schoolchildren, are entitled to buy at state prices 2 kg of meat, 1 kg of sausagemeat, 600–700 g of butter, etc. Although this is not enough to meet all the needs of most families, it does at least guarantee a certain nutritional minimum. The rest is obtained at consumer co-operative society shops or at the collective-farm market according to the family's income.

ix) Finally there are *Beryozka* shops which sell scarce, good-quality, mostly imported goods, which can be bought with special cheques generally obtained by Soviet citizens in exchange for foreign currency or as part-wages for officials working in foreign trade, the Ministry for Foreign Affairs and other government departments associated with foreign countries, and also some people working in the arts.

The above list is obviously incomplete but it clearly indicates the multi-faceted nature of this trade and its variety of form and method.

In principle, the large number of trade channels is one expression of the pluralism of economic relations that we must aim at. In complementing each other, the various kinds of trade vie for 'the purchaser's rouble' and so enable people to satisfy their needs when goods are in short supply in the state trade network. But this is only one side of the coin. The other is that not all these channels are open to all social groups and strata. In some cases it is people living in the richer and more prosperous republics (e.g. the Baltic and Belorussian Republics) that find themselves in a privileged position. In others, it is people working in important government departments or senior officials in central, ministerial or local authority bodies. Moreover, certain trade channels are open to one or other social stratum not simply because of economic factors but for quite contradictory administrative reasons.

Because of the closed character of some trading networks which belong to government institutions, comparatively isolated markets exist that service different social groups. These markets offer their customers a variety of products at divergent prices, which means that some privileged persons can buy good-quality goods more cheaply than shoddy goods available on the open market. In this way the sale of consumer goods and services effects a hidden redistribution of incomes in favour of social groups which have access to privileged channels of supply. As a result, each rouble spent by people in these groups has a greater purchasing power than the ordinary rouble. In poorly supplied regions the rouble is actually devalued since it is not possible to buy anything with it. For this reason, the present multiplicity of trade channels leaves many groups dissatisfied and creates social tension.

Obviously, this area of social life is in need of normalization and this must be done by the new social policy. The *Beryozka* shops came in for a lot of unfavourable criticism. Being nice and bright, they attracted the involuntary attention of passers-by who could go in and see the rare imported goods and ask their price in roubles. But if anyone tried to buy something, then it had to be explained that a rouble earned in an ordinary factory or institute was not accepted there but a different kind of rouble, called a 'cheque'. And people earning these 'cheques' could buy things that were not available to others. Naturally, such a system caused resentment and humiliated people who earned 'ordinary' roubles by seeming to indicate that they were second-class earnings. The government decided to close down the *Beryozka* shops as from 1 July 1988. This was welcomed by the general public. It represented a particular but fairly serious step towards strengthening social justice and changing over from administrative to economic management methods.

What should be done about the segmentation that has developed in consumer markets so as to ensure that they gradually merge into a complex, multi-channel but integrated market which functions in accordance with economic logic? The main way to achieve this is by overcoming the general shortages of consumer goods. All these 'special shops' or 'counters', hidden 'distributors', 'coupons', buffets and canteens that only serve certain selected groups are not just a whim. If they didn't exist, in some places production would have to come to a halt because the other channels of supply simply do not function properly.

Shortages of goods may be absolute or relative. Under conditions of absolute shortage it is impossible to satisfy people's minimal requirements, e.g. to feed them, not allow anyone to starve, provide a roof over their heads, and supply essential clothing and footwear. Relative shortage, however, means that the supply of goods is insufficient to satisfy demand based on purchasing power. Absolute shortages can only be overcome by producing more goods but relative shortages which occur more frequently can be eliminated by regulating price levels. The higher the price, the less the demand for a product. Therefore, price increases are enough to ensure that even the scarcest of goods can be found in the shops. Incidentally, it is precisely this situation that we have on the collective-farm and street markets where everything is available but at very high prices. In state shops beef (usually frozen) costs 2 roubles per kilo while on the collective-farm market best (fresh) beef can be bought at 7–8 roubles per kilo. Moreover, in most towns meat is not freely available in state shops, while there is plenty in the markets. Retail price policy is, therefore, an important way of normalizing the market, re-establishing its uniformity and overcoming shortages.

Socialist social relations make it possible to deliberately fix prices to diverge from their social cost, which is usually considered to be an advantage of the system. In fact, the prices of such goods as vodka, tobacco, etc. are fixed far above their cost in order to restrict their consumption. On the other hand, the prices of children's things, books, and records are fixed below cost. This is done to make them easier for people to buy so as to create a wider readership, for example, and raise cultural standards.

The low prices charged for basic foodstuffs (meat, bread and milk) have a different origin. In fact, their production costs have been growing for decades as technological progress in agriculture has been extremely slow while wages have increased relatively rapidly. At the present time, the production costs of meat, butter and some other products are more than double the state retail prices. The difference is made up by an annual farm subsidy on butter and milk amounting to tens of thousands of millions of roubles. Since it does not make sense to retain the old prices for meat and milk in the new economic circumstances, economists have more than once suggested to the government that these prices should be raised to make production profitable and that wages should be raised in compensation. However, no action has been taken for fear of social unrest. Moreover, the public has become convinced that stable prices for basic foodstuffs, housing, and other social benefits are almost the main characteristic of socialism. They have therefore regarded any price rise, including, for example, economically justified price rises on consumer goods together with compensatory wage increases, as an attack on their living standards and social justice. It will be a complex socio-psychological task to overcome this stereotype of social consciousness and convince people of the validity of fixing economic prices for foodstuffs that are in short supply.

Any substantial divergences in retail prices lead to fresh problems. Take, for example, the price of spirits which has now been fixed at what is essentially a prohibitive level. Since only well-off people can afford to buy vodka and cognac in state shops now that prices have been increased, purchases have dropped substantially. But the demand of poorer people to consume alcohol remained, so when prices rose many families responded by producing their own liquor. As a result in the state shops a litre of vodka now costs about 20 roubles, while a litre of equally strong home brew costs about one rouble to make. I say nothing about the enforced substitution of vodka and other spirits by similar liquids manufactured for industrial use and which are harmful to health.

Holding the price of consumer goods at below cost also has serious negative consequences. Thus the artificially low prices of meat, milk and bread create shortages by increasing the real demand for these goods. Low domestic prices lead to an uneconomic use of products which often incorporate a significant amount of foreign exchange. Thus, many villagers feed their pigs and calves with bread as this costs them less than commercial feeds. People buy more bread than than they can possibly eat and then throw away the stale bread because it costs practically nothing. Low state prices for meat that is in short supply present opportunities for economic swindling. Meat, for example, that is supplied to state shops for sale at 2 roubles a kilo is in fact passed on for sale in co-operative shops at 4 roubles a kilo and the difference is pocketed by the people organizing the deal. Although low food prices keep the price of basic necessities low, they also reduce any incentive to work hard and well.

Finally, it is not possible to provide the whole population with meat and milk at state prices. The only people who can buy these products at the right price and with a range of choice are the inhabitants of some large towns at the expense of those living in other towns and villages, the inhabitants of central regions at the expense of all the others, workers in some privileged offices at the expense of all other workers, top management at the expense of ordinary employees. All this corrupts socialist justice instead of strengthening it. By artificially maintaining low prices on goods in short supply a special mechanism is created for effecting the hidden redistribution of incomes, which destroys proper income relativities.

From the economic point of view, the best way of adjusting prices to social costs is to take account of world market prices. Since the retail price system that has developed in our country is based on completely different principles, there is a real need to reform it. It is, of course, impossible to change the prices of consumer goods without affecting real incomes. Even if wages, pensions, and benefits are increased to offset higher prices, many groups may suffer a loss of income. Improving the structure of wages in social production presupposes some adjustment to the incomes of individual producers and co-operators. By that I do mean adjustment, not equality, which takes into account differences in intensity, quality, and creativity as well as social conditions of work. Taxation must act as the main economic lever for regulating the incomes of small-scale producers and the tax system itself must be reformed. This means that the complex reform of wages, income tax, retail prices, and service charges, as well as state pensions, grants and benefits, has become a matter of urgency.

The main aim of this reform is practical implementation of the principle of socialist justice, i.e. securing a better and more consistent distribution of consumption according to the quantity, quality and efficiency of work. In all the years of Soviet power there has not been a reform that so openly and directly affects the interests of all groups of the population without exception. Defining the overall necessity, specific directions, and possible variants of the reform, analysing the probable economic and social consequences of each variant, and selecting the best variant is an incredibly complex and responsible task. Decisions must not be taken in a hurry, and yet delay in carrying out the reform has its dangers since the prolongation of economically unjustified distribution relations could lead to a cooling-off in people's attitude to restructuring. The decision on strengthening socialist justice cannot and must not be allowed to remain a mere good intention. 'The eyes fear it, but the hands do it', people sometimes say about a difficult piece of work. In this case, the complexity of the task that needs to be tackled in theory and practice is frightening, but it just has to be done. And the necessary work has already begun: teams of specialists are preparing numerous variants for the reform, comparing one with another and working out optimal solutions.

As I see it, the comprehensive reform of distribution relations must include the following main elements:

i) Lowering state retail prices of goods whose prices now greatly exceed costs (cars, some items of clothing and footwear, crockery and consumer durables). This measure is capable of increasing consumption income by some 8–10,000 million roubles.

ii) Increasing state retail prices of goods that are at present being sold below cost thanks to state subsidies. This measure will reduce budgetary expenditure and cut consumption income by approximately 50–60,000 million roubles.

iii) Abolishing income tax on wages which has by now lost its economic and social significance, as well as the single-persons tax. Income tax was introduced several decades ago with a view to evening out the incomes of low-paid and highly paid workers. Wages below 60 roubles were not subject to tax at all, wages between 60 and 100 roubles were taxed at a rate of 7–8 per cent, and wages over 100 roubles at 13 per cent. The vast majority of people now earn more than 100 roubles a month and pay the state 13 per cent of their wages, so the redistributory function of the tax has fallen away. In fact, since the tax is deducted at source and transferred to the state budget, this operation which entails a certain amount of effort is quite pointless. Either wages should be paid in full without any deduction of tax (which would largely offset any price rises) or they should be cut by 13 per cent. The first variant is probably preferable.

iv) Wages, pensions, grants and benefits should be raised by at least as much as the recipients would lose as a result of the first three measures. In other words, full compensation should be made for food price rises through price cuts on other goods, the abolition of taxes and increased money payments.

v) Further opportunities should be created for individual and co-operative businesses. Income tax declaration forms should be introduced for people employed outside the state sector. Progressive taxation should be introduced so that individual and co-operative incomes corresponding to average wages in social production are not taxed, incomes that are two or three times greater than this are taxed at 15–20 per cent, and higher incomes are taxed at 30–50 per cent or more. It is important that taxation should be structured in such a way that incentives are not destroyed but, at the same time, no group can get rich illegally through business swindles or taking advantage of market forces. A market should also be created for goods and services that people want and which are at the moment distributed outside market channels, sometimes on particularly favourable terms or free. These include allotments or gardens belonging to second homes in the country, state housing, holiday travel vouchers and a number of other things. This question will be discussed in more detail in the following section.

In conclusion, the necessity for the comprehensive reform of prices and incomes is dictated by economic considerations and the general logic of restructuring economic management. However, the social consequences of such reform are so great and diverse that they are capable of outweighing the economic result. The situation has grown particularly serious as a result of very large budget deficits and the rapid rise in consumer prices. People are becoming extraordinarily irritated by the constant price rises and the disappearance of the cheaper range of goods from the shops. In these circumstances any talk of reforming retail prices evokes a negative response and is a cause of great anxiety. This makes implementing the reform problematical, at least for the time being.

THE DEVELOPMENT OF SOCIAL GUARANTEES

Consistent application of the principle 'From each according to his abilities, to each according to his work' is the main but not the only component of socialist justice. Marx and Engels themselves observed that this principle contains a certain 'bourgeois' element, apparent in the equivalence of relations between the individual and society: whoever has given a certain amount to society should receive the same amount from society in another form. Socialist society must, however, not only concern itself with those who are capable of work but provide social protection for all its members. Consistent application of socialist justice implies the interaction of two social mechanisms: the economic motivation of the workforce and social guarantees. While the first is designed to overcome workers' passivity in securing a high standard of living for their families, to heighten people's economic responsibility for their own well-being and to improve their work, the second is designed to secure the social protection of citizens, the unconditional observance of the universal right to work, financial maintenance in illness and old age, and the satisfaction of basic social and cultural needs.

This explains why more than a quarter of total consumption in the USSR is distributed not through payment for work in state and individual production, but through the channels for social expenditure. This is done in three ways: a) through monetary payments to various groups of non-working people, b) through investment in the social infrastructure, and c) through social services that are provided without charge or on a concessionary basis. Let us examine the principles for allocating social expenditure in each of these ways.

In 1986 the population of the Soviet Union was about 282 million, and the annual average number of industrial workers, office employees, and collective farm members was 131 million. The remaining 151 million was made up of children and juveniles, young adults who had not yet started work, pensioners, housewives, the chronically sick and the disabled. More than half of the population, therefore, took no part in national production but was in need of a basic income and state support. One would think that many of these could be supported out of the wages of working members of the family. However, firstly, these sources are not always sufficient to satisfy needs; secondly, economic dependence upon other members of the family is often psychologically hard to bear; and thirdly, a number of people who are incapable of work live on their own and do not have a family. Finally, giving the working members of a family responsibility for fully maintaining those who cannot work is socially unjust to those who have more dependants. Sociological surveys that we conducted in Siberian villages showed that only a half of present differentials in per capita family incomes were due to differences in earnings. The other half was due to differences in the number of dependants that working members of a family supported. This indicates the need for planned state provision of benefits to the non-working population in the form of pensions, grants or allowances.

The bulk of this kind of expenditure has gone on retirement pensions which are provided to men from the age of 60 and to women from the age of 55 (in sectors where working conditions are particularly hard, they are paid five years earlier). In 1986 nearly 50,000 million roubles were paid out for this purpose (nearly twice the amount a decade earlier). In the future, this sum will be even greater as a result of the ageing of the population and the increase in average pensions.

The positive features of the Soviet system of pension provision are its universal character, low age qualification, short length of employment needed to qualify for full pension (25 years for men and 20 for women), guaranteed amount of pension and graduated pensions. The average level of pensions has been rising: in 1970 it amounted to 53 roubles a month, in 1980 it was 72 roubles, while in 1986 it was 89 roubles. Collective-farmer pensions increased from 14 to 48 roubles per month in the same period.

However, the present system of pension provision has grave weaknesses that are growing with the passage of time. In the first place they are fixed, irrespective of rising prices, and this forces down real incomes. There is also a fixed upper limit of 120 roubles a month. In 1956, when the pension law was passed, this was high but now, as a result of the sharp rise in average wages, more than half of all pensioners receive the 120 roubles. This means that even here we come up against that same 'levelling off' which acts as a disincentive to workers of pre-retirement age to maximize their earnings with the aim of improving their future pensions. Also, the present system of regulating the amount of work a pensioner can do has no justification. Most are allowed to work for no more than two months in a year, otherwise they lose their pensions. Only in places where there is an acute shortage of labour are pensioners allowed to work the whole year without loss of pension. As a result, a significant number of pensioners still capable of work are precluded from making a contribution to production. However, the provision of social guarantees including pensions should expand personal incomes, not reduce them. Otherwise, these guarantees themselves lose their humanitarian character, become an arena of unnecessary administrative regulations and unnecessarily complicate people's lives.

Over the past few years the Soviet state has taken a number of measures to improve pension provision. In 1986 there was an increase in pensions for people who had worked in agriculture. In addition, employees who had retired more than ten years earlier and whose pensions were less than 60 roubles a month received an increase. Today they receive the same pensions as workers with similar occupations and qualifications who are now retiring. Special supplementary payments have been introduced for single pensioners who have no families of their own, etc.

These one-off measures, however, do not provide an all-round solution. It is therefore intended to carry out a total reform of pension provision in the near future. Ideas are being worked out by specialists and practitioners and are under discussion. Once formulated, the draft proposals will become the subject of nation-wide discussion before the final version of the law is enacted. For the moment then we can only talk about the key measures for improving pension provision which will be reflected in the reform. These are a general increase in the average pension so as to narrow the gap between pensions and wages; eliminating differences between rural and urban populations, and between state-sector workers and collective farmers; introducing 'deferred pensions' whereby every additional year at work increases the future pension; creating a mechanism whereby pensions will automatically rise in step with retail price rises; further lowering the pensionable age for some categories of workers; abolishing the ceiling on pensions; and giving people the right to 'earn' increments to their future pensions by means of special deposits while they are still working.

Apart from retirement pensions, the state provides a variety of other benefits. Nearly 15,000 million roubles per year are spent on social insurance, e.g. sickness benefit, benefits for mothers off work looking after sick children, and maternity leave. Benefits are being systematically improved. For example, in 1987 the length of paid leave for working mothers to look after sick children was increased from seven to fourteen days. Mothers with four or more children now receive monthly allowances. Families whose incomes do not exceed 50 roubles a month per person, children whose father is doing military service, families of deceased servicemen, people disabled from birth, and several other groups receive monthly allowances.

Most students at technical colleges, specialist training colleges, colleges of further education, and universities receive state grants, which are paid in accordance with examination results and are distributed by student organizations. Until 1987 student grants were very low (30–50 roubles a month). They have now almost doubled but are still insufficient to meet the needs of young people. Most students, therefore, either have help from their parents or earn extra money, sometimes in the vacations. Students' work is of great benefit to society for they not only receive wages but also gain valuable experience of life and the social toughening-up process. In 1985, 764,000 students worked on building sites and the work they did was valued at more than 1,000 million roubles. Not all students, however, are able to find work. And constant distractions from study have an effect on their academic achievement. In the future, therefore, student grants must be increased.

The second area of state expenditure on social needs is investment in the construction of housing and public buildings i.e. development of the social infrastructure. Here, too, there are a number of problems associated with socialist justice and, therefore, with social policy.

The financing of social infrastructure is allocated, on the one hand, between different regions (republics, regions, towns and villages) and, on the other, between different sectors (housing and personal-service establishments, education, public health, pre-school establishments, cultural institutions, etc). However, in neither case are planning decisions soundly based.

First, let us look at the allocation of investments between the different sectors providing services and amenities to the general public. For many decades persistent imbalances in this area have complicated the lives of millions of people. Housing construction has far outpaced the creation of a network of services and amenities, and people moving into new housing areas have to wait a long time for their own local shops, day nurseries, schools, post offices, etc. to open. There is usually a time-lag of eight or ten years before the full range of services and amenities becomes available to people moving into new homes. Why is it not possible to provide the full range of facilities that people need in their own area? They are built in the end, after people have had to put up with a lot of inconvenience.

Two reasons are usually put forward to explain what has become established practice. The first is that people are badly in need of housing: some families do not have a roof over their heads, while others live in extremely cramped conditions. First and foremost, therefore, people have to be provided with housing, and must put up somehow with a lack of amenities. But how, one asks, can working parents 'put up with' a lack of kindergartens, schools, clinics, and shops? For it is obvious that blocks of flats built 'on an open field' do not of themselves constitute normal living conditions.

The second argument points out that it is both easier and more profitable for builders using industrial methods to construct houses than it is to build schools or leisure centres. They therefore fulfil the construction plan in terms of volume (again, the notorious 'gross output' target) and only then, when they have no choice, do they start to build schools, shops, public libraries, etc. Here we come up against a typical feature of the economic mechanism that has operated until recently – the 'sellers' market' which foists on consumers not what they need but what it is more profitable to sell. As I see it, it is this second argument that is the more telling. Restructuring economic relations will therefore have to ensure a more balanced development of the social structure.

We now turn to the regional allocation of social investment. There is for the moment no question of equality or justice in this field. By far the greater part of investment in social infrastructural construction is made in the capitals of the Union republics and other large towns. Medium-sized towns receive significantly less, and the smallest towns and villages are in the worst position. This investment pattern is based on criteria set by the State Planning and State Construction Commissions and these vary according to administrative status and size of population.

Let us take as examples towns like Minsk and Novosibirsk, each of which has about one-and-a-half million inhabitants. It might have seemed that since they have populations of the same size they would be able to claim an equal standard of infrastructure. Minsk, however, is the capital of a Union republic, while Novosibirsk is only a provincial centre, and the standard laid down for its infrastructure is therefore much lower. No-one comparing the level of development and living conditions in the two towns would agree that the marked difference between them is socially justified. The principles laid down for financing social infrastructure will have to be radically reviewed.

It is also incorrect to adhere too rigidly to existing criteria for financing infrastructure according to size of population, although they are important. People who live in the country, for example, obtain many of the services they need in small towns which serve as regional centres. When developing the social infrastructure of these towns, account must therefore be taken, not only of those living in the particular town, but of people living in the surrounding villages. This is not done at the moment.

There is yet another problem. The rural population is getting smaller and there is a certain amount of difficulty obtaining sufficient manpower to work in agriculture. Our press is full of accounts of how small villages are dying, and arguments about the need to preserve them, both as centres for agricultural areas and as a valuable heritage, bequeathed to us by our fathers and grandfathers. Villages with a declining population, however, are transferred into the lowest group as far as the provision of services and amenities is concerned. As a result not only are new public buildings not constructed but some of the existing ones have to be closed down. Meanwhile, the assertion that villages 'have no future', and the fact that no new social facilities are being built, acts as a fresh impetus to the migration of young people. Gradually, because of this distortion of demographic structure, there will be only old people left in the villages, and in time they will disappear altogether. Planning the development of the social infrastructure must therefore be tackled on a case-by-case basis taking into account all the circumstances and not merely the formal criteria on which present allocations are based – administrative status and size of population.

Another aspect to the question of allocating social infrastructure is administrative in nature. The development and running of services for the general public are financed through two channels: a) through local authorities and b) through ministries and departments responsible for particular sectors of the economy. In the vast majority of towns there are the usual town, district, and provincial schools, hospitals, outpatients' clinics, kindergartens, shops, and so on, serving all groups of people, and there are amenities belonging to ministries that can be used only by people working for the particular ministry. More often than not the ministries build flats, kindergartens, restaurants, medical establishments, leisure centres, rest homes, children's holiday camps, etc.

Amenity funds held by ministries are worth nearly as much as those managed by the local Soviets. In other words, funds available for the provision of services and amenities are almost equally divided between local authorities and ministries. In the case of new towns which are being built as part of a major industrial project by a particular ministry, the provision of social amenities by that same ministry may make sense. However, in towns with a number of different industries, it is an anachronism and leads to social conflict. This is because social amenities which are exclusive to a particular ministry are located in residential areas where everyone needs these services. They are told, however, that the kindergarten (clinic, swimming pool) can be used only by those who work at a particular place – a research institute, university, etc. Such a situation is obviously regarded as unfair since the idea of universal equality is deeply ingrained in the consciousness of our people, and the fact that people working for a particular ministry have more rights than everybody else is a contradiction of that idea.

In an attempt to correct this injustice, the authorities in some towns have, as it were, 'socialized' the amenities belonging to different enterprises and opened up access to them more equitably. In Barnaul, in the centre of Siberia, besides regional and town hospitals, there were some ministry hospitals attached to the railway, the engine plant, the tyre factory, etc. The regional Soviet reached an agreement with the enterprises and the appropriate ministries to introduce a degree of specialization into the various hospitals. The hospital belonging to the tyre factory, for example, specializes in different types of surgery, the engine-plant hospital specializes in cardiology and haematology, and the railway hospital in gastrology. In this way, patients now attend hospital depending not on where they work but on the nature of their illness. This is not only more just, but ensures better treatment and enables medical staff to become better qualified.

It would seem clear from the above that investment in social amenities which is centrally allocated on the basis of universal criteria does not adequately meet people's needs because it does not take into account either differences in the national, demographic, social or vocational make-up of regional groups or their social awareness or differences in ideas about where the need for construction for social and amenity purposes is greatest. The present system for developing the social infrastructure is, on the one hand, insufficiently democratic and, on the other, inconsistent with the ideas of economic reform since, under the new conditions, the amount of funds available for social development will depend on an enterprise's economic efficiency. The revenue collected by local Soviets which determines their possible level of social investment will likewise depend on the income earned by enterprises in their area. In fact social construction will be decentralized and this will obviously entail many problems that we are not yet aware of. As regards the centralized system for allocating investment on the basis of fixed criteria unrelated to economic performance, this will obviously come to an end under the new conditions.

The third area of social expenditure is state expenditure on education, culture, the health service, and sports facilities which are provided either free of charge or on a concessionary basis. The development and operation of these services cost the state quite a lot of money, while people use the services they need free or at a fraction of their real cost. The difference is made up by the state out of funds set aside for social expenditure.

What are the socio-economic arguments for providing various services on concessional terms or free of charge? Why, for example, is medical training free, while training to be a hairdresser or beautician has to be paid for and is comparatively expensive?

Experts agree that the principal social reason for the free (or subsidised) provision of specific services must be that society is more keen on their expanded use even than those who take advantage of them.

Let us look at education. Soviet society has a strong interest in improving the level and quality of education of young people, in extending and deepening their knowledge and in impressing on them the need constantly to improve their level of cultural, scientific and technological information. However, by no means everybody wants to study. Even with free and compulsory secondary education a number of young people do not see any value in the acquisition of knowledge and they cannot be made to learn by force. If education had to be paid for, however, the number of people reaching secondary and higher levels would fall at the expense of those who are very able, want to study, but do not have the necessary financial means to do so.

A similar situation exists in the health service. Socialist society is interested in maintaining optimal standards of physical and mental health for all its members, from children to the elderly, from inhabitants of the capital to the populations of outlying districts. However, different social groups have different incomes and their ability to pay for medical help differs accordingly. If it had not been for the free health service, many illnesses would have remained undetected, the country would not have been able to deal successfully with epidemics or extend average life expectancy from the 32 years of 1913 to today's 69–70 years. It is not just a matter of financial capacity, however: a timely visit to the doctor presupposes a certain cultural level, a knowledge of medicine and hygiene, and an appreciation of the value of health in enjoying to the full all that life has to offer. This is not always the case. People absorbed in family, business or creative interests often do not pay enough attention to a deterioration in their health and go to the doctor too late. That is why the health service is not only free, but is also active: it does not wait until the sick person applies for help, but tries gradually to move the centre of gravity from making sick people well to preventing healthy people falling sick. To this end, preventive check-ups are made. All types of medical services are provided free. There is a nation-wide network of special clinics, specialized sanatoria, etc. Patients can stay in TB sanatoria without charge for many months and even years until they are completely recovered.

Soviet people also enjoy a number of concessionary benefits in the cultural field. Thus, in the best theatres in Moscow or Leningrad a ticket to a first-night performance costs not more than 4–5 roubles, a ticket for the cinema costs 50–70 kopeks. The price of a daily newspaper is 4–5 kopeks, a weekly is 20 kopeks, and an annual subscription to a serious monthly magazine or journal is 10–12 roubles. Books in the Soviet Union are several times cheaper than in the West, and school textbooks are supplied to most pupils free. All this reflects the achievements of socialism in the development of social guarantees and social protection of all members of society.

However, it would be incorrect to suppose that the free provision of essential services has only positive sides to it. No object in nature exists without a shadow. In just the same way, it is not possible to organize social affairs without entailing certain negative consequences. They exist even in the free (or subsidized) provision of social services.

Thus, the free provision of financially costly services disturbs normal economic processes in the non-productive sphere. The most important sectors have neither developed nor improved their work or their corresponding service sectors, they do not produce any income but simply increase budgetary expenditure. Under conditions of slow economic growth, this creates great difficulties and may lead in the end to a curtailment of their financial and technological resources and a drop in the wages of their employees. As a result, they fail to meet public demand and are less able to offer quality services in the fields of medicine, education and culture.

Inadequate services prompt those who have the opportunity and the power to obtain a privileged position in gaining access to the services they need. As a result, a network of exclusive hospitals and clinics developed to serve the upper echelons, special mechanisms were created to enable young people to attend the best universities and further education colleges, and special forms of cultural provision for the 'elite' grew up.

People without access to 'closed' services but fairly well-off (those working in distribution, public catering, car servicing, skilled workers and the upper strata of the intelligentsia) have done their best to obtain good services by paying for them either with favours in return or with money or costly presents. There is a resultant competition between clients who are endeavouring to obtain services free and those who pay for them, illegally but at quite a high cost. Originating in the Caucasus, this practice spread comparatively rapidly to towns in the European part of the country, including Moscow, as a result of which medical treatment that is officially free is now in fact paid for. This is how a doctor describes the system that has developed: [10]

> . . . a rouble to the old woman sitting at the entrance to the ward
> – she will bring in a shopping bag of food and other things. A
> rouble to the nurse – and she will bring a bedpan. A rouble to
> the orderly – and she will bring you a night-shirt or pyjamas that
> fit, another rouble – and slippers appear, yet another – and the
> sheets are changed. Have a word with the sister – and, for about
> ten roubles, when she is on night duty she will look after your
> aged relative properly.

In hospitals where such practice is widespread only patients who can pay well can hope for good treatment.

Free provision has also led to the uneconomic use of scarce social services by clients. 'Easy come, easy go', as the saying has it. For example, I have seen people leaving excellent sanatoria long before treatment has been completed. And they were always the ones who had managed to get vouchers to stay there without paying the full price but at a 70 per cent discount, or completely free. For the majority of these people, sanatorium treatment was not necessary: it is just that the enterprise where they worked provided them with a voucher and sometimes paid the journey to the health resort, so they would go, stay for a while in the sanatorium, and leave. Meanwhile, it is not easy for most patients who need one to obtain a voucher, even at the full price: sometimes people wait for them for years. Free provision unjustifiably lowers the prestige of the services concerned, devalues their social worth, and may give rise to a careless, indifferent attitude to their use.

Thus, the negative aspects of free provision of social and cultural services include an extreme imbalance in their distribution among social strata and groups, the hidden redistribution of social expenditure to the benefit of more influential and better-off groups, corruption in the fields of education, medicine and culture, and the under-developed economic basis of sectors that cater for people's personal development and welfare as compared to the production sector.

Aware of these facts, many of our own economists and sociologists have come to the conclusion that the provision of social services on a paying basis should be extended. I would emphasize that there is absolutely no question of discontinuing the free provision of ordinary services, based on the level of economic development that has been actually achieved. The issue is how to expand rapidly those services that people need, in some cases at their own expense. We need a system in which people can satisfy their need for various services not only to the extent provided by the state but over and above that level, according to their own preferences, needs, and pattern of choice. Such an approach does not represent a deviation from socialist principles as is sometimes thought in the West. On the contrary, it ensures, firstly, that some fresh air is let into the bad atmosphere that has developed with regard to the free provision of many services in short supply and, secondly, that opportunities for spending one's income will be further democratized.

Today, in fact, it never enters anyone's head to interfere in the purchase of food, articles of clothing and shoes by individual families; that is rightly considered to be their own affair. Most families, however, cannot spend part of their wages in paying for better medical attention or obtain a voucher to a popular holiday resort but have to stick to services that are free but are far from being top-rank.

In Moscow there are now more than a hundred medical co-operatives, where at a reasonable price it is possible to have a consultation with qualified specialists, undergo diagnostic examination, use the services of masseurs, acupuncturists, etc. However, the demand for these fee-paying medical services greatly exceeds the capacity of the new institutions.

In conclusion, I shall touch upon another serious problem associated with social expenditure and that concerns the almost free provision of flats in state-owned housing blocks. The rent for these flats is calculated on the basis of 13 kopeks a month per square metre (an average of 5–6 roubles for a flat) or 3–5 per cent of a family's income. One would think that such a system would be something to be proud of: the citizen's right to be provided with accommodation is secured by the Constitution and in addition it costs practically nothing. However, the reality is more complicated.

Above all, the question arises as to why housing is considered a service which society is more interested in, it seems, than its own citizens. Since the 1930s the housing problem has been one of the most difficult facing our society. The average living area per person is about 14 square metres, while in most European countries it is 25–30 sq.m., and in the USA more than 50 sq.m. The most widely-used formula for flat occupancy is 'x − 1' or 'x − 2', indicating that the number of rooms is one or two less than the number of members in the family. A considerable number of people living in towns still live in multi-occupancy flats where families occupying one or two rooms share kitchen, bathroom and toilet with other tenants. The decision taken at the 27th Party Congress to provide every family with a separate flat will not, according to expert estimates, be carried out before the year 2000. A fifth of the urban housing stock still lacks basic domestic amenities – mains water, sewerage and central heating. In every enterprise and in every organization there are long waiting lists for accommodation and people often have to wait years. All this demonstrates that public housing is one of the services in shortest supply, for which people are prepared to make sacrifices, for example, by changing a highly-skilled job for one that is less interesting, less highly regarded and less well-paid but that holds out the promise of a flat. What is the explanation for this scarce service being provided free of charge? There is no comparison with medicine, education or the enjoyment of cultural facilities.

The exclusion of housing from market relations, i.e. the absence of a free housing market, does have a number of undesirable consequences. Because earnings cannot be spent on improving living conditions, the motivating power of wages is weakened, and there is less incentive to work harder and more efficiently. The fact that the state allocates limited resources to housing construction and that it is extremely difficult to build a house independently, delays the eventual solution of the housing problem and increases the gap between size of family income and the quality of their accommodation – the number and size of rooms, comfort and convenience, etc. Low rents, which on average cover only one third of maintenance and service costs, not to mention depreciation, mean that the housing sector is a consistent loss-maker in need of ever-increasing state subsidies.

Further, state housing varies considerably as to size, building finish, convenience, location, etc. Rents, however, are fixed according to the number of square metres per flat irrespective of differences in quality. As a result, that part of social expenditure which is used to subsidize low rents is distributed on a very unequal basis among various social groups. Families occupying top-class flats receive the biggest subsidies while most people get significantly less, and those living in individual houses or co-operative blocks build, repair and maintain them at their own expense, and are not subsidized at all.

Finally, the free provision of services that are in extremely short supply leads to the emergence of a variety of 'shadow' mechanisms in the allocation of housing. The press has published examples, not only of housing being provided for bribes or in exchange for expensive services, but also of the activity of organized criminals who have amassed fortunes through the allocation of state flats.

It has become common that when families exchange flats of unequal value, those who have formally 'gained' from the exchange pay the 'losers' a large sum of money. This means that market relations have illegally 'crept' into the public housing sector in a very ugly way. For people are 'selling' flats that they have not bought but obtained for nothing. This means that they obtain a speculative income from selling their flat.

Another example of the 'shadow' economy is the letting of state-owned flats at rents many times higher than the official level. Thus, the rent for a bed-sitting room in Moscow is not less than 100 roubles per month, while official tenants pay the state a maximum of 5 roubles a month. This happens when people go to work in another town for some time and rent out their accommodation, or when people who once had a large family and were allocated a large flat now have a considerable amount of room to spare. Once a family has been allocated a flat, it has guaranteed permanent tenancy and does not have to move to comply with any points system determining allocation that may be in force. Consequently, while some families have less than 6 square metres per person, others have 25–30 and more. If rents corresponded to costs, most families with too much room would apply to exchange their flat for a smaller one. However, taking advantage of the free accommodation, they derive a considerable amount of income from their excess living space.

On the basis of these arguments, an increasing number of experts now support the creation of an open housing market. The first step in this direction would be fixing state rents at a level that fully covers running costs and maintenance, and makes the public housing sector profitable rather than loss-making. Rents must also be substantially differentiated according to the quality of the flat. Since housing co-operatives, not to mention the individual sector, are already marketed, fixing economic rents for state housing would be a step in the direction of socialist justice. Taken on its own, this mechanism threatens to force down living standards. The planned character of a socialist economy, however, enables any such drop to be offset by a rise in wages and pensions and by increased state expenditure on the development of medicine, education and other public service sectors.

As can be seen, the principle of socialist justice is not confined to giving everybody the chance to work according to their abilities and to receive according to their work. In addition, it allows for the creation of a mechanism to provide and allocate services and benefits that are not directly derived from working. We have learned from experience that free provision does not always give the best results. It is justified only with regard to the necessary minimum in housing, the health service, education and culture that can realistically be given to every member of our society. Any service or benefit provided above that minimum should as a rule be paid for out of earnings. Changing the historically established system of allocating social expenditure is complex not only in the economic but also in socio-psychological respects, since it must be based on the restructuring of public perceptions. It also constitutes an essential part of the process of social renewal and cleansing that is taking place in our country.

I have discussed social policy in the narrow sense of the word, i.e. the series of measures that are aimed at ensuring social justice and raising living standards. The next chapter is devoted to problems associated with the formulation of a societal policy providing support for the forces of social renewal and driving out the forces that are slowing down the movement towards socialism.

The Social Management of Restructuring

4

SOCIAL FACTORS ACTING AS A BRAKE ON RESTRUCTURING

In the Introduction to this book I discussed the fact that the re-structuring of social relations in the Soviet Union is having a difficult passage. The concept of restructuring as a *social revolution* is more of a statement of principle on the part of our political leaders than an on-going process. While changes achieved so far in the press and in regard to openness can with some reservations be called revolution-ary, modernization of the economic management mechanism which underpins all other changes is very much a compromise. Officials in most ministries stubbornly persist, no matter what, in retaining their full power over enterprises. Thus, in 1988 the number of planning and standard-accounting indicators imposed on enterprises was even greater than in previous years.[1] In spite of political deci-sions, the obligation on economic organizations to report to Party and Soviet bodies continues to increase.[2] When orders placed by the state are ubiquitous, there is no question of enterprises selecting a profitable range of output nor of a broad development of contractual relationships, etc. Here is just one comment made by an enterprise manager on how ministries are behaving:[3]

> The whole output range was defined as a state order, but so as finally to destroy the enterprise's autonomy, the range was also broken down by product. This kind of plan has nothing to do with restructuring but is a blatant and completely unjustified diktat . . . Actions like that undermine people's belief in change and discredit the economic reform undertaken by the Party.

The practice of unilaterally fixing the amount of profit that has to be transferred to the ministries is no less detrimental to restructuring. Not only is the standard rate set at a higher level than before, but the total amount is variable as ministries assume the power to take more profits, allegedly in the interests of the industry as a whole. Such a practice destroys the very basis of economic reform – the creation of personal motivation to improve the quality of work and output.

Customer-enterprises are still rigidly bound to particular suppliers and are thus deprived of any economic room for manoeuvre. The much-criticized external 'funding' of production inputs remains in force, which helps to create artificial shortages and pile up unwanted stocks. Formalistic attitudes still exist in relations between ministries and between them and the enterprises under them. The practice of selecting top officials from a list of people approved by the Party apparatus still exists and contradicts in principle the Party's aim of carrying out a thorough democratization of management, the election of managers and their increased answerability to the workforce. All this shows that the central ministries and local authorities remain a stronghold of administrative and bureaucratic methods of management.

Attempts to introduce new forms of economic activity – co-operatives, leasing, etc. – have met with great opposition. Thus in the summer of 1988 the Supreme Soviet passed an extremely radical law on the development of co-operative forms of activity. In late December, however, the Presidium of the Supreme Soviet issued a decree severely limiting the areas of activity open to co-operatives; in fact, they annulled a number of the statutes of that law. This unconstitutional act is an example of the opposition to restructuring by the machinery of government.

There is a similar state of affairs with regard to social policy which is intended to strengthen and develop socialist justice and achieve a more rapid improvement in living standards. Firstly, if this is to happen economic development must take place. Any social measure, whether it is improving pension provision, reforming the wages structure, or speeding up housing construction, demands considerable state resources which can only be provided as a result of economic growth; and this is still far from adequate. Secondly, and no less important, any thorough-going attempts to reform the social arena (e.g. to supplement the state medical service with a co-operative one, to fundamentally restructure schools, to change the system for supplying goods to the general public) are confronted with powerful opposition from conservative elements in the relevant ministries and government departments. A recent example is of the Ministry of Health banning co-operative clinics which in the short period of their existence had managed to become very popular with the public because they offered better services than the state system.

The tendency for executive authorities to water down the fundamental ideas of restructuring has a negative effect on public consciousness and generally undermines confidence in its success. According to a survey conducted by the Institute of Sociological Research of the Soviet Academy of Sciences in 1987, only 16 per cent of respondents expressed the opinion that restructuring was making good progress; 31.4 per cent thought that it was proceeding slowly and with great difficulty; and 32.3 per cent that it was not making itself felt at all. (The remaining 20.3 per cent had difficulty in replying or did not reply.) People considered the main reasons for the slow progress of restructuring to be the continued existence of formalistic attitudes, the gulf between word and deed, and the bureaucratic character of social relations. Eighty per cent of respondents noted that they had personally encountered this kind of formalism. The reluctance of officials to take responsibility for tackling pressing problems was noted by 57 per cent of respondents, their apathy and inertia by 47 per cent, the failure to discipline officials for allowing formalistic attitudes by 42 per cent, and the incompetence of responsible officials by 34 per cent.[4]

Particular mention should be made of the fact that from 1987 onwards optimism about restructuring began to decline. Thus, according to research conducted by I. V. Ryvkina, from 1980 to 1986 the number of top managers and administrators in industry and agriculture in the Altai region who supported radical restructuring increased from 12 to 39 per cent, while in 1987 it fell to 31 per cent. Research carried out by Zh. T. Toshchenko shows a similar trend. In 1986 more than half of all workers questioned thought that if they worked harder they would be paid more. A year later only slightly over a quarter of the workers and only 21 per cent of managers expressed that opinion. A quarter of all workers and a third of the managers expressed doubt on this point and the remainder thought they would not be paid more. When compared to 1986 only half the number of people in 1987 noted positive achievements in the work of the authorities and social organizations.[5] Public opinion about the success of restructuring is thus not only not notable for its optimism, but shows a tendency to take an increasingly poor view of the situation.

The difficulties encountered in restructuring, its slow progress and the periodic alternation of successes and failures are only to be expected. Politicians and specialists foresaw the exceptional difficulty of implementing the reforms and gave advance warning of this. Among the circumstances making the restructuring of social relations difficult, the following were mentioned:

i) The huge size of the country and the diversity of social and economic structures, working and social conditions in the different republics and regions; the physical and social distance of the periphery from the centre; the multi-tier system of managing society which hinders any feedback between the political authorities and the general public.

ii) The recollection of previous unsuccessful attempts to improve economic management methods; the consequent lack of faith in the measures being undertaken today; an assumption regarding the possibility of a complete reversal causing socio-political inertia on the part of many officials.

iii) The lack of major economic resources to give an initial impulse to economic development. The contradiction between propaganda-inspired expectations of a rapid end to consumer-goods shortages and growing social and economic difficulties that inevitably accompany every large-scale reform.

. These circumstances are really important. The main difficulties, however, are associated with the fact that restructuring affects individuals' vitally important and interacting interests. Projected and current measures taken by the Party affect these interests in different ways, satisfying some and infringing upon and restricting others. The groups who gain and those who lose from the changes in social relations are not mere bystanders but the basic social forces involved in restructuring. In deciding particular problems and in choosing certain lines of conduct, they do not overlook what is to their own advantage or disadvantage. The final outcome of this interaction between groups with different, even conflicting, interests decides the course of restructuring.

As I see it, the following aspects of restructuring have the greatest effect on the position of social groups:

i) Consistent separation of the functions of Party, state and economic management. An end to political supervision of enterprise operations. Concentrating the Party's attention on resolving strategic problems affecting society's development, strengthening the Soviet Union's position in the international community, creating a new economic and political mode of thought, and selecting and training key personnel. Concentrating the attention of government on achieving the comprehensive social and economic development of the regions, satisfying people's physical and social needs, and strengthening civil rights and socialist justice.

ii) The extension of openness in social affairs and activation of the mass media, which will gradually remove the social barriers that previously separated the self-elected elite from the mass of ordinary working people. An associated increase in the complexity of management and a fundamental change in the conditions of managerial work.

iii) The growing awareness by broad sections of society of the incorrectness of many theoretical positions that had previously seemed immutable, a radical change in the interpretation of major historical events and key issues in philosophy, political economy and sociology. An emerging demand for new social science concepts that adequately reflect historical reality and the particular features of the present stage in the country's development that are capable of giving restructuring the right direction.

iv) The transfer of a significant portion of powers regarding the ownership, management and use of public property from higher to lower authorities, and an increase in their autonomy and consequently their accountability.

v) The development of enterprise self-management, the election of managers by the workforce instead of their appointment 'from above', greater answerability by top managers to their workforce in the decision-taking process. More open management and a bigger role for public opinion.

vi) A greater correspondence between wages and the quantity and quality of output, on the one hand, and the costs of production, on the other. The more widespread practice of different forms of contractual and leasing relations. Greater wage differentials between profitable and loss-making enterprises and within an enterprise between highly-skilled and unskilled, conscientious and bad workers.

vii) The removal of restrictions and especially prohibitions on all useful economic, organizational and technological initiatives on the part of the workforce. The development of the co-operative form of work and the consequently greater opportunities to increase personal incomes by extra work.

viii) An increase in the social value of creative work, the development of scientific, technological, and socio-economic experimentation and a more intensive and efficient exploitation of people's intellectual potential.

ix) The redeployment of some redundant workers from the production sector and management and administration and their retraining and placement in new jobs. The growing problem of employment in those republics where there has been a low level of geographical mobility, particularly in mining and in agricultural areas. Possibly greater difficulties for women with young children in obtaining work. A probable reduction in these circumstances of a high rate of turnover of key personnel and a higher standard of discipline at work and with regard to production.

x) The development of co-operative trading and free street markets selling a variety of goods and food which will help satisfy consumer demand. An increase in the number of producers of consumer goods and the emergence of competition for customers' roubles; and a reduction in and eventual elimination of shortages. The abolition of special channels for supplying privileged officials and the creation of a national market open to all sections of the public.

xi) A closer correspondence, essential in the change-over to economic management methods, between the retail prices of consumer goods and their social value, an increase in state prices of meat, dairy and bread products, a reduction in the prices of consumer durables, clothing and footwear, rent differentials according to the quality of accommodation and its location, and a significant increase in chargeable services. The greater dependence of a family's living standards and conditions on its own efforts in order to stimulate a higher rate of participation in the labour market.

This is obviously not an exhaustive list of the most important areas where restructuring affects the position of social groups. But it is sufficient to permit a partial assessment of its far-reaching and complex social consequences.

In order to provide effective leadership of the course of restructuring, it is important to know which classes, strata and groups stand to gain or lose by certain measures. This in turn requires a proper understanding of the country's social structure. However, Soviet social science is weighed down by a multitude of dogmas in this area, unsupported by either serious theoretical work or empirical analysis.

Ever since the 1930s, official documents, academic writings, and social science textbooks have been using what is known as the 'tripartite formula' to define the social and class structure of Soviet society, consisting of the working class, the peasantry and the intelligentsia. The differences between these groups were regarded as inter-class and systemic, while all remaining differences were viewed as inner-class (or non-class) and secondary. It was customary, for example, to classify differences between various operational and skill categories of workers and collective farmers and between the hierarchical strata of the intelligentsia as inner-class, and differences between nations and peoples, between rural and urban populations, and between agricultural and industrial workers as non-class.

However, empirical research shows that this 'formula' does not correspond to the realities of life.

i) At present the position of collective-farm peasants is almost indistinguishable from that of the rural section of the working class. From the social point of view state-farm workers are much closer to collective farmers than to industrial workers. The social divide between workers and peasants is therefore narrower than that between the rural and urban populations.[6]

ii) The social differences between the collective-farm peasantry and the industrial working class, which were immense a few decades ago, are also disappearing comparatively rapidly and are now less significant than differences between operational and skill categories within each group.

iii) The differences between very highly-qualified workers and non-administrative or non-managerial engineers and technicians are rapidly decreasing. As regards the character of their skills and knowhow, their rights and duties, and their living standards and way of life, there is no appreciable difference between these groups. In fact, in a number of industries as much as 10–15 per cent of the workforce has had a higher education, i.e. formally belong to the intelligentsia.[7]

iv) The intelligentsia as a stratum is extremely heterogeneous. It comprises genuine 'proletarians of mental labour', the intellectual elite, and the country's political leadership.

v) The 'tripartite formula' of the social structure does not cover many groups which do in fact exist in society and play an important part in restructuring. These include, for example, managers at different levels of administration, distribution and service sector workers, individual entrepreneurs, co-operators, office employees, 'shadow economy' operators, etc.

These all point to the need to formulate a more relevant description of our social structure. This will be more complex than the structure of Soviet society in the 1920s and early 1930s since development leads to an increased complexity of the system in question and to a greater degree of pluralism rather than a greater uniformity of its components and linkages. Therefore the tired old dogma that the development of socialist society will be characterized by 'complete social uniformity' is incorrect. On the other hand, the idea that social differences can eventually lose their class nature and acquire a new content is a real possibility although it will not be a simple thing to achieve. Even in this case, however, social structure will become not simpler but more complex, a process that has been observed in practice despite expert assertions to the contrary.

To determine the real structure of our society, it is appropriate to use the methodology for studying social differences which potentially underpins Lenin's definition of class. In the Introduction I cited the criteria that Lenin proposed for defining social classes. These are: place in the social organization of labour, relationship to the means of production, and the share and sources of social wealth that are acquired. Lenin considered these criteria in their totality but I would emphasize that each one, even when considered independently, possesses a not inconsiderable power of differentiation. Using these criteria, it is possible to identify groups that do not always have a class character but which play an important part in the functioning of society.

In fact, the qualitative features of the contribution made by different groups to the development of society is reflected in their role in the *social organization of labour*. This role determines their specific place in the system of legislative and executive power; the functional area of activity (management, production, distribution or exchange of tangible goods and services, social services, cultural provision, education and training, etc.); and type of job (i.e. the correlation of executive and operational functions, mental and physical, complex and simple elements).

Relationship to the means of production is determined by a) forms of property and b) the methods and forms of ownership, distribution and use of the means of production and objects of labour. This aspect of the social position of groups can be evaluated with the aid of such indicators as participation or non-participation in formulating state economic strategy and the economic management mechanism; the totality of powers with regard to taking decisions concerning the social means of production (e.g. their distribution, redistribution, sale and purchase); economic forms of making use of social property; ownership of social and individual means of production (land, plantations, cattle and poultry, business premises, transport facilities, agricultural and other stocks). Further factors determining the relationship of different groups to the means of production are a) the kind of technical equipment used in production (state-of-the-art, value, social prestige, scarcity) and b) the possibility of free or concessional use of means of production used on the job for work 'on the side' or for personal use (chauffeurs, tractor drivers, stomatologists, etc).

The share of social wealth received by different social groups is indicated by the volume and sources of the goods and services they consume and the social and cultural benefits that they enjoy. The sources of these may be wages earned in social production, incomes from entrepreneurial activity, inherited wealth, benefits financed out of social expenditure funds, including those resulting directly from one's job. This aspect can be described by such features as the general level of current income and the value of accumulated and/or inherited wealth; the relationship between various sources of income; the presence/absence of unearned and illegal income; provision of housing, and consumer goods and services; the value and selection of goods obtained free or on a concessional basis.

Although there are many factors affecting the position of groups, most of them are interconnected. Thus, the part played by a particular group in the organization of social work determines its relationship to the means of production, while taken together these features in their turn affect the structure and volume of goods and services that are received. The socio-economic position of social groups, therefore, is determined by their qualitative characteristics with their roots both in the past and present structure of our society.

In a more fundamental work, which is at the present time being prepared for publication,[8] an attempt has been made to construct an integrated account of the social structure of Soviet society based on Leninist criteria. However, the groups discovered by this method number some dozens. The aim of this section of the present book does not call for a fully detailed description of the social structure and will deal only with those differences in the positions of groups that determine their differing attitudes to restructuring. I shall therefore, firstly, refrain from examining those social groups whose behaviour does not exert an appreciable influence on the course of restructuring (unskilled factory and office workers, pensioners, school students, de-classed elements, etc.) and, secondly, I shall as far as I am able enlarge on my initial description of the social structure.

I would name the following social groups as being the principal forces of restructuring and as determining its development:

i) The stratum of the working class that is most advanced in terms of job skills and in social and political terms.

ii) The basic (largest) stratum of workers with average skills who operate equipment of an average technical standard.

iii) The stratum of workers who have been corrupted by the long-term practice of receiving unearned income and who are unaccustomed to high-quality and intensive work.

iv) The collective-farm peasantry who can be divided into the same strata as the above.

v) The scientific and technological intelligentsia (engineers, technologists, and natural scientists).

vi) Managers and economic administrators in the production sector.

vii) Senior officials in trade and service sectors.

viii) Co-operators and small entrepreneurs.

ix) The social and humanitarian intelligentsia (teachers, doctors, journalists, writers, artists, social scientists, etc).

x) Officials nominated by the Party apparatus in the machinery of political government, i.e. Party, state and public bodies.

xi) Political leaders.

xii) Participants in organized crime (the mafiosi), incorporating the corrupted section of officials in the trade and service sectors, operators in the 'shadow economy', and the socially and morally corrupted section of factory and office workers.

In the following section I shall try to isolate the particular characteristics that mark the present position of these groups and to describe their interests and their attitude to restructuring.

THE INTERESTS OF SOCIAL GROUPS

The *working class* is by far the largest group in Soviet society. As the formal joint owner of state property, it can take decisions about the means of production through the system of self-management and, most important, it can use them directly in the course of work. The principal source of income for workers consists in a) wages from their workplace and b) benefits paid for out of social funds. Wages vary according to the complexity, level of skill, how hard or detrimental to health the work is, and other social qualities of labour not directly associated with its final outcome. As a result of the change-over to the new conditions for managing the economy, wages are beginning to be determined to an increasing extent by the final outcome of labour.

The restructuring of economic and socio-political relations is on the whole in the workers' interests. They gain from the removal of official restrictions on working overtime, the democratization of production management, a more businesslike and efficient resolution of social questions, a more rapid pace of housing construction, wider powers for the workforce in its struggle against formalism and bureaucracy, and greater satisfaction of the demand for goods and services.

Restructuring does carry certain minus factors for the workers, however, and these must not be forgotten. These are faster price increases for basic food products and services and possible rent increases for housing over and above the guaranteed state minimum, etc. A fairly complex range of problems will also arise as a result of the likelihood of redundancies. The closure of unprofitable enterprises and the efforts of many workforces to achieve the same or a greater level of production with less manpower will inevitably lead to the dismissal of some workers. This is the natural consequence of restructuring, the 'social price' that must be paid for the country's accelerated rate of growth and for overcoming its backwardness.

The perspectives that restructuring opens up for particular strata of the working class are not the same in every case. I shall first examine the stratum comprising the best educated, qualified, and creatively and politically active workers, capable of taking initiatives. They are as a rule employed in advanced-technology sectors of the economy: precision tool engineering, flexible automation, complex sectors of the chemical or bio-chemical industries, the machine-tool industry, computer technology, etc. With skilled and efficient use of advanced technology (often imported and therefore in particularly short supply) they produce complex and top-quality output that is in demand both at home and abroad. Excellent qualifications and the ability to use technology that is unique in its complexity and efficiency ensures that this section of workers earns wages that often exceed professional salaries, have good living conditions and access to good medical care, and enjoy a high status combined with self-confidence and an active participation in society.

I believe that members of this group have more to gain from restructuring than others. Firstly, under the system of administrative commands they basically 'took orders' and were unable to do genuinely creative work, with the result that their potential was not fully realized. Secondly, they have a keener interest than others in putting an end to the 'levelling-off' system, i.e. in obtaining a proper and just reward for high-quality and conscientious work as opposed to unskilled and careless work. Thirdly, they have a particular interest in the organization of small groups of contract and leasing workforces, economic associations, contract teams and small co-operatives, where their creative potential can be fully realized. Finally, this section of workers, who are noted for their socio-political activity, are usually the driving force in social organizations and workforce councils and in the struggle for greater openness in management, the election of managers, etc. As regards the social difficulties of restructuring, these affect highly-skilled workers least of all. This stratum of the working class can therefore be regarded as a source of support for the Communist Party's efforts for reform.

The same, although to a lesser degree, can be said of the large stratum of *average skilled workers* with an average level of technology at work. They also show an interest in the sub-contracting and leasing forms of organising production. Many of them are, it is true, accustomed to being paid more for time spent at work rather than final output. By separating the conscientious from the careless workers much more sharply than before, the new system of economic relations will turn out to be a dead loss for some of them compared to the former state of affairs. Once they have learned to work better, however, they will be able to increase their standard of living appreciably. At the moment many of these workers do extra work on a co-operative or family basis. They have both the possibilities (necessary skills, materials) and the vital need for extra earnings, as their income level is lower than that of the previous group.

Gaining from the generally more rapid pace of social and economic development, this large stratum of workers will also soon begin to experience personally the impact of the new conditions and the acceleration of technological progress. Some of them will have to look for new jobs. In large towns this will not present any problems, at least in the immediate future, but the new jobs will in all probability not be as good as the previous ones. In small towns, however, and in the countryside, the situation can be more complicated. The greatest difficulties will be experienced by workers who are no longer young and have low levels of skill and who have lost the ability to learn new job skills, and also by people with restricted mobility (mothers with families at home, and elderly people).

On the whole this basic stratum of the working class undoubtedly has more to gain than lose from restructuring. It therefore contains many supporters and allies of restructuring. It is, however, notably less active and displays less initiative than members of the first group and is used to carrying out orders rather than acting according to its own understanding of things. To become active champions of an idea, people must have a thorough grasp of its significance and act upon their own perceptions, in accordance with their own values, needs and interests. The majority of ordinary workers, however, do not yet really have a thorough understanding of the concept of restructuring, have not grasped the interconnectedness of its measures or that it is in their own vital interests. It should be mentioned in this connection that, alongside leading workers who form its backbone, the working class includes a not inconsiderable number of people with low educational levels, few skills and a limited outlook who concentrate on their own interests. As well as supporters of restructuring, therefore, this section of the working class includes many socially passive people. Some of them adopt a sceptical attitude and have no faith in the mass media ('We've heard all this before. It didn't succeed then, and it won't succeed now'). Others are quite uninterested in the changes that are going on, considering that restructuring economic management is a matter for the leaders and experts. Yet others have a conservative turn of mind and are inclined towards the values of 'the good old days'.

There is a third stratum of workers who deserve attention. Under the previous system it occupied a particularly good position and therefore has a cautious attitude to restructuring. Although fairly heterogeneous, it does have one typical feature – it is accustomed to receiving unearned incomes and unjustified privileges and benefits. Being able to take from society more than they give has a corrupting effect on people. It is therefore characteristic of this stratum to put personal and group interests above the interests of the workforce or society as a whole.

Who in particular belongs to this stratum? Firstly, people who work in exceptionally prestigious and privileged organizations and so traditionally enjoy more congenial working conditions, higher wages and more social benefits not based on high levels of output but on the particular character of their place of work. This applies, for example, to the position of personal chauffeurs to senior officials, medical staff in special sanatoria or medical institutes for the privileged, etc.

Secondly, people who have skills that are in short supply and who can thus demand high wages that they themselves consider just, irrespective of their work output.

Personally I would also include in this stratum those who are patently bad workers and who in effect turn good raw materials into rejects. People like this should be made to pay for the materials they waste rather than be paid wages but, unfortunately, there is a whole legion of them. They build houses that fall down round the occupants' ears, light fires on factory premises, crash trains, put agricultural produce into storage to rot, and are paid for doing it.

The fourth type of worker consists of people who earn a bit 'on the side' (most of them are employed in car maintenance, catering, personal and domestic services, the state trading sector, collective-farm markets, etc.). 'Extra charges', 'palm-greasing', 'tips' and not infrequently even direct extortions from customers make up, if not their main income, in any event a significant part of it.

Related to these is the fifth type of worker making a living from the petty and sometimes large-scale theft of supplies and goods. Light industries, food industries, construction and agriculture are the main victims of the 'activity' of these workers.

On the whole the privileged stratum of the working class, to some degree bribed and corrupted by higher-level groups, does not show much interest in restructuring. The worst section of them (chauffeurs who stick portraits of Stalin on their windscreens) are openly conservative, if not reactionary. The better part, who understand the impropriety of their position and the unfairness of the privileges they enjoy, maintain a passive attitude and adopt a fatalistic view of restructuring. 'If they take some privileges away', they say, 'it will be from everybody, not just me, and that won't be too bad.' Taken as a whole, they tend to be opponents rather than supporters of restructuring, but they have no strong convictions and do not represent a powerful social force.

Clearly, it is not just the bureaucracy that forms a braking mechanism on restructuring. Members of the working class are also involved and on an appreciable scale.

The collective-farm peasantry is the next largest social group in Soviet society. The principal feature of its position is the free use of land provided by the state and the co-operative ownership of the remaining means of production by the workforce. Since by definition they are on full economic accounting, collective farms should have the power to take independent decisions about the means of production and to enjoy freedom of economic activity. Income distributed among the collective farmers must be generated as a result of the economic activity of the workforce, i.e. as part of its gross income. The basic ideas of transforming economic relations by restructuring, therefore, are completely in keeping with the principles of agricultural co-operation.

In fact, however, over many decades all features of real co-operative relations have been relentlessly driven out of the collective-farm sector, from freedom of choice about the basic direction of production to the distribution of income. A steady 'étatization' of collective farms has taken place, turning them into quasi-state farms, with the same bureaucratic management structures and the same economic results.[9] I am convinced that, if 30–40 years ago the collective farms had been given the opportunity to work under economic conditions in keeping with their character, then today this country would not only not be suffering from shortages of food, but would be exporting it to other countries.

For collective farmers, restructuring means a return to the original ideas of co-operation, the 'de-étatization' of the collective farms, their freeing from unprofessional bureaucratic control, the regeneration of collective-farm democracy, the development of self-management, the restoration to the workforce of the power to select the most profitable economic structure, and efficient forms of production.

The change-over by collective farms to full economic accounting will not, of course, be a straightforward process without any conflicts. It does, after all, entail the ending of state subsidies and a change-over from guaranteed wages (irrespective of results) at rates comparable to those paid at nearby state farms to the distribution of income actually earned by each workforce. The change-over to the new conditions will inevitably bring to light differences in the economic situation of collective farms that is obscured by existing relations. It will open up good prospects for development for some farms but threaten others with liquidation.

There is no doubt that the long-term strategic interests of collective farmers coincide with the aims of restructuring. The matter is rather more complicated, however, when it comes to their immediate interests. Although the previous economic relations were inefficient, restricted farms' freedom of action, resulted in unnecessary losses, etc., they did cover any losses incurred and ensure reasonable wages even on the weakest farms. Although collective farms were in practice deprived of any economic powers, they did not, on the other hand, bear any responsibility for the results of their work or take any economic risk.

A typical picture of stagnation? Undoubtedly. But people had got used to it, and tolerated it: they had, after all, lost the habit of running the farm on their own and taking economic risks. Restructuring therefore causes feelings of anxiety and apprehension among a considerable number of collective farmers. The more energetic, creative, confident and qualified section of collective farmers (like industrial workers) support restructuring, willingly enter into workforce contracts and achieve far better results than before. The more inert section of collective farmers (particularly those working on farms with a poor physical, technological and social base) doubt the possibility of standing on their own feet without financial assistance from the state. There is also a broad section of collective farmers who have not grasped the essential meaning of restructuring, which seems to them to concern only 'the bosses'.

More than a third of collective-farm output is produced on peasant individual plots on land provided by the collective farm, with privately-owned means of production and family labour. The state's attitude to these smallholdings has changed radically more than once – from helping their development as 'a part of socialist farming' to their compulsory abolition as 'survivals of bourgeois property relations' and back again. By opening the doors to all forms of individual and family business activity, restructuring is giving the peasant homestead a 'second chance'. Collective-farm families contract to fatten up several dozen bullocks, pigs and other livestock either on their own premises or in farm buildings they have themselves repaired. The collective farms provide them with feed, litter, and veterinary services, and then buy the livestock on previously agreed terms. Under this system, the individual sector in fact merges with the public sector and peasant families, collective farms and society all benefit from the arrangement. A policy that is directed at making full use of resources in the individual sector of production is in the interests of the peasantry and enjoys its wholehearted support. This policy is not, it is true, even now being carried out by all local authorities. In fact, many of them obstruct the development of individual holdings, regarding them as the source of 'petty bourgeois' relations contrary to the spirit of socialism.

On the whole, the collective-farm peasantry has as much to gain from restructuring as industrial workers. Its advanced section constitutes the social basis for transforming the economy, while the vast majority are allies of restructuring.

The scientific and technological intelligentsia is the stratum that consists of middle management, engineers and technicians, and natural scientists. Its functions lie in the organization of production, the stimulation of scientific and technological progress, and the design, application, construction and efficient use of production equipment. The socio-economic position of this stratum does not at the moment match its social role. There are more engineers and technologists than the country needs and their level of skill falls far below world standards. In fact most of them do not work in their specialization at all but as relatively unskilled employees, doing clerical work, etc. Their work is devoid of any creative content, their wages are low and their social prestige negligible.

The most highly qualified, creative and capable section of the scientific and technological intelligentsia suffer more than other groups from administrative and bureaucratic methods of management. Their work is fettered by endless instructions and they wait for years and decades for their discoveries and inventions to be put into practice. In some sectors they earn less than ordinary workers and they have few opportunities for earning more, while the creative component of their work is hardly reflected in their pay at all.

This determines their ambivalent attitude towards restructuring. For highly qualified and creative professional workers restructuring holds out the promise of significant gains in the form of opportunities to implement new ideas, earn higher incomes, and enjoy greater social prestige. Many specialists are now joining sub-contracting workforces and co-operatives producing high-technology goods. Most of them support the policy of greater openness and democratization.

On the other hand, the social awareness of this stratum of the intelligentsia is heavily tinged with scepticism with regard to restructuring. Engineers and technologists too often encounter bureaucratic distortions of the ideas underlying restructuring from its quasi-supporters, and formalistic versions of its content as trendy words and slogans are mouthed to cover up practices that remain unchanged. While in sympathy with the concept of restructuring, which is in their interests, many professional experts do not believe that the braking mechanism can be destroyed.

There is also a fairly large group who have become accustomed to cushy jobs, good pay and the absence of responsibility for their work. These people either never had any professional skills or have lost them. They are not capable of working efficiently and therefore prefer to sit out their time under the old, familiar conditions until they retire on a pension.

Into the *senior management* group I put the directors and chief specialists of enterprises and enterprise groups, construction and transport organizations, state and collective farms, and the heads of factory workshops, departments, etc. This group is responsible for the efficient management of operations and the scientific, technological and socio-economic development of production. It is accorded wide powers to take decisions not only about the means of production but also about the utilization of manpower.

Senior managers receive high salaries and numerous bonuses, enjoy a wide range of privileges, and receive a variety of benefits from social funds. Apart from that, they can manipulate the use of inputs and products not only for social but for their own individual purposes. Their living standards are significantly higher than any of the groups considered so far, but their work is extremely complex and intensive, entailing great physical and nervous strain. I need only mention the unrestricted working day, endless checks by dozens of supervisory bodies, the administrative and bureaucratic style of relations with government departments, imbalances between production plans and available resources, incorrect deliveries of materials and equipment, etc.

The changes in the working conditions of managers as a result of restructuring tend to be contradictory. On the one hand, the opportunities for economic, organizational, technological and social creativity are increasing considerably. Together with the workforce under them, managers are becoming the real masters of those sections entrusted to them and are free of many of the restrictions that previously tied them down. The change-over from the appointment of managers 'from above' to their election by the workforce strengthens their position and improves their relations with senior management. The less rapid turnover of core workers and a stronger work discipline are having a positive effect on output.

But this is only one side of the question. The other is associated with the need for a fundamental change in methods of leadership away from the traditional carrying out of instructions 'handed down' from above towards taking independent, at times risky, organizational and technological initiatives. The need for better managerial skills and personal qualities is increasing in the new conditions, while managerial jobs are becoming more and more complex and responsible. This is enough to make a number of managers take up a conservative position and not be in too great a hurry to implement changes in management methods. It must also be admitted that the first attempts at switching enterprises to the new system were not sufficiently well thought out, which increased the number of managers dissatisfied with restructuring and caused a certain lack of co-ordination and some confusion. While they are in favour of the concept in principle, they consider that it is being put into practice with an unsure hand and that many 'novelties' being introduced are in fact strengthening administrative-command management. Hence their scepticism and lack of faith in the final victory of restructuring and their equivocal position.

The material position of managers capable of adapting to the new conditions will improve as a result of restructuring since the 'ceiling' for efficiency bonuses for achieving good economic indicators, introducing new technology and increasing exports will rise. However, their earnings will depend to an increasing extent on the results achieved by the workforce and so salary differentials will increase within a sector.

Restructuring affects the interests of managers far too powerfully and directly for them to remain indifferent to it. But their attitude is ambivalent. Firstly, it varies considerably depending on their social and personal attitudes and their mode of socio-economic thought. Secondly, they can distinguish better than anyone else between the theoretical concept of restructuring and actual changes in economic relations, approving the former in principle but often condemning the latter.

The next group comprises *top officials in the distribution, public catering, and personal and domestic service sectors* and in organizations distributing goods and services out of public funds. Although there is no special relationship to the means of production, they do occupy a very particular position in relation to the provision of goods and services. Although they do not by any means own them, they do have extensive powers in distributing them and the chance to manipulate them for their own ends.

The wages of this group are not above average. However, according to sociological research, which is confirmed by many accounts appearing in the press, they own a vast amount of property in the form of second homes by the sea, foreign cars, gold, valuables, works of art, stacks of cash, etc. A significant, if not the main, part of their incomes is illegal, acquired by 'playing the scarcity market' – speculation, bribe-taking (e.g. in allocating housing), so-called 're-grading' (when low-quality goods are sold at higher prices), the switching of goods from state to co-operative shops where they are sold at higher prices, etc.

This group's prosperity is the direct result of administrative and bureaucratic methods of management that cause consumer shortages. No less significant is the weakened state of socialist justice, the merging of the traders' elite with the corrupt section of the Party, Soviet and legal and police authorities, the lack of openness on the part of management, and the atmosphere that has prevailed for a very long time in which the powers-that-be go unpunished and can get away with anything.

Restructuring cuts the ground from under the feet of this group. Economic accounting and self-financing encourage enterprises to keep a strict account of sales revenue. The change-over from the central supply or funding system to the free sale of production inputs destroys the monopoly position of those who previously distributed them. Openness and the constant development of democracy helps lead to the disclosure of swindling that has been going unpunished for years. Finally, co-operative and family businesses create competition for the state trading, public catering and service sectors, and the more they develop, the stronger this competition will be.

The old system is coming to an end. The section of this group that is deeply 'rooted' in the previous system will resist the change-over in every way it can. Above all, it will try to discredit the very idea of restructuring in the eyes of working people. After all, in a number of towns shops are empty while food is lying in railway stations, wholesale warehouses and even in the back premises of shops. One would be justified in thinking that officials in the distribution sector are doing this on purpose to undermine people's faith in restructuring and to make them think that it has no future and is bound to fail. On the initiative of the trade unions, groups of workers have been getting together in many towns to carry out checks on shops and warehouses. In areas of greatest shortage significant supplies of extremely scarce goods have been discovered, carefully hidden from the public.

The honest, morally sound section of this group has the potential for reformation and renewal, the possibility of doing an honest job in return for a normal wage. On the whole, however, the situation here is not very good. In the distribution sector a fairly well-developed, firmly-established and self-perpetuating system has grown up which provides its workers with illegal extra incomes. It is therefore not easy to find supporters and allies of restructuring in this group. There are even fewer quasi-supporters than in most other strata. This sector of distribution and exchange (covering everything from the means of production to personal and social services) will probably remain one of the firmest strongholds of conservatism in our society for a long time to come.

Small co-operatives and individual producers constitute one social group. Their role in the social organization of labour consists in the provision, on their own initiative, of goods and services that the public needs, mainly with the use of resources that are not available to the public sector. Small socialist entrepreneurs aim at plugging the 'chinks' and 'gaps' that systematically open up in operations between large enterprises and government departments. Small-scale production is distinguished by its flexibility, adaptability and sensivity to the needs of the consumer. It has no need for endless agreements regarding co-ordination at different levels of authority and is therefore much quicker to exploit new technological and economic ideas. Its special role goes with its special relationship to the means of production, which are either co-operatively/personally owned, leased from the state or bought from the state on credit.

Small producers independently own, control and make use of the means of production themselves. Their income is obtained from the sale of their goods or services at prices that depend on supply and demand. Co-operatives (or individual entrepreneurs) cover their costs and put money aside for development out of their receipts and then consume the rest. In principle, this system of income creation and distribution calls to mind the collective-farm system, except that small co-operative incomes are less stable since they are more dependent on the market. For this reason incomes are more dependent on the entrepreneurship of each particular workforce and are much higher on average. On the other hand, small entrepreneurs lose out in comparison with other groups as regards social benefits (housing allocation, pension, sick pay, etc.).

New forms of co-operative and individual/family business have been gaining strength. In the spring of 1988 there were more than 1,400 different types of co-operative working in Moscow alone – from the production of scarce spare parts for large enterprises to 'introductions with a view to marriage'. The ability to identify the precise areas where public needs are not being satisfied is a rich source of income to the co-operatives. People with creative minds have many ideas of what can be done with comparatively little outlay. A fairly broad section not only of existing but of potential co-operators have an interest, therefore, in the development and extension of small-scale entrepreneurial activity.

All these people are allies of restructuring, which not only allows them to increase their income but to realize their potential much more fully. The more progressive wing of this group regard their activity, not just from their own personal point of view, but from the point of view of society as a whole, as practical involvement in restructuring, i.e. they are among its ideological supporters. Its other wing, however, is concerned only with getting rich quick without a backward glance at morality or even the law. Consumers have many complaints regarding the quality of goods and services provided by the co-operatives, which are moreover very expensive. Unscrupulous people, rising to the surface like scum on stagnant water, give a bad name to what is undoubtedly a progressive process of regeneration and development of co-operation. Their 'support' has a bogus character, which puts them in the category of quasi-allies of restructuring.

The position of the *social and humanitarian intelligentsia* (teachers, doctors, artists, and academics in the humanities and the social sciences) has much in common with that of the scientific and technological intelligentsia. Their position in the social organization of labour, however, is different: they are instrumental in forming spiritual and moral values, they preserve and develop culture and provide education and training for new generations. By the nature of their work, this group is far removed from the distribution and use of the social means of production. Their sources of income are the low salaries they receive from their main place of work, various supplementary earnings (usually small) and comparatively high payments for books, articles, concert appearances, etc. which are earned by the most successful part of the group. By way of what might be regarded as compensating doctors and teachers for the low social evaluation attached to their work in the stagnation period, it became common practice for them to be paid personally for services at a fairly high level (private coaching, consultations). In this way, patients' sincere gratitude for their restored health became interwoven with an organized system of demanding extra payments at set rates for the hospitalization of patients, carrying out examinations and operations, post-operational care, etc. Although this is by no the practice in all hospitals, it became a fairly common practice.

The position of the social and humanitarian intelligentsia in the period of spiritual stagnation and social decay was bad in both material and spiritual and moral respects: humiliatingly low wages, a low social status and the impossibility of individual creative work in teaching, medicine, literature, the arts and sciences. They were faced with two alternatives: either 'to dance to the music' or to try to do their professional duty creatively under difficult, sometimes intolerable, conditions. They have suffered more than other groups from the suppression of democracy and openness, the distortion of socialist relations, and the decline in public morality.

We see many people in this group today who held on to their socialist values throughout all the difficulties of the previous era and thereby prepared the ground for restructuring. As Alexander Gelman has said, the moral nucleus of the people did not die:[10]

> It was transfixed with terror and defencelessness in the Stalinist era but, by curling up and clenching itself into a ball, it kept its inner quality. Otherwise there would have been no 20th Congress and no restructuring today.

We may regard singers and poets like Bulat Okudzhava and Vladimir Vysotsky, progressive social scientists, writers and journalists, as its initiators, ideologists, and prophets, courageously speaking out against bureaucratic distortions of socialism. The most radical members of the humanitarian intelligentsia are now fighting for recognition of restructuring as a democratic revolution, destined to put Soviet society on the road to socialist construction. They act as

THE INTERESTS OF SOCIAL GROUPS 175

ideologists, interpreters and creators of restructuring, and initiators of its wider and deeper development. The main section of the social and humanitarian intelligentsia welcome restructuring, in the first instance because of the growing freedom for spiritual creativity, the development of openness and democracy, and open discussion in the press of urgent social problems which makes their practical resolution possible. They are in the forefront of an active campaign for the moral and social regeneration of society.

In giving due recognition to the intelligentsia's struggle against the phenomena of stagnation, one must not close one's eyes to the fact that such a situation could not have developed unless some of its members had played their part in it. The conservative section, who previously upheld the old dogmas, cannot fundamentally change their views at the wave of a magic wand. Nostalgic for the past, this section regard the transformation of social relations not as an advance but as a deviation from socialist principles, they become indignant at the 'excessive' development of openness and the over-frank revelations of the past as if this would destroy youthful ideals, etc. The ill-famed letter sent to the editors of the newspaper *Sovetskaya Rossiya* by Nina Andreyeva is a good example of such views. Although most of Andreyeva's supporters speak in favour of restructuring, they cannot in fact accept it and take up a conservative position. It should also be borne in mind that the majority of social scientists and teachers in the ideological disciplines are intrinsically tied to their earlier statements and publications. Now that it is becoming obvious that these were mistaken, many of them are experiencing a genuine crisis and try to prove that at least some of the ideas that they had been putting forward were correct. This is the real basis of the conservatism of a section of the social and humanitarian intelligentsia. Many of these people are, as it were, standing at the crossroads between views and values held in the past and those propagated today or else they adopt a sceptical attitude as though they cannot allow themselves to believe in the possibility of a serious change in social affairs.

Finally, alongside the supporters and opponents of reform, there are many people without any principles at all. They make passionate declarations of faith in restructuring in public, then they go back to their offices and do very little about it. It seems that the social and humanitarian intelligentsia is the most heterogeneous of all the strata that have been examined.

Senior officials in the administrative apparatus (the so-called *nomenklatura*) implement executive state and Party power in the political and economic arenas, acting as a power group on behalf of the owners of socialist property – the people. The living conditions of this group are much better than for the rest of the population.

In addition to their wages, they enjoy many material, social and cultural privileges.

Under the previous system of social relations, these officials wielded enormous political power. Rapidly proliferating, this group dominated the whole country and became systematically separated from the mass of ordinary working people by increasingly strict social and political barriers. The command style of management of lower-level bodies, the unquestioning carrying out of orders from higher levels of authority, the resolution of most problems in a formalistic manner, minimal direct contacts with ordinary people, and the misuse of official positions for personal gain were all fairly typical behavioural characteristics.

The position of these officials is fundamentally changing under the new conditions. Many of their functions are becoming redundant now that the administrative and bureaucratic management of production is being abolished, the powers of enterprises are being extended, and workplace democracy is being developed. Both the sphere of influence and the size of the political apparatus are being reduced. Some of these officials are therefore losing their high-status and remunerative jobs and are faced with having to return to the production sector where new job skills and considerable physical and mental energy are required. This prospect is clearly not an inspiring one for those who are still too young to be thinking in terms of a pension.

Those officials still working in the apparatus are also faced with difficult problems. Under the new conditions the very content of political leadership has to be changed. Gelman has rightly commented on this, emphasizing that[11]

> the Party must learn to operate by using its ideological and spiritual authority. And this is the sort of moral authority that people can only submit to voluntarily.
>
> When it is possible to issue orders, nobody will try to convince. When it is possible to issue orders, all the complexities of life and action are unceremoniously simplified and reduced to schemes or dogmas. It was precisely the command principle of action that caused mass over-simplification ... This is one of the reasons for opposition to democratization – many Party workers are just not capable of coping with complex tasks and do not have the necessary qualities. But everyone wants to do what they can do. And if they cannot do something, then they say that it is not necessary to do it, that it is harmful and dangerous to the principles of socialism.

It has to be added that these officials still staunchly uphold the ideology of stagnation. Many of them believe that only command methods of management are effective, dream of 'the firm hand' and 'the old order', do not understand the possibility of combining plan with market, and await the return of the good old days.

Unfortunately, the conservatives still make up the majority of the senior administrative apparatus. Their left wing, albeit unwillingly, are nevertheless prepared to go along with democratization, but the right wing are openly reactionary. They do not wish to give way on even trivial points and ignore sharply critical articles written about them in the national press. In this connection, it is worth mentioning that people employed in the apparatus who oppose restructuring are not making a bad job of adapting to the conditions of openness. They have realized that, even when clear and convincing proof of their unsavoury activity appears in the press, this is not after all a catastrophe or the end of their career because questions discussed in the press are finally resolved by other mechanisms – in top-level offices and without the use of openness.

The fact that openness is not sufficiently effective and is excluded from certain levels in the administrative apparatus is one of the main reasons for the difficult progress of restructuring as a whole, and its almost complete absence from a number of republics, regions and government departments. The process of destroying the old and developing new relations is being obstructed by conservative and reactionary political leaders. The quasi-supporters of restructuring working in posts controlled by the Party apparatus represent a not inconsiderable danger. Although they give the appearance of being active and take a leading part in formulating guidelines and instructions, in practice they are negating the efforts of genuine supporters of restructuring.

The role played by these senior officials is determined by the fact that, although they have a conservative outlook, they wield great political and economic power (and will continue to do so for a long time to come). They play the title role in the social mechanism of putting a brake on democratization. The neutralization of this group is therefore one of the crucial strategic problems of social management.

All this, of course, does not mean that officials in the Party and state apparatus do not include progressively-minded and qualified specialists who not only support but creatively develop and deepen the concept of restructuring and actively contribute to putting it into practice. This is usually done, however, not in the interests of the group but against them, on the basis of higher values.

The group comprising the *political leaders of society* includes the higher echelons of Party and state authority – members and candidate members of the Central Committee of the Communist Party, deputies of the Supreme Soviet, ministers in charge of

Union ministries and departments, Soviet Army generals, prominent diplomats, Party and Soviet leaders in the republics, regions and large towns, and other people of similar rank. These are the country's highest representatives, the leaders of its political life. When assessing the composition of this group, it must be borne in mind that most of its members simultaneously hold responsible posts in several ruling bodies: thus, members and candidate members of the Party Central Committee are at the same time Supreme Soviet deputies, Party leaders in the republics and regions are also members of the Party Central Committee, and so on. As a result, they form the integral ruling nucleus of the Communist Party and the Soviet state.

The clear predominance of the centralist over the democratic principle in running our society has meant that the top political leadership has an extremely important role in determining the future direction of the country's development and in solving its current problems. This feature of our social and political structure is a result of the inadequate development of democratic institutions in Russia (not to mention most of the southern republics), the lack of any reliable system for studying public opinion so that it can be taken into account in governing the country, and the long-established predominance of the administrative-command style in the interaction between different 'storeys' of the administration. Throughout the whole of its history Soviet society has been characterized by its great concentration of political power. This was particularly strong in the Stalinist period. In the years of restructuring the political system has been somewhat liberalized and has begun to address people and their problems. There have not so far, however, been any fundamental changes in the distribution of political power between various social structures or between their vertical links. This explains the intense interest shown, both at home and abroad, in the personalities of the Soviet political leadership.

This group works out the strategy of economic and social development, determines its long-term objectives, selects effective ways of achieving them, and formulates an international policy that strengthens the Soviet Union's position. The formation (appointment, promotion or demotion, dismissal) of senior officials in the apparatus of political government is another important prerogative.

This group occupies an extremely high material and social position, which is in keeping with the maximal level of responsibility and complexity of its work. The main feature of its position, however, is the political power it wields over large areas of social life and the control it exercises over the fate of millions of people. Such a position combines extraordinarily wide (almost unlimited) powers with a high degree of moral and political responsibility. It is not everyone who can manage to fulfil such functions and, as we have seen, not everyone does.

The interests of members of this group are predominantly political and can be divided into social and personal components. The principal social interest of these political leaders is to lead society out of its inertia and stagnation, increase the pace of social and economic development, build up the country's strength and provide a reliable defence capacity. This is understandable. Firstly, to govern a country that is in the process of dynamic development and has a highly developed economy carries greater prestige and is easier than governing one that is technologically and socially backward. Secondly, however firmly established power may be, its stability depends to a significant extent on the mood of the people, which is affected by living standards and conditions and by how quickly they are improving. As a result, the socially-orientated interests of the political leaders basically coincide with the interests of society.

The personal interests of the members of this group are chiefly evidenced in their efforts to maintain and strengthen their official position and power. It would be naive to think that the struggle for power, which permeates all human history, loses its social roots and comes to an end under socialism. Information that is now being widely publicized about the power struggles during the 1920s and 1930s and in the years that followed demonstrates that such an opinion is quite wrong. However, leaders can maintain and strengthen their position in two ways: either by highly efficient work and the successful resolution of complex political problems or by the creation of fairly powerful groupings whose members support one another through social and family connections. Those who use the first way need broad political, economic and social understanding, great civic courage, unshakeable willpower and a very deep conviction of the historical inevitability of restructuring. The people recognize that Mikhail Gorbachev, his closest aides, and some other political leaders have these qualities.

Within the ranks of the group under consideration, however, there are still quite a number of people who were formed in the period of social stagnation and who became used to issuing administrative commands and expressing their superiority over their subordinates in a very crude way, and were constantly aware of their absolute power and their freedom to act with impunity. These people do not support new ways of doing things and most of them do not measure up to the new demand for political leaders with high levels of qualifications and personal and social qualities. Many of them have committed acts in the past that the people cannot forgive or forget. Having lost their former activism and neither desirous nor capable of understanding the spirit of the times, this section of the political leadership preach conservative values. While formally supporting restructuring, in practice they continue to employ the old methods of leadership and are constantly throwing a spanner in the works when attempts are made to democratize society. For the moment, therefore, there are quite a few 'conservation areas' which remain untouched by the current reforms. A fairly intensive process of replacement within the leadership has improved the situation, but it is happening very gradually.

So far I have been considering groups that are differentiated by their place in the social organization of labour and their relation to the means of production. These groups are interconnected by relations of specialization and co-operation, leadership and implementation. The world of organized crime (the mafia), which is small in number but extremely influential and dangerous, has quite a different character. It combines the dishonest section of people working in the distributive and personal service sectors, operators in the shadow economy, and the corrupt section of the ruling apparatus, including the judicial and police authorities. We are not talking here about pilferers, small-time speculators and bribe-takers but about powerful cliques of criminals who established a regime of lawlessness on 'protected' territories and maintained it for many years. Some members of this group have been exposed, taken to court and sentenced. Others are in hiding, but they cannot let themselves wait passively for something to happen, since for them restructuring means not merely a loss of status and power but a loss of their liberty. Restructuring has no more implacable and utterly unscrupulous enemies than these. We are not dealing here merely with conservatives but with out-and-out reactionaries who have no trace of socialist or even remotely social values. Given the chance, they would put our society on the road not only to capitalism, but to bureaucratic feudalism.

I wish to make the reservation here that the account I have given of our society's social structure and the interacting elements that determine the progress of restructuring is not validated by representative sociological research but is more in the nature of a hypothesis. It is based on material drawn from the Soviet press and specialist publications, letters sent to me by readers in response to articles that I have written, ideas gained from various discussions and conversations with people belonging to different social groups and, finally, the result of incomplete and unco-ordinated pieces of sociological research conducted at different times and in different regions. More systematic and methodologically reliable research into the social structure of Soviet society is a thing of the future.

A STRATEGY FOR THE SOCIAL MANAGEMENT OF RESTRUCTURING

So far I have looked at people's attitudes to restructuring as a function of their position in society and their membership of a particular social group. Actually, however, it depends on other factors as well.

Thus, for example, a person's educational level and qualifications, knowledge of current events, working and political career, intellectual outlook, and awareness of individual, group and social interests, are all of great significance. As a general rule, the more politically and socially developed a person is, the more positive and effective is his or her attitude to restructuring. The advanced section of the population attaches most importance to its fundamental direction and historical necessity, while the more inert section usually refers only to its own narrow experience of contact with restructuring, which is often not typical.

Generational differences related to personal formation at different historical periods exert a considerable influence on attitudes to restructuring. At first glance it would appear that the younger generation should include more supporters of radical social change and fewer conservative-minded people. However, this is not borne out by reality. According to my observations, two age groups are now notable for their social activism: people not older than 35–38 years and not younger than 55–60. These groups managed to take a real 'breath of freedom' while they were still young (up to 32 years of age) – the first group after 1983, and the second after 1956. The intervening generations who were adolescents and young adults during the years of social stagnation were in many ways lost to society. They are marked by social pessimism, have little faith in socialist values, take a sceptical view of the possibility of positive change in economic relations, and adopt a passive attitude in social matters.

Subjective attitudes to restructuring also depend on the creative expression of personality. Usually creative people are very energetic, hold radical political convictions, and long to bring about revolutionary change. The opposite personality type is more inert and passive.

Just as important is a person's personal experience of participation in economic and other reforms, the extent of their involvement in the previous system of social relations, the level and maturity of their social ties, and their level of satisfaction with the position they have achieved. Finally, individual attitudes to restructuring depend to a great extent on such human qualities as honesty, decency, social conscience, sense of compassion, etc.

For these reasons one can find people of every class, social stratum and group who not only have different but sometimes opposite attitudes. Workers standing side by side at benches, scientists working on the same problem, and officials employed by the same department, are often on 'opposite sides of the barricade' as far as their convictions are concerned. Thus, differences in attitudes to restructuring have a dual character: social groups that make up the structure of society are distinguished by attitudes that are very typical of each particular group, but in each of these groups one can find people with other attitudes, although in varying ratios. The following types of attitude of interest to us can be listed as follows:

i) The *ideologists and initiators of restructuring*. This group consists of people who are deeply convinced of the need for a radical, revolutionary transformation of social relations inherited from the past. They understand that there is no acceptable alternative and that deviation from the political line currently laid down or any delay in restructuring (not to mention its 'silent curbing') threatens the fate of socialism in the Soviet Union. They understand that to democratize economic and political relations completely, to free society of phenomena alien to socialism, to re-assess the country's history and its present position honestly and openly, is the only possible way to stop the trend towards greater scientific, technological and social backwardness and maintain our country's leading position in the modern international community.

The members of this group are known for matching word with deed: they not only speak in favour of restructuring, they fight for it in practice without sparing themselves. They are the flagships of restructuring who are willing to tackle highly complex problems, overcome major difficulties, and show others the way forward. They are not a large group numerically but their historical role is tremendous.

ii) *Supporters*. This larger group consists of people who share the concept of restructuring put forward by the initiators, who frequently develop it in a creative manner and try hard to put it into practice. They are the most progressive, energetic and creative section of Soviet society, prepared to contribute to the full extent of their ability and capacity to help in their country's renewal and prosperity while at the same time raising their own standard of living and improving their way of life. They are people of democratic and humanist convictions who are committed to the ideas of socialist justice. When they encounter the braking mechanism they usually battle against it but, because their actions lack co-ordination, they do not always win. Many of them are experiencing great difficulties and disappointments but as a rule their convictions remain unchanged.

iii) *Social allies.* I would put into this group people who are not convinced supporters of the integral concept of restructuring (sometimes because they are not familiar with it and in other cases because they have doubts about, or do not agree with, one or other of its tenets) but who nevertheless have a personal interest in certain aspects of the reforms taking place. These could be, for example, the development of co-operative and individual businesses, the establishment of joint ventures between Soviet and foreign companies, greater enterprise autonomy and more workforce powers, more open management, faster scientific and technological progress, etc. This group's attitude to restructuring is less stable and reliable than that of the first two groups because it depends to a far greater extent on the difficulties they encounter in their attempts to pursue their interests. If they are met with formalism, bureaucracy, deception, and corruption and if they are unable to develop and prove their own point of view, some of these potential allies become disillusioned and retire from the field.

iv) *Quasi-supporters.* This group consists of people who have neither principles nor strongly-held political beliefs. They are prepared to serve any master, affirm any 'truths' and organize the people to tackle any task so long as it is 'in keeping with the times', finds favour with the bosses and leads to their own promotion. Judging by their pronouncements, these people should be among the fervent supporters of restructuring. But if they noticed that the political atmosphere was changing, they would immediately fall silent and completely change their views. In favourable circumstances, the members of this group can be useful. However, their lack of principle combined with their opportunism and careerism does contain a large element of danger. Unfortunately, the presence of representatives of this group in the leadership is a very real and unwelcome fact.

v) *Observers.* This group comprises people who support the concept of restructuring in principle but have a very negative experience of previous attempts at social reform. People like this believe that restructuring is necessary but that society has neither adequate forces nor organizational resources to combat a bureaucracy that has exceptional power and no intention of surrendering it. However much the initiators, supporters and allies of restructuring may try, therefore, it will be halted by opposing forces and put into reverse. In such an event people who firmly and unreservedly commit themselves to restructuring will most likely suffer politically and at the very least lose their jobs. With this in mind, members of this group prefer to watch from the sidelines, not without sympathy for the supporters of restructuring but without any particular faith in their ultimate victory. This group's position is not very stable and depends to a significant extent on how restructuring actually develops. Every success lessens this group's scepticism, and every failure increases it. The group is an important social reserve for restructuring.

vi) '*Neutrals*'. These are the socially inert section of the population who have no particular attitude to what is happening in the country. Wrapped up in their own personal or strictly family affairs, without much education or experience of social issues, they are distinguished by their social passivity. This group does not take an interest in the overall direction of restructuring, is not aware of its historical significance, and often brushes aside information about current events in the mass media. It contains many conservative-minded individuals who stick to the old lifestyles just because they are used to them and never allow any new ideas to enter their heads. Because of its social passivity, this group's behaviour does not do restructuring any harm but it does not do it any good either and on the whole it helps to put a brake on social development.

vii) *Conservatives*. These are mostly people whose personalities were formed in the period when democracy was suppressed and the administrative-command style of management flourished. Their psyche bears the indelible imprint of stagnation. Most of them are still convinced of the omnipotence of 'His Majesty the Plan', the unsocialist nature of market relations, and that the Second World War was mainly won by Stalin's genius, etc. Forced to adapt themselves to the new conditions, these people are prepared verbally to accept the necessity for certain changes and often use the vocabulary of restructuring. Within their own narrow circle, however, they regard the concept of restructuring as anti-socialist. In practice, this group makes every effort to obstruct social transformation, to prevent restructuring from gathering the necessary momentum and to prevent the situation arising when restructuring will be irreversible. The conservatives are the prime movers in the braking mechanism and because they form part of the administration represent a considerable threat to restructuring.

viii) *Reactionaries* have more cogent reasons for not accepting the ideas of restructuring than conservatives. Conservatives oppose these ideas with the dogmatic notions of Stalin's 'barrack-room socialism', while the reactionaries oppose any socialist values on principle. Most of them live purely for the sake of grabbing as much as they can and do their best to get their hands on as much as they can of the public's money without regard for any legal or moral considerations. Another section, corrupted by their unlimited power over many thousands of people, are doing their best to regain or retain this power, which has provided them with a special 'elitist' lifestyle and legal impunity. The contradiction between this group and societal interests has become antagonistic. At the historical level the answer to the question 'who will win out?' is not in doubt, but at the present time the struggle between reactionaries who are vested with power and the supporters of restructuring is ruthless.

One also comes across other attitudes to restructuring. For example, there is a section of young people who cannot tell the difference between bogus and real values, who blindly follow pseudo-leaders and 'innovators' in the belief that they are fighting for restructuring while they are in fact harming it. One example of this is the *Pamyat* ('Memory') association, which has become a stronghold of reaction, obscurantism and anti-Semitism. The principal types of attitude, however, are those already described.

What, then, is the relationship between social groups which are distinguished, on the one hand, by their objective position in society and, on the other, by the nature of their personal views and convictions? To answer this question we shall construct a table in which the rows represent social strata and groups and the columns represent types of attitude to restructuring. If we could place the adult population in its different constituent elements, the overwhelming majority of cells would certainly be filled in. However, one cell would contain millions of people and others only tens. I shall attempt to describe what in my estimation is the probable distribution of representatives from each social stratum according to type of attitude to restructuring, and will pick out those elements in the table that are most significant. The social strata and groups are ranked in descending order of support for restructuring. Types of attitude to restructuring are also ranked according to less positive and more negative activism.

To simplify the table the following changes have been made to the list of social groups and strata presented in the previous section of this chapter. Firstly, the advanced stratum of industrial workers have been combined with the similar stratum of collective farmers because their attitude is the same; secondly, for the same reason the mass of ordinary workers has been combined with collective farmers; and, thirdly, the groups comprising political leaders and top managers have been combined. The hatched cells indicate that the positions are typical, while the blank cells show that they are comparatively rare.

The table can be read by row or by column. In the first case, we see the familiar pattern of different attitudes to restructuring shown by each social group. If we examine the columns, however, we can see which social groups are major sources of recruitment of people who take various positions on restructuring. We shall look more closely at this second aspect.

Table: Typical positions of members of social strata and groups in relation to restructuring

Social strata and groups	Initiators	Supporters	Allies	Quasi-supporters	Observers	Neutrals	Conservatives	Reactionaries
1	2	3	4	5	6	7	8	9
Advanced workers and collective farmers	▨	▨	▨	▨				
Political leaders and senior management	▨	▨	▨		▨		▨	
Social and humanitarian intelligentsia	▨	▨		▨	▨		▨	▨
Co-operators, lease-holders and small entrepreneurs		▨	▨	▨				
Ordinary workers and collective farmers			▨	▨	▨	▨	▨	
Scientific and techno-logical intelligentsia		▨	▨	▨	▨			
Party-nominated officials in the administration		▨			▨		▨	▨
Top officials in distri-butive and service sectors					▨		▨	▨
Workers with unjustified privileges					▨		▨	▨
Participants in organized crime (mafioso groups)								▨

As can be seen from the table, the initiators of restructuring are progressive political leaders and top managers, the radically-inclined section of the social and humanitarian intelligentsia, and advanced workers and peasants.

Supporters are the largest group. They are found in every social stratum except the most conservative, which indicates the broad social base of the reform. Workers, peasants, co-operators and small entrepreneurs are allies of restructuring. Quasi-supporters are found in all groups of the intelligentsia carrying out administrative functions. Political camouflage is of no use to workers, peasants and craftsmen.

The position of interested observer is typical of most groups. Least represented are the groups whose activity demands a fairly definite position in relation to restructuring. They are political leaders and top managers, officials nominated by the Party apparatus, advanced workers and collective farmers, and small entrepreneurs. A neutral attitude is characteristic of the most inert and passive section of manual workers.

Like supporters of restructuring, conservatives appear in almost all groups. They are found least often in the ranks of advanced workers and collective farmers and of small entrepreneurs who would not have committed themselves to restructuring if they had conservative views. As regards the reactionaries, they are concentrated in a limited number of groups which must be watched particularly carefully in the course of managing restructuring. These are a) the corrupt section of workers in the Party and Soviet apparatus, b) officials in the distributive and service sectors, c) the section of the working class that has been bought over by the first two groups, and d) participants in organized crime who consolidate the preceding groups.

As can be seen, the picture is fairly complex. Society is split up into groups that differ substantially (sometimes diametrically) in their attitude to restructuring. The struggle between social forces that stand for or against changes in social relations has a daily airing in the press, giving rise to strong feelings and lively discussions. Society is being increasingly drawn into restructuring, the groups of 'neutrals' and 'observers' are gradually dwindling, and the conflict between convinced supporters and consistent opponents is becoming more and more open.

On the other hand, although attitudes are determined by membership of a particular stratum and group, they are not, as we have seen, completely rigid. In this connection, the general disposition of social forces around restructuring tends to fluctuate. Moreover, what is called for is a strategy of management not by the usual, if complex, process of evolution but through a revolution which radically changes the basic social and political structures and leads to a complete redistribution of power, rights, duties and freedoms between classes, strata and groups.

With regard to the question as to which of the possible paths towards further social development will be the battle-ground, I am once again completely in agreement with Gelman, who points out the three main directions that in theory our society could take: the revolutionary-democratic, the liberal-conservative and the openly reactionary ('back to Stalin'). After noting that the last variant is only remotely possible because people have learned a lot, have changed as a result, and will not therefore allow it to happen, he pays particular attention to the dangers present on the liberal-conservative path with which political activists of the old type want to replace the revolutionary democratization of society. In describing the differences between these three development paths, Gelman writes[12]:

> Democratization envisages the redistribution of power, rights, and freedoms, and the creation of a whole number of independent management and information structures. Liberalization, however, means retention of all the basic features of the administrative system in a milder variant. Liberalization represents the half-clenched fist. It is the same hand, however, and at a moment's notice can be made into a fist again. Outwardly, liberalization can at times look like democratization, but it is in fact an inadmissible substitute.

In fact the real historical alternative is not the '*to be or not to be*' of restructuring, economic reform and the democratization of society. Forces that are completely against it are not very great. The real alternative is *what is to be* the nature of restructuring: revolutionary (radical) or evolutionary (liberal-conservative). The future of the people lies in the balance, depending on which of the two is in fact implemented. If it is the first, then the world, after having witnessed the Japanese, Chinese and other 'miracles', will be given the chance of seeing the 'Soviet miracle' of a sharp rise in growth rates and the rapid transformation of a technologically and socially backward country into a great modern and dynamic power. If the second way is chosen, however, then the gap between the Soviet Union and the advanced capitalist countries which has grown wider over the preceding period can become irreversible and this once great country will lose its position, shut itself off behind a new 'iron curtain', begin to repress the democratic opposition and turn into an isolated outpost. This alternative is too serious to allow us to wait fatalistically to see which forces will gain the ascendancy. What is needed is a well-thought-out strategy capable of steering the restructuring process on to a historically progressive course.

This strategy must keep inter-group conflict to a minimum and lower social tensions so that the objectives that have been set are achieved at the lowest possible social cost. This means that as few people as possible should suffer from restructuring and that their losses should be as light as possible. If this is done, restructuring will help consolidate society rather than fragment it and will regenerate social values rather than lead to their degeneration. But it is a matter of judgement. With the interests of the democratic and the reactionary sections of society in direct opposition, adhering too rigidly to the policy of easing conflicts could weaken the ideas of restructuring. It is in this context that I believe it is necessary to examine all the phenomena that reflect the slow progress of restructuring and the dissatisfaction felt by working people with the results achieved so far. A policy entirely orientated towards social compromise and a fear of doing anything against the interests of groups who are impeding restructuring can become a very serious brake on the far-reaching development of this process.

All this illustrates the complexity of working out an effective strategy for the management of restructuring. Above all, it raises the question as to which groups it should target: those which are defined by their social position in society or by their subjective attitude to restructuring? The position, problems and difficulties facing groups of the first type are more or less clear and it is therefore easier to work out measures that can improve their attitude to restructuring. From the point of view of their subjective attitudes, however, these groups are heterogeneous. The second type of groups are easier to target but they are difficult to identify: even a comprehensive sociological opinion poll of the adult population could not resolve this problem since there is not a single conservative or reactionary who would admit to being one. Where measures directed at social groups fail, it could be useful to formulate measures addressed to groups with different ideological positions in relation to restructuring.

In the rest of this chapter I shall confine myself to a brief description of possible measures directed at social groups occupying various positions in society. The aims of this strategy are to strengthen and activate the groups that make up the social base of restructuring, to limit the role and functions of groups of the opposite persuasion, and to help bring about a better ratio between 'democrats' and 'conservatives' among those who determine the fate of restructuring. To this end, firstly, the tasks to be undertaken with respect to each group must be defined and, secondly, the resources which can be used must be specified. I shall start with the groups and strata that are a potential source of support for a radical variant of reform, but which are in need of further reinforcement and strengthening.

i) *Political leaders*. As has already been mentioned, this group is heterogeneous. Alongside ideologists and initiators of restructuring, it contains conservatives and even reactionaries. One of the tasks to be done, therefore, is to renew the personnel which would give it a younger profile, radicalize its political and economic thinking and raise its professional qualifications and social and moral qualities. This can be achieved, firstly, by systematically improving the level of knowledge about the social sciences (history, economics, law, sociology) in the upper echelons of power; secondly, by training in advance a pool of future political leaders (taken mainly from the production and service sectors rather than the administration) and, thirdly, by democratizing the policy of selecting personnel, in particular, the method of promoting political leaders, taking more account of public opinion, holding competitions between candidates based on an examination of their programmes, and publishing candidates' political biographies showing not only the different jobs they have held but also their policies and actions at turning-points in history. Such measures as limiting the stay in office of leading politicians to not more than two terms and openness regarding the work done by higher management bodies will also contribute to improving the quality of the leadership. Putting these measures into practice can turn this group into a genuine alliance of like-minded democrats under whose leadership restructuring will proceed at a much faster pace.

ii) *Senior management*. This group plays one of the central roles in the restructuring of economic relations. They can be fairly sharply divided into those who 'want to and can' and those who 'cannot and therefore do not want to'. Substantial changes have to be made in management personnel. In the last analysis only those who can prove their ability to manage production efficiently, understand new economic ideas, and correctly interpret and introduce new concepts and who can take calculated risks and win should be allowed to keep their jobs. Those managers whose most valuable possession is their armchair and whose principal skill is pandering to the boss must be got rid of, and the quicker the better. If economic accounting and self-financing are introduced in earnest and not just as a formality, managers will automatically be divided into the two 'factions' mentioned above. The election of managers by the workforce can contribute towards the renewal of management personnel but again only if this is done properly and not just on a formal basis (as often happens). At the moment, however, in addition to economic and democratic mechanisms for improving management personnel, an appropriate policy for the selection of senior personnel in ministerial departments and local authorities must be developed. Unfortunately, they are themselves contaminated with bureaucratic attitudes and therefore cannot effectively cope with this complex task.

The active participation of managers in restructuring can also be encouraged by measures such as a) extending the economic powers of enterprises and introducing full economic accounting, b) providing legal and political guarantees to protect managers who have decided upon implementing the ideas underlying restructuring despite instructions restricting their activity, c) modernizing the system for raising qualifications in special faculties at universities and colleges and in the Academy for the National Economy, and d) extending direct international contacts with the managements of foreign companies and participation in mixed enterprises.

iii) *The working class* has not been the principal initiator of restructuring. It does, however, play a decisive role in determining the road to be taken. In Chapter Three I tried to show that restructuring is being carried out in the interests of the people as a whole and, above all, the working class and the peasantry. But not everyone realizes this. There are in the working class, alongside active supporters of restructuring, a not inconsiderable number of passive and indifferent people who are in no hurry to define their social position. The success of restructuring, particularly in reaching the stage of being politically irreversible, depends to a decisive extent on working class activity. That section of workers who at the moment have no interest at all in restructuring must be aroused from their social apathy so that they at least begin to take an interest in what is going on around them and form their own opinions about key questions. Workers who watch current changes with interest but some mistrust can and must be turned into active supporters or at least allies of restructuring.

There is no doubt that openness plays an important part in solving these problems, since it activates the social and political consciousness of all social groups without exception. But openness on its own is not enough. Constant press accounts of disgraceful practices and lawless actions bring home to workers the need to assist restructuring, not just by producing more but by taking a direct part in the transformation of social relations. Effective forms of organization must be found into which these efforts can be channelled. Some have emerged spontaneously: these are informal social initiatives ranging from the *Perestroika* clubs in Moscow and Leningrad to the all-Union 'Memorial' movement for erecting a monument to the victims of Stalinism. The appearance of such initiatives is a sign that 'the temperature in the boiler is rising' but the actual 'head of steam' that has been raised is not yet very effective. The Popular Fronts in Support of Restructuring, which are financed out of people's own money and not from state funds, have been significantly more effective. The local branches of these Fronts themselves decide where to apply their efforts and yet have a formal social and political status. In the future they should be empowered to oversee the implementation by local authorities and ministerial departments of all-Union decisions on restructuring.

iv) *Collective farmers.* Soviet power worked hard to turn peasants into hired workers rather than owners of land. It is now necessary to retrieve what is not entirely lost, i.e. to attempt to return to the collective farmers such particular peasant qualities as knowledge and understanding of the land and farm animals, love of farm work, attachment to their own home territory, and the ability to run a farm diligently and make a profit. The first step in this direction could be the 'de-state-farm-ization' of the collective farms, which 25–30 years ago were transformed by a stroke of the bureaucratic pen from collective to state farms in order to make them simpler to control. In Latvia and the other Baltic republics experience has been gained in converting the 'higher' form of agricultural enterprise back into the 'lower' form, i.e. the re-organization of state farms into collective farms. This has been giving good economic and social results. This measure will reduce the size of the working class, and the peasantry will increase, which was commonly considered to be a retrogressive step. In fact, however, this structural change will, on the one hand, bring about the formal reunification of two extremely close social groups – the collective farmers and the state farm workers – and, on the other, restore the traditionally industrial character of the working class. But that is not the point. The main thing is that agriculture should be given an organizational and economic form most appropriate to the particular character of this sector. Under socialism it is the co-operative form that does this.

Collective farmers must also be given the authority, if this is decided at a general meeting, to divide up their farm into smaller, economically rational units. The overwhelming majority of giant farms are inefficient, as has been demonstrated the world over. A new way of organizing collective farms into associations of primary agricultural co-operatives should also be tried out experimentally.[13] In this case small co-operatives become autonomous economic units, while the administration of the collective farm is formed and financed 'from below', making it leaner and more efficient. Finally, leasing and family contract work in social production must also be developed and collective farmers' individual landholdings must be expanded. Carrying out these measures will affect the vast majority of collective farmers and indeed the entire rural population, will spark off new energy and transform the majority of these groups into supporters and allies of restructuring.

v). I shall look briefly at the *intelligentsia*. Its most progressive section is a driving force for restructuring. The more restructuring gathers momentum, the fewer indifferent members of the intelligentsia there will be and the more involved and active they will become. I would mention just two serious problems associated with this group. The first is the extraordinarily low level of professional training attained to date by a significant number of engineers, agronomists, doctors and teachers. This indicates that the intelligentsia, in the full sense of the word, is very much smaller than the number of people who have degrees. It is therefore right that the excessive number of specialists working in the economy should be reduced and the less qualified should be found jobs where there is a high level of technology. This measure will raise both the salaries and the status of those specialists retaining their jobs.

The second consideration concerns social scientists and teachers. It is no secret that the social sciences in this country have not stood up well to the test of restructuring. The traditional dogmas have been destroyed, and it takes time to construct a new theory. It is easier for researchers because they can immediately apply themselves to a new search for truth. For teachers, however, it is more difficult for they have to answer students' questions today, and most of them do not know what to say. It is my opinion that a large number of social science teachers are not able to cope with this critical situation, are incapable of changing their modes of thought, and will have to be pensioned off. The others will seek and find answers to the disturbing questions on their own. But for society as a whole this is not a solution. In a period when social relations are being radically transformed, it needs as never before a social science theory that is methodologically sound. For this reason goal-orientated work is being developed on a wide scale, ideally on a competitive basis, i.e. by forming teams of scientists working in parallel on the same problems. At the same time an increasing number of social-science students and post-graduates are studying abroad. For example, in 1989 20 young sociologists will be setting out on a two-year period of study at various universities in the USA, and another 20 will be attending a three-month course at Manchester University in the UK. This practice is becoming more common.

This is how things stand with groups that have a particular interest in the radical variant of implementing restructuring. But what approach should be adopted to the strata that are slowing down the progress of restructuring? Obviously, groups in organised crime must be exposed, tried and sentenced with all the severity of the law. There is no question of any particular social strategy with regard to these people. It is another matter when it comes to groups whose activity, although not criminal, does nevertheless slow down the progress of restructuring. I have already explained which groups these are.

i). *Officials nominated by the Party apparatus working in the political administration* are the main vehicles of administrative and bureaucratic methods of leadership and outdated economic and political thinking. Most of them seem simply unable to accept, let alone implement, the measures put forward by our political leaders. The following basic tasks can be laid down: a) severely reducing their number (to at least a half or a third), b) appointing younger people and replacing staff with people from outside the apparatus, and c) putting an end to the social and even physical gap that has been created over the years between members of this group and the vast majority of ordinary people (accommodation in special housing and districts, the use of special shops, restaurants, personal service establishments, clinics, treatment at special sanatoria and hospitals, special airport and railway waiting rooms for 'deputies', and so on and so forth). As I see it, senior officials doing exceptionally important work with no set working day have a certain moral right to obtain consumer goods without queuing for them. It is important, however, that the privileges accorded to such people are open and above-board and are not hidden from the public, and that the choice and price of goods supplied to them are not better than those obtainable from state shops. Only then will this specific stratum really understand the needs and problems of the general public and be able to identify with them. Under these circumstances also, the manager's armchair will lose half its attraction, and people suitable for the job will come to work in the machinery of government.

I would also identify the following important measures aimed at raising the social quality of this group: firstly, a substantial limitation of the powers wielded by the apparatus, secondly, the democratization of procedures for training, checking the credentials, and promoting senior officials and, thirdly, the organization of effective ways of raising their qualifications, the elimination of provincialism in political views, and the development of social and economic thinking open to new facts, ideas and concepts.

ii). *Workers in the distributive and service sectors.* I have already discussed the section of this group that is associated with large-scale swindles and theft. In this section I am examining a group comprising many millions of workers which is in a very specific position. In receipt of a patently depressed wage, which seems to have been deliberately calculated on the assumption that it would be supplemented by other incomes, this group has the opportunity and is compelled to engage in improper activities – overcharging or underweighing, under-the-counter dealing, the sale of scarce goods to 'their own' customers at inflated prices, etc. It is commonly thought that it is not possible to earn an honest living in trade: you are forced to cheat whether you want to or not. As a result, the whole area of trade, public catering and personal and domestic services is like a cancerous growth corrupting adjacent parts of the social organism. In most other socialist countries, however, and even more so in capitalist countries, trade is just as decent and respected an occupation as working at the factory bench or in the field.

The existing system has led to the corruption of a large section of people employed in this sector. They are used to supplementing their incomes and are reluctant to give it up. Without their help, however, and their honest efforts to contribute to the success of restructuring, its impact will not be felt by its main customer – the public. Shops are standing empty, and will continue to do so, even when there are goods in stock.

How can we make commerce decent and learn to trade 'as they do in Europe' – the way Lenin wished? The principal way to do this, of course, is by increasing production of the goods that people need and by overcoming shortages. But that takes time. Meanwhile, I believe that the pluralism of trading organizations should be increased so that they can compete with one another for the customer's roubles. There is a future for enterprises selling their goods in their own shops; there is a future for local consumer associations fostering co-operative trade; there is a future for leasing out small shops, cafés and restaurants. The development of these forms of trading and services will, firstly, create competition between sellers which is a habit we have lost and, secondly and no less importantly, will increase the number of supporters of restructuring in this conservative group.

These are some preliminary ideas about a social strategy for managing restructuring. Many thoughts, appraisals, conclusions, proposals and discussions are currently being put forward. My hope is that in the future special economic and sociological research projects will show which of them are correct, which need amendment and which are simply mistaken.

Political Conditions for Success

5

DEMOCRATIZATION AND OPENNESS

Restructuring has reached a critical stage. It can go one of two ways. Either it will assume a revolutionary character with the active support of the people and sweep away all obstacles on the road to the renewal of society or, if people become disillusioned with results, its supporters' strength will begin to weaken, social resources will become exhausted, and the opponents of restructuring will gleefully announce its failure and a return to the previous system. In my opinion it is hardly likely that the progressive section of society, stirred and inspired by restructuring, will want, or be able, to submit to defeat. It is more likely that in one form or another the struggle will go on. As a result, a very much sharper confrontation between social forces will ensue whose final outcome is unpredictable, while the social cost would be enormous. This is one of the reasons why the present stage of restructuring is holding world attention. Its progress is not easy: victories won by progressive forces are sometimes followed by counter-attacks from the conservatives, the high tides of democratization and openness by ebb tides.

Somewhat simplifying the alignment of social forces described in the previous chapter, the upper echelons of authority may be said to be directing and initiating restructuring, the bureaucratic stratum of officials nominated by the Party apparatus has a significant braking effect, the advanced strata of the intelligentsia and the workers are in sympathy with restructuring and are doing all they can to consolidate its successes, while most ordinary working people are slowly rousing themselves from their social lethargy and are in effect only now beginning to take up their own position as citizens. As a whole, workers' and peasants' understanding of the need for social change is growing. Increasing numbers realize that there is no way back and that the growing difficulties can only be overcome by advancing steadily and sticking firmly to the policy that has been decided. Mass political activity, however, has not yet reached the stage where restructuring is irreversible. For this, far greater personal identification with the new idea is required and people need to be included to a much greater extent in the practicalities of transforming social institutions and establishing new forms of social activity. History shows that freedom, democracy, social justice and economic prosperity are not handed to people on a plate, but fought for by their own efforts. The revolutionary restructuring of Soviet society cannot be carried out 'from above'. It can and must be carried out by people themselves, with a clear understanding of their own interests and ready to fight for them.

Gorbachev understands this better than most. Critically interpreting the experience of his predecessors, he attributes the failure of the reforms of 1950–60 primarily to the fact that they were undertaken 'from above' without any wider involvement of working people. Vital decisions, materially affecting people's circumstances and fates, were taken *in camera*, without any consultation whatsoever with the people concerned. In addition, putting these decisions into practice was entrusted not to those with an interest in progressive changes but to the bureaucratic apparatus who had directly opposite interests. Not surprisingly, most of the original intentions of the reformers remained on paper. With this in mind, Gorbachev attaches great importance to the democratization of society as the most reliable way of involving people and making them more active. He maintains that 'democratization of society is the very soul of restructuring and its progress will determine the success of restructuring itself . . . and the future of socialism as a whole'.[1]

The situation is complex because for decades any form of spontaneous political or social action was stopped or even punished – sometimes quite severely. In time this resulted in complete alienation not only from political organizations but from politics generally. Most people did not want to have anything to do with it. Typically, for example, if someone said in the course of a friendly conversation 'It's a political matter', the others would interpret these words as a direct signal that the subject was closed. To discuss political questions was dangerous but to undertake independent political action was dangerous 'to the nth degree'. As a result, people's interests, needs and values necessarily became very parochial, private and trivial.

Things have now changed but previous attitudes to politics, particularly to innovations originating from the authorities, will make themselves felt for a long time to come. This should give no cause for surprise. Rain-soaked wood does not light at the first match, but demands both skill and patience from the person lighting the bonfire. The same can be said about activating people; the democratization of society is the 'oxygen' that will enable it to catch alight very quickly. As one of the independent objectives of restructuring, democratization is at the same time the key to success in all other areas. Only the steady democratization of social relationships will link the interests of the upper echelons of authority to those of ordinary people with a voltaic arc of such power that nobody will be able to extinguish it.

It is unfortunate that neither Russian pre-revolutionary nor Soviet politics developed strong traditions of genuinely democratic relations. People have paid the price for centuries of serfdom and autocratic tyranny and decades of lawlessness under Stalin and Brezhnev. They either did not have the chance to acquire or have lost the culture of political and national tolerance, social dialogues conducted with mutual respect, collective attempts to find a compromise, and sensible agreements reached by striking a balance between conflicting interests. The low level of political culture has led to measures to extend democracy being perceived by certain groups as the right to fight for their interests by any methods including undemocratic ones. The publicist Boris Vasilyev characterizes this distorted idea of democracy as follows:

> The orders suddenly came that from such-and-such a date it was allowed. But it [democracy] should, above all, be perceived as certain things not being allowed. It is not allowed to break the law, violate the Constitution, dismiss a worker at the boss's whim, or raise prices without reason: it is not allowed to forbid, to hold back, not to allow. Democracy is always observance of the law, while we in our simplicity think that it is only the possibility of saying or writing whatever comes into our head.

In view of the long predominance of lawlessness and the shaky state of the legal system, Gorbachev points out with some insistence the connection between democracy and the rule of law;[2]

> Democracy is not the opposite of order. On the contrary, it is a higher level of order which is not based on unthinking obedience and the blind carrying out of orders but on wholehearted initiative and participation in society by its members.
>
> Democracy is not the opposite of discipline. On the contrary, it is conscious discipline and a certain level of organization on the part of working people based on a feeling of being the real masters of their country, on a collective approach, and a feeling of solidarity of interest and effort between all citizens.
>
> Democracy is not the opposite of responsibility, it is not permissiveness and the absence of control. On the contrary, it is self-control by society itself, based on trust, civic maturity and an understanding of social responsibility. It is the unity of rights and obligations.

All this might seem to some Western readers to be stating the obvious but people who live in the Soviet Union face a long process of learning the habits of genuine democracy. This in itself is not a terrible thing – it would be worse to remain in our previous situation. Every instance, however, of abuse or unwise use of a citizen's democratic rights resulting in a weakenening in the rule of law is interpreted by conservative forces as evidence that these measures are 'premature' and that society is 'unprepared' for democracy. The opponents of restructuring believe that the public should first be prepared for democracy within the framework of a totalitarian regime and only then granted rights and freedoms. This is nonsense, of course. Just as it is impossible to learn to swim without entering the water, so is it impossible to learn to operate under democratic conditions without practical experience of those conditions. The inevitable initial social disturbances, the over-reactions and the sharpening social conflicts resulting from an inadequate culture of democracy, all these are 'infantile disorders' which society has to go through sooner or later. And better sooner than later.

The current democratization process is complex and many-sided and very far-reaching. I would define its two most important directions as follows: firstly, the further development of openness and, secondly, the democratization of political institutions, the strengthening of legality, and the development of pluralism in social and political affairs. In this section I shall be discussing the first of these directions.

Although democratization represents only one component of restructuring, and openness only one component of democratization, the concepts 'restructuring' and 'openness' are often used together as if they meant the same thing. This is understandable, for the development of openness has been the most important achievement of restructuring. So far Soviet society has had its greatest success in that direction.

Western correspondents often ask why a generally accepted term like 'freedom of the press' is not used to define openness. Actually, however, openness is a much broader concept than freedom of the press. I would define openness as a social atmosphere and political climate where there is maximal frankness on the part of the authorities in relation to members of society. The nature of socialism assumes frank and equal dialogue between social groups having different interests but the same goal. For the dialogue to be on an equal footing, the public must be in full possession of all the facts needed for making decisions. Openness also means that the public must be honestly and fully informed about everything that is going on at home and abroad: about successes, economic failures and problems; social differences and the position of different groups; top-level inner-party struggles; the state of the natural environment in specific towns and regions; expenditure on armaments and defence costs; the size of the national debt; the activities of the KGB and the Ministry of the Interior, and a great deal more.

In countries with strong democratic traditions, public information about key aspects of living conditions and the quality of life is taken for granted if not always provided, but there is no such tradition in the Soviet Union. Although they act in the name of the people, the authorities are more accustomed to doing so without their participation rather than with it. They do not bother to discuss lines of action or results with people they are meant to be serving. The following is an extract from the resolution 'On openness' passed by the 19th Party Conference:

> Without openness there can be no restructuring, no democracy . . .
> Openness is the natural atmosphere for the existence and progress of democratic, humane socialism . . . Conference considers openness to be a developing process and emphasizes that its steady growth is an indispensable condition for expressing the essentially democratic nature of the socialist system, its treatment of people, and the involvement of individuals in all matters affecting society, the state, and the workforce. Conference considers openness to be an effective guarantee against any distortions of socialism, a guarantee that is based on popular control over the activity of all social institutions, authorities, and administrative bodies.

The Party's position on developing openness is very clear-cut. Nevertheless, every real step in this direction is hard-won.

The number of sources where people can find the information that interests them about the way the country is run have grown considerably over the past three or four years. Most important, the curtain hiding the country's historical past – the dramatic 1920s–40s, the stormy 1950s–60s and the stagnating 1970s – has been drawn aside. One by one, though at no great speed, archives are being opened up to which access has been completely barred, even to historians. The public can satisfy their thirst for knowledge about any period in Soviet history by reading appropriate newspapers and journals. Only a few years ago libraries used to allow readers access to periodicals relating to the previous three years only – a fact, astonishing in its frankness and cynicism, which shut people off from information about events that they themselves had lived through. Current newspapers and journals have become an extremely valuable source of information. Many of them regularly discuss the 'blank spots' in our history, provide interesting new assessments of historical personalities, and compare and contrast different points of view on particular moments in our past as well as our present and future. All this creates a growing demand for a better understanding of what has happened in the past and for an evaluation of the correctness of various decisions and the comparative effectiveness of alternative development paths, etc. This in turn will help ordinary citizens to mature and to become aware of their own responsibility for the country's development and make them both want and be prepared to take its future into their own hands.

The second factor in the development of openness was the publication of whole sections of social statistics that were not previously available. In the Stalinist period such statistics either did not reflect the true state of affairs or were not even compiled. They began to improve during the 'thaw' but with the onset of the 'stagnation' period the statistical yearbooks began to 'lose weight' before our very eyes. More and more sections were cut out: data were no longer published not only about such sensitive subjects as crime and suicide, but also about average life expectancy, mortality, marriage and divorce, and the birth rate. Information about the direction and volume of migration flows was treated as a state secret. Now all these 'secrets' have come to an end. For the first time for many years social statistics are available for discussion. It has become clear, however, that the sources of information that the Central Statistical Office can 'open up' are very limited indeed. Necessary data relating to most of today's issues simply do not exist. Methods of obtaining, collating and processing them have yet to be worked out, which will take quite some time.

The third factor in the development of openness is the fundamental change in the mass media. Newspapers and radio and TV broadcasts used to be full of praise for non-existent achievements, which was extremely irritating. In this connection, the following 'Radio Yerevan' joke was going round in Khrushchev's time: 'Question: How can my family get lots of food? Answer: Simple. Just plug your fridge into the radio.' This was a fairly perceptive reaction to the situation at that time.

Now, however, the press publishes a mass of material directed against the bureaucrats and mafiosi who are slowing down the progress of restructuring. Newspapers and magazines are naming names, time and place, and are demanding that central and local authorities discuss things democratically and deal with problems justly. They systematically recall issues that have already been raised, follow things up, and demand straight answers to questions that are worrying people. Television programmes that discuss major and difficult problems with people belonging to different interest groups – government departments, enterprises, jobs, age-groups – are extremely popular. The Leningrad radio programmes 'Public Opinion', 'The Fifth Wheel', '600 Minutes' are very successful, as are the TV programmes for young people – 'Points of View', 'Stairway' and 'The 11th Storey' which broadcast interesting and impartial information on traditionally taboo subjects. Long-standing restrictions on criticism of recent Party and government decisions have been lifted. Such criticism now begins at the stage when programme proposals are being discussed and continues after final decisions have been made by those in charge. This shows that a more democratic and healthy situation now exists.

'Areas not open to discussion' are gradually being abolished, i.e. areas of public life about which nothing is published and which are not talked about. A few years ago there were many such areas: the presence of Soviet troops in Afghanistan, the share of military expenditure in the budget, Jewish emigration, protest meetings about government decisions, human disasters, the personal attitudes and differences of opinion between political leaders, etc. It used to be considered impermissible to intervene in the affairs of republics and cities that came under the personal jurisdiction of Political Bureau members – Shcherbitsky (Ukraine), Rashidov (Uzbekistan), Kunayev (Kazakhstan), Aliyev (Azerbaidzhan), Grishin (Moscow), Romanov (Leningrad), and others. These restrictions have now been lifted or at least relaxed and there are fewer 'no-go areas'.

But openness is not just a matter of keeping people informed about what goes on in the 'corridors of power'. It also allows them to express publicly at meetings and demonstrations their own opinions about actions taken by the authorities and decisions they are planning to take or are actually implementing and to obtain satisfactory explanations from them. This is a sign of the development of criticism 'from below' and hard-hitting and frank discussions between 'managers' and 'managed' about the development of society. The following issues, for example, could be the subject of such discussions: Nagorno–Karabakh, which is still a burning issue here; whether Union republics can or should change over to economic accounting and self-financing systems and how they can do so, even perhaps by establishing their own currencies; the redistribution of legislative powers and rights between central and Republican governments; the constitutionality and effectiveness of certain resolutions and decisions taken by the Presidium of the Supreme Soviet, and many more.

The development of openness is making the life of apparatus officials less stable and comfortable. They have to deal not only with workers, collective farmers and the intelligentsia who are unaccustomed to political struggle but with press, radio, and television reporters who have in the new conditions become the real vanguard of restructuring. No mercy can be expected from these people and, bending to circumstances, the bureaucracy often finds itself having to enter into a dialogue with the public, for in the new conditions anyone who blatantly ignores openness can lose their job. Open political dialogue between social groups is the fourth factor in the development of openness.

The fifth factor is the growing and deepening social and cultural relations between Soviet society and the rest of the world. Radio broadcasts to the Soviet Union from Western countries are not being jammed for there is no longer any point. They used to inform Soviet people about things that they could not find out from sources inside the Soviet Union and prompted a critical attitude to the actions of the Soviet authorities. Now the Soviet press and television perform the same function with a better background knowledge and in greater depth. In the circumstances our interest in Western broadcasts has noticeably diminished. We are fairly well informed about the facts relating to our own lives, although we are still interested in the views of Western specialists and journalists on restructuring. It is difficult to understand a socio-political system thoroughly when one is living within it. In this sense an objective view from outside can be very useful.

Thanks to restructuring and openness, Soviet people can now receive television broadcasts direct from most Western countries. The international 'tele-bridges' which are becoming freer, more relaxed and interesting with each broadcast are very popular. Foreign travel into and out of the Soviet Union is growing rapidly. International firms are setting up in the Soviet Union which means that in the course of business our people come into close contact with workers from other countries. Person-to-person meetings between people of different countries, the Soviet Union and the USA for example, are becoming a tradition. Beginning in 1985 in Chautauqua, USA, they have taken place every year alternately in each country. The hundreds of people who take part in these lively, warm and friendly meetings will not soon forget them. Of particular importance are the exchange visits between groups of children and teenagers who get used to seeing their contemporaries as friends rather than potential enemies, get an undistorted impression about their way of life, their values, etc. Mention should also be made of the greater exchange of films, books published in translation, and so on. All this shows that Soviet society is becoming more open to people from other countries as well.

The development of openness, however, is not going smoothly since it runs against the interests of powerful groups who would find it much more convenient to keep their activities secret. Under cover of an official or Party 'secret', things can go on, and in practice have gone on, that would not survive the light of openness. A great many barriers are therefore being placed in the path of restructuring by government departments and local councils, and it meets with outright opposition from the bureaucracy. Many leaders cannot and do not wish to give up their habitual ways of stifling 'criticism from below' and still refuse to tolerate their colleagues expressing independent opinions. As a result, openness is not yet complete. The main brake on its further development is the state of inertia shown by officials in the Party and Soviet apparatus, ministries, enterprises and organizations, their fear of openness, their inability and unwillingness to deal with 'the public', their misgivings as to the possible consequences.

Many Party committees are still trying hard to exercise complete control over the press by assuming monopolistic powers of decision over what should and should not be published and reprimanding editors for publishing 'inappropriate' material. There is even a theory in the peripheral regions that there are two sorts of openness – one for the central and one for the provincial press (to the benefit of the former, of course). There have been cases of central newspapers that contain very critical reports about certain local authorities being withdrawn or destroyed in those areas without ever having reached the subscribers.

There is still not enough openness in the judicial system. According to the Constitution, hearings in all courts must be open to the press without restriction. Despite this, journalists are constantly being denied access to court proceedings. A sociological survey of judges showed that there is a reason for this. Only 60 per cent of them considered that openness contributed to the effective administration of justice. Fifty per cent were prepared to provide journalists with information about the case, and 46 per cent were prepared to allow them to attend sittings on the same basis as ordinary members of the public. Only 13 per cent of judges would not pay attention to the press tape-recorder, although it is not forbidden by law to take recordings out of the court-room.

The following is a good example of the strange things that the struggle against openness can lead to. Following complaints from people living in Sverdlovsk about the poor quality of their bread, a commission arrived from Moscow wanting to sound out public opinion on the matter. For this purpose questionnaires were circulated to several shops. The directors of the factory supplying the town with bread promptly assembled a team of officials and ordered them to descend on the shops in question and complete the questionnaires themselves. They were advised to sign either with false names or with the names of friends and relations who would not give them away. For greater operational efficiency the team was assigned a special bus. The directors succeeded in extracting half the negative replies that filtered through. In this way the 'public opinion of the citizens of Sverdlovsk' was obtained. An account by one of those who took part in the operation was printed in *Literaturnaya gazeta* on 1 April 1987.

However, having enjoyed a taste of openness and freedom, people have changed. For many, openness has become the breath of life. The frequent attempts to restrict or completely reverse restructuring, therefore, usually meet with opposition. Protest meetings and demonstrations spring up, complaints appear in the press, petitions signed by thousands are delivered to the Party Central Committee, and slogans and appeals are indelibly painted on the walls of buildings. The bureaucrats have to give way because 'the public', once it has become aware of its own interests and is ready to fight for them, is a powerful force.

The resolution 'On openness' passed by the 19th Party Conference opens up broad prospects for the further democratization of society. It contained proposals that Party forums and meetings should be open, that the public should be kept fully informed about the work of leading bodies of the Communist Party, local Party organizations and their committees, and that the mechanism for promoting top officials should be substantially democratized. Members of elective Party bodies are supposed to have the right of free access to meetings of committees accountable to them, including the Central Committee. They will be given the right to make use of documents, reports and data that are available to officials servicing Party committees. Particular emphasis has been placed on the need to create legal guarantees of openness and to draw up legislation defining the rights and duties of the state, officials and citizens in putting its principles into practice.

It is appropriate to conclude this discussion of openness with the following words by Mikhail Gorbachev:

> Democratization and openness are not just the means for achieving restructuring. They are the achievement of the very essence of our socialist system. We must learn to live in conditions of openness and constantly make a critical analysis of what has been done, what our successes are, what has been achieved and what our mistakes have been. Openness and criticism – these are the means of control by the people, by society over all its processes . . . In answer to the question whether there are any limits to openness, criticism and democracy, we say firmly: if openness, criticism and democracy are in the interests of socialism, in the people's interests, they have no limits.

RESTRUCTURING POLITICAL INSTITUTIONS

Openness and the fostering of political awareness among ordinary people cannot on their own make restructuring irreversible. The country's democratic future must be guaranteed by reliable political institutions that will not only enable citizens to obtain and discuss information of importance to them but participate in government and use their authority in a real way.

To make it easier for the Western reader to understand our problems, I shall briefly describe the present political power structure here. According to the Constitution, the Soviet of People's Deputies forms the basis of the political system. In the opinion of authoritative jurists, however, Soviet society in fact lives under a three-tier power system.[3] Its elements (in decreasing order of real power) are a) the Party apparatus, b) ministries and government departments, and c) the Soviets of People's Deputies. The concept of popular representation is not applicable to any one of these authorities since essentially this would mean that all of them are set up and function as a result of free, universal, equal and direct elections by secret ballot. The main condition for this to happen is, firstly, the real possibility of putting forward candidates who represent all social groups and, secondly, control by the electorate over the activities of their elected representatives including the power to recall those whose performance is unsatisfactory.

Let us look at what happens in practice. The Party leadership which exercises a maximal degree of power is set up on the basis of inner-party rather than popular representation and cannot therefore take the place of the Soviets. Elected officials comprise only a small part of the Party apparatus, most of which is made up of officials who are appointed by higher grades in the Party leadership and are in practice accountable only to them. In addition, Party elections are not direct but multi-tiered which is far from democratic.

Second place is occupied by the ministries and government departments, of which there is a fantastically large number – about 900. The many-million-strong army of bureaucrats employed in the ministries and state committees bear no relation at all to popular representation. Wielding immense power, they represent only themselves and their own interests. In issuing countless compulsory instructions and directing people's every step, the ministries are in fact usurping the power of legislative bodies and trampling them underfoot.

The Soviets of People's Deputies, unlike the first two power institutions, have a formal claim to the role of representative bodies. However, until recently elections to these bodies have been a mere formality since people have had to 'choose the best' – of only one candidate. Also, the Soviets wielded no real power since they were severely restricted by the local Party leadership, ministries, and enterprises and by their own administrative staff which had unlimited opportunities for interpreting in their own way decisions taken by deputies. Issues that are of vital importance to the people are formally decided by the Soviets of People's Deputies, while in practice this is done by members of staff servicing the executive committees, i.e. the bureaucratic apparatus.

This is the situation that radical political reform has to change. It has to transform this firmly established, traditional and complex system. And the principal protagonists in this revolutionary transformation of the power structure are bound to be those who will lose power as a result. The 19th Party Conference stated that the decisive direction of reform was to ensure that the supreme power of the Soviets was the basis for socialist statehood and self-government throughout the country. The same thought is expressed in the short but pithy political slogan, 'All power to the Soviets'.

Successful political reform means, firstly, that a significant amount of power enjoyed by Party bodies and by ministries and departments must be transferred to the Soviets and, secondly, that procedures for the setting up and functioning of the Soviets themselves must undergo radical democratization. The first task is very much more complicated than the second since it cannot be done without restructuring the Party and the ministries, i.e. the two 'whales' on which the country's administration rests.

I shall begin with the government departments. Economists consider that the basic task is to achieve a drastic reduction in their numbers, not so much to achieve savings in the use of public resources as to compel them to change their functions and to deprive them of the opportunity of giving orders to enterprises, organizations and citizens. While agreeing in principle with the necessity for this measure, jurists do emphasize its inadequacy. They point out the necessity for a more clear-cut legal definition of ministerial activities and a restriction of their power by law. It is proposed, for example, to introduce compulsory registration by the Ministry of Justice of all statutory laws that exceed the narrow competence of departments. This would enable the Ministry of Justice to refuse to register acts that run counter to the Soviet Constitution and existing laws, which it cannot at the moment do. Creating a special Committee of Constitutional Control has a similar object. In the present legislative muddle, even government decisions often contravene earlier laws that have not yet been rescinded. As a result, 'multiple law' is added to 'multiple authority'.

It is also important to maintain a balance between the economic powers of sectoral administrations (industrial ministries), on the one hand, and regional Soviets, on the other. The share of public resources that each has at its disposal cannot be compared. The ministries have everything, and the regional Soviets have nothing. In their practical activities, therefore, the Soviets are completely dependent upon the charity of the ministries that own the enterprises in their regions. Even in some large towns, not to mention small ones, ministries own not only the total housing stock but also the social infrastructure, including public transport. Decisions about the social development of such towns are taken by the management of large enterprises, not the Soviets. Under these circumstances, people's deputies can usually only observe and make requests.

To break away from this situation, it is proposed that the ministries should pay a tax to the Soviets, which would take on full responsibility for the comprehensive social and economic development of their region and represent the interests of local people. Government departments and enterprises would just be responsible for developing production, the Soviets of People's Deputies for the social infrastructure and the maintenance of good living conditions.

The overall redistribution of power between sectoral and regional administrations presents some considerable difficulty. The proposed separation of the functions of Party and state power, however, is even more difficult. The present division of functions means that the Party takes decisions but is not responsible for their implementation, while the Soviets carry out the orders of the Party and are fully accountable for the effect they have. In other words, the Party apparatus has all the rights, while the local Soviets bear the full responsibility. No rational arguments, of course, can be put forward to support such a 'division of labour'. It has come about because the Party committees, having absolute power, have gradually been able to acquire extensive rights and to free themselves of obligations, which they have placed on the Soviets' shoulders. It is not surprising that, without a radical restructuring of political power, attempts to obtain a more satisfactory division of functions between Party and state bodies were doomed to failure.

The issue is now placed in the context of comprehensive political and legal reform that envisages both a clear-cut division of functions and the internal reorganization of each institution in accordance with the functions it has taken on. This allows one to hope that the issue will finally be resolved.

According to the documents of the 19th Party Conference, the Soviet Communist Party must be transformed from an organization directly managing society into a political vanguard of working people, responsible for developing the strategic ideas of development and an ideology responsive to the new conditions. It should also be responsible for the training, selection and promotion of its leading personnel and for broad organizational work among the people. It is intended that in future Party committees will not take decisions containing direct commands to state and economic bodies. Instead, their political line will be put into practice not by issuing orders but through the activity of communists employed in various areas of society. The Party's authority will be based, not on its power but on the skill, honesty, authority and practical activity of its members.

Such an important change in functions will inevitably necessitate restructuring the Party's own internal organization and its forms of work. The main direction of this restructuring is the thorough democratization of relations between communists. In practice, this will largely be done by drastic cuts in salaried staff – that stronghold of bureaucracy – and in shifting the centre of gravity to the work of primary-level organizations. We often seem to forget that the Party is not a million professional functionaries, but first and foremost about 20 million communists working in factories, collective farms, schools, hospitals, research institutes, etc. Till now the administrative machinery of Party committees has operated in the name of communists while monopolistically appropriating their authority and issuing them with commands. The situation must now change. The Party apparatus is being reshaped to accord with stronger political leadership at the new stage of restructuring and is being reorganized and reduced in size. It must give up its leading role to local Party branches in the administration, factories, collective farms, and institutions. The industrial departments of the Central Committee and lower Party committees which duplicated the functions of the Soviets and were always giving orders to government departments and enterprises have been abolished. There are proposals to reduce the regional network of Party organizations and consolidate them in larger units by abolishing district committees. In all, a cut in the Party apparatus of not less than 30–50 per cent is to be expected. This will free primary-level Party organizations and their elected bodies from petty guidance 'from above' and will enable them to work more independently and actively.

The style of membership organization within the Party needs to be fundamentally changed, including the admission of new members. In Brezhnev's 'stagnation' period the mechanism for recruitment was taken to ridiculous lengths. The apparatus did not regulate the political, practical and moral qualities of Party members so much as their formal social and demographic composition (by age, sex, social position, education, nationality, etc.). Industrial workers, irrespective of their personal qualities, had no difficulty in joining the Party. Professional people, however, used to wait for years until their branches received their quota for accepting them into the Party, by which time they had often changed their minds. This practice completely distorted the idea of the Party as an alliance of politically like-minded people.

It is now proposed that acceptance into the Party will be democratized, that the centralized quota system will be abandoned, and that non-Party people will be involved in vetting candidates. It has been decided to limit the holding of elective Party office to two five-year terms, which will hit the existing system of nominating officials fairly hard. After ten years, Party workers must either transfer to a higher post or take another job, preferably in their former occupation, possibly in the very same workforce that they left. They will thus have an incentive not to cut themselves off from their former colleagues and to conduct themselves more democratically and with greater humility.

The changes I have talked about are not fantasy but today's reality. Re-elections in Party branches have already taken place, and elections to regional, town and district committees are in full swing. What the results will be, whether the decision to separate the functions of Party and Soviet will be successfully realized, time alone will tell. One would like to believe that the slogan, 'All power to the Soviets', will ring out again with its original revolutionary socialist fervour.

How will the Soviets change, once directly administrative functions have been transferred to them, the Party has begun to influence them only through the activity of its members, and ministries and departments have given them a fair share of economic power? The Soviets will have to assume responsibility for making legislative decisions on vital issues concerning state, economic, social and cultural matters and in practice transform themselves into genuine institutions of people's power.

In concrete terms, what needs to be done to bring this about? First and foremost, the existing electoral mechanism must be radically democratized. For more than 50 years the Soviet people have taken a merely formal part in elections. Candidates were confidently nominated 'from above' rather than proposed 'from below' on the initiative of the electorate. Heaven help us if some workforce, given the honour of nominating a candidate to the Soviet, decided to display any independence. I remember the commotion there was in Akademgorodok, Novosibirsk, a few years ago when the staff at an institute which had been instructed to nominate the Vice-President of the Siberian Division of the Academy of Sciences as a candidate to the Supreme Soviet 'had the temerity' to propose somebody else. It was not a question of whether the proposed candidate was better or worse, but of the unheard-of degree of disobedience which showed the 'political immaturity' of the staff. The electorate now insist on their right to select candidates. They want several candidates to be nominated for each seat, each of them to defend his or her programme in a real election campaign. They believe that both the final election and the selection of the candidate should be carried out by secret ballot, while the voting procedure and election results should be subject to democratic supervision to prevent any falsification.

An element new to the political system will be the election of a third of Supreme Soviet deputies, not from area constituencies but directly by social organizations – the Communist Party, the Communist Youth League, trade unions and co-operatives, women's organizations, professional associations, etc. The Association of Professional Arts Unions, for example, which incorporates the Unions of Writers, Artists, Film Workers, Composers, Theatre Workers, Architects, etc., has been allocated 11 seats in the Supreme Soviet. Many more candidates than that, of course, were nominated for these seats and an election campaign was carried on among them. This campaign resulted in the election of the best representatives of the creative intelligentsia to the highest body of state power. Under a purely constituency system, representation of this and other social groups in the Supreme Soviet was more a matter of chance. It is, however, important that public organizations should not put forward their own officials, as often used to happen.

The second condition for transforming Soviets into genuine institutions of people's power is their consistent separation from executive bodies and the reinstatement of their supremacy. There were a number of reasons why officials have had much greater power than those who represent the public interest. The first is that most deputies carried out their duties only during brief sessions held three or four times a year, while permanent officials worked throughout the year. Draft legislation approved by the Soviets was prepared by the staff who were fully informed on every issue and were professional administrators. People's representatives, however, did not usually have time to study information and discuss draft decisions. More often than not, therefore, they only 'rubber-stamped' prepared documents. As a deputy in the Novosibirsk Regional Soviet (1968–70), I had personal experience of this.

The second reason for the virtual subordination of Soviets to their executive committees was that until recently executive committee officers (chairperson, deputy chairperson, departmental heads and to some extent their deputies) were also simultaneously people's deputies. It was thought that having the status of deputies, i.e. being able to take part on an equal footing in the sessions, raised their social prestige and made the work of legislating easier. In fact, such a system strengthened the position of the Party-nominated apparatus. The officials-cum-deputies were in fact irremovable in the period between elections and could use their authority as deputies in their day-to-day work. Another aspect of the system, however, was the fundamental inequality between deputies who were permanent officials and deputies who had other jobs elsewhere. The officials were absolute masters of the Soviet: they prepared draft laws, presented them at sessions, answered questions and, of course, steered through the clauses they considered necessary. The other deputies felt unsure of themselves and also somewhat guilty that they had not had time to prepare for the session, and therefore either kept quiet or mechanically voted 'for'. Deputies' speeches were planned in advance by the executive committee officials. As regards the groups of deputies who were supposed to exercise control over the activity of the executive bodies between sessions, they were in fact totally dependent upon the apparatus and in no position to control it.

Following the 19th Party Conference decision, from 1989 both chambers of the Supreme Soviet will work in permanent session, and their members will be released from their regular employment and will be able to pay full attention to their legislative work. Officials employed by the all-Union and Republican Councils of Ministers (with the exception of their chairpersons) will not stand for election to the Soviets to which they are accountable. As regards local Soviets, their workload is much lighter and their deputies number millions. It is not necessary to release them from their basic employment. Each local Soviet will therefore elect a presidium from among its members who will carry out their duties on a full-time basis throughout the year. They will also supervise the work of the full-time officials. Sessions will last much longer than now and for that period deputies will be released from their normal jobs. The holding of elective office and posts subject to confirmation by Soviets will be limited to two terms. This should ensure the necessary rotation of office-holders and put a check on bureaucratization.

This reform, proposed or already undertaken, means introducing into our political system some elements of the parliamentary model. The regular working of the two chambers of the Supreme Soviet, the creation of a Permanent Commission on key issues, the release of deputies from their regular employment, the creation of a Committee of Constitutional Control, the introduction of the practice of questioning ministers – all these features will bring Soviet power closer to the west European parliamentary system and improve the political culture of our society.

There is another question associated with the reorganization of political power that is the subject of heated discussion both here and abroad. Why, after announcing that Party and state power must be separated, did the 19th Party Conference, and then the Supreme Soviet, recommend that the position of chairperson of a Soviet should as a rule be held by the first secretary of the corresponding Party committee? This surely means the concentration of higher Party and Soviet power in one person, which at first glance is a direct contradiction of the original idea. This idea was first put forward by Mikhail Gorbachev in his address to the conference. It had not appeared in the Central Committee theses published a month before and most deputies were apparently quite unprepared for it. As a visitor to the conference, I witnessed the heated discussions around this point that took place in the lobbies afterwards. To be honest, I was myself in a 'state of shock': the necessity of separating Party and state power seemed indisputable to me and the new proposal ran counter to that idea. A great many people thought the same way. More far-sighted and experienced politicians, however, were already saying that it was not only the correct but the only possible decision since it opened up the real possibility of transferring the powers of the Party authorities to the Soviets. In time I came to realise the correctness of this way of thinking and can therefore argue in its favour.

The Party apparatus now has practically unlimited power. Neither the extent of this power nor its style of work is regulated by law. The Party apparatus can at its own discretion decide everything or nothing. We have seen what this can lead to in practice. Rules must therefore be written into Soviet law regulating the functions of the Party apparatus and its relationship to the state and society and compelling it to 'share' its power with the Soviets. But how can this actually be done, when that power is now in the hands of the Party apparatus? History contains very few examples of power being given up voluntarily. But here we have the idea of integrating the functions of Party and state, at least on a temporary basis, in a single institution of power where rights are balanced with duties and 'managers' are politically accountable to the 'managed'. In this case powers must be redistributed, not between particular social groups and individuals, but between political institutions while individuals move between posts, which is socially less painful.

In this way, the secretaries of Party committees will not be appointed by the chairpersons of the corresponding Soviets and will not even be elected by a small number of communists on a particular committee but will become deputies as a result of the direct choice of the electorate. In any event, this is what should happen. For the moment, it is true, an interim decision has been taken regarding the election of chairpersons by Soviets, i.e. by indirect vote. Public opinion is insisting, however, that chairpersons of all Soviets without exception – from local Soviets to the Supreme Soviet – should be elected by universal, equal and direct suffrage in a secret ballot and with the obligatory selection of several candidates for each seat.

Good leaders respected by the people will pass this test with honour and will acquire the status of elected representatives. Party leaders who lose the competitive campaign would obviously also have to give up their Party posts, which will improve the quality of its leadership. In the last analysis the combination of Party and state power will make both accountable to and controllable by the people.

As E. Ametistov put it:[4]

> There is no doubt, that this kind of restructuring will strengthen the position of the most progressive and energetic section of the Party apparatus, that most devoted to the ideas of restructuring, and will strengthen their role in state bodies. It will cut the ground from under the feet of the Party bureaucracy and will virtually destroy their base. There will thus be a direct link between solving the delicate question of separating the functions of power, and strengthening the nucleus of Party members in Soviets of People's Deputies, ministries, institutions and enterprises.

These are some of the most important features of political reform in the Soviet Union. Some difficult and distinct problems remain outside the scope of this description, such as those associated with the creation of a society based on the rule of law, i.e. where law is an inviolable force and any deviation from it will entail inevitable penalties; the struggle to increase human rights and freedoms based on rules and guarantees provided by the Constitution; the widescale development of new public organizations that will play an increasing role in restructuring and exert considerable influence in changing the work of such traditional organizations as the Communist Youth League, trade unions, etc.

As with the restructuring of economic relations, political and legal reform needs an appropriate social strategy. Its most important aspect concerns groups with different attitudes to restructuring. The main object of such a strategy is gradually to change supporters into initiators, allies into convinced supporters, wait-and-see onlookers into allies, those indifferent to social problems at least into interested observers, conservatives trying to slow down restructuring into people who are loyal to it. The political processes that have already been described above will make it possible to achieve these objectives. To make them even more effective, however, several additional measures must be taken, some of which I list as follows:

i) The complete abolition of the undemocratic *nomenklatura* system whereby the Party apparatus nominates people for important posts, since this slows down and distorts the natural rotation and renewal of top leaders; formation of the upper echelons of authority with due regard for the democratic choice of the people and ridding it as quickly as possible of corrupt elements, conservatives and reactionaries. Greater openness regarding the political conduct of Party and Soviet leaders, thus enabling people to form their own independent opinions about the effectiveness of their performance. In-depth reporting about the work of Party committees, Soviets, and their executive committees in the press, on radio and television. Central television programmes about Plenary Sessions held by the Party Central Committee, the Supreme Soviet and the Council of Ministers, which will clearly show, on the one hand, who are consistent fighters for restructuring and, on the other, who are only quasi-supporters whose actions do not match their words.

ii) The tidying-up of existing legislation so as to remove the many contradictions and ambiguities that lay laws open to different interpretations. A sharp curtailment in the number of cases of law-breaking by office-holders regardless of their seniority and the institution of legal proceedings against bureaucrats whose activities harm the country. An increase in public confidence regarding the soundness of current measures, in particular, the commitment by the state to encourage co-operative and individual businesses and to promote the development of contracting teams, leasing of land, etc. The creation of legal guarantees for all those managers and administrators who act as pioneers in generating new social relationships and often prove almost defenceless against accusations of infringing old instructions.

iii) The creation of favourable political and ideological conditions for the organizational consolidation of supporters of restructuring, irrespective of whether they are Communist Party members or not. General support for the broad movement of Popular Fronts in Support of Restructuring. The establishment of an all-Union Popular Front in Support of Restructuring based on Popular Fronts in the republics and large cities headed by well-known journalists, political figures, academics, social experimentalists, leading workers, co-operators, etc. Without claiming to be a second party and with a strong nucleus of Communist Party members, the Popular Front could act as a serious and highly regarded opponent of Party organizations on certain issues. The Popular Front must be allowed to organize its own finances provided by voluntary contributions from ordinary members of the public and organizations, publish its own periodicals, and run programmes on central and local television.

iv) An end to the political suspicion at present shown by the authorities towards movements taking social initiatives, which as a rule bring together the most lively and sensible sections of young people. The affiliation of socialist-orientated clubs and social initiative movements to the Popular Front and their provision with both practical and organizational help and moral support. The provision of premises necessary for their work and help in facilitating such forms of political activity as organizing mass meetings, demonstrations, personal meetings with political leaders, etc. The establishment of contacts for the exchange of ideas and discussions about moral values between members of social initiative movements and Communist Party and Communist Youth members so as to integrate all forms of activity that are in the spirit of restructuring.

I have named only some of the measures that could bring about a more rapid, radical and effective implementation of restructuring. If due attention is paid to specific proposals put forward by the large number of people interested in the revolutionary transformation of Soviet society, even greater successes can be achieved.

I should like to conclude my account of the events now taking place in our country with the words that express my civic and professional credo: restructuring is vitally necessary, it is making headway, and it must succeed.

1989 As the First Year of the Radical Restructuring of Soviet Society: A Postscript 6

The fifth chapter of this book was written at the end of 1988, and was full of anticipation of great political changes. Yet, the changes that actually took place in the Soviet Union in 1989 exceeded all expectations.

This first year of genuinely radical restructuring of our society was dramatic in the extreme. It began with the need to deal with the consequences of the catastrophic earthquake in Armenia. There followed the unprecedentedly fierce election campaign, the tragic events in Georgia, the first Congress of People's Deputies, which kept the adult population riveted to their televisions for a total of 95 hours, the first session of the new Supreme Soviet, the formation of a new government, sharpening inter-ethnic confrontations in a number of Union and Autonomous Republics (the Baltic, Uzbekistan, Moldavia and Transcaucasia) and finally a virtually countrywide strike by coal-miners. And all this within the space of twelve months. Things are changing at such a pace in various parts of the country that it is difficult enough to keep track of them, let alone control them.

In this brief postscript cum update I cannot go into all the above events in detail. I should like to touch upon three important ones: the election campaign, the Congress of People's Deputies and the first session of the new Supreme Soviet. These events may offer a natural cutting-off point to this book, and one which to the Soviet people at large and to me personally represented a moment of major significance and high drama in the political history of the Soviet Union.

At the end of 1988 the date for the election of People's Deputies was fixed for 26 March 1989. The new electoral law differed substantially from the previous one – in the main it was more democratic. A Congress of 2,250 People's Deputies, occupying a very much higher position in the hierarchy of state power than the Supreme Soviet of old, was in itself a new concept. The elections were to be conducted primarily on the basis of a contest among

several candidates who would present and defend their own programmes. A third of the deputies were to be elected from local
constituencies of roughly the same population size, a third from
national constituencies, thus ensuring equal representation of each
Republic, and a third were to be nominated and elected by public
organizations, for example the trade unions, the Academy of Sciences, the Communist Party Central Committee, etc., each of which
would be allocated a specific number of seats.

Although the new electoral law had a number of serious weaknesses it nevertheless gave the electorate some opportunity of
expressing its wishes and in many regions full advantage was taken
of this opportunity. The election campaign took the form of a bitter
contest between the radically-minded section of the population on
the one hand and the Party and Soviet bureaucracy on the other.
The first group put forward deputies prepared to support policies
aimed at social renewal, while the other did all it could to secure
representation for its own social group in the highest state authority.
To this end it exploited all the loop-holes in the new law.

The battle had already begun at the stage of nominating candidates by enterprise workforces and public organizations legally entitled to do so. In many regions the list of institutions 'entrusted' with
putting forward a candidate had been drawn up by the Party district
committees. However, politically active workforces which had not
appeared on the list held meetings and put forward their own
candidates. Attempts were also made to hold impromptu meetings
of tenants or local residents and to put forward candidates by means
of collecting signatures on a petition but this was eventually declared
illegal. Many thousands of candidates were put forward at this stage
– from one to 20 per seat. There was also considerable duplication.
Academician Andrei Sakharov, for example, was proposed by as
many as 55 separate institutes of the USSR Academy of Sciences,
Boris Yeltsin by many enterprises in Moscow and the Urals. I
myself was proposed by three types of organization – the trade
unions, the USSR Academy of Sciences and professional societies
or associations, e.g. the Soviet Sociological Association.

The next step was the sifting of the many candidates put forward and their official registration. This was done by constituency
electoral meetings and, in the case of public organizations, their
central committees and conferences. These bodies had to hear all the
candidates put forward in a particular constituency, consider their
programmes and decide by secret ballot who was to be registered
and who taken off the list. This procedure in effect turned the direct
election of deputies into an indirect one because the most radical
and 'awkward' candidates were eliminated at this stage. This was
done using different strategems and under various pretexts. Often

inadequate premises accommodating only 600 to 700 people were provided for the electoral meeting and the hall was packed out with especially chosen people of the right persuasion several hours before the beginning of the meeting. Those who unsuspectingly turned up half an hour early simply could not get into the hall while the meeting proceeded according to the pre-arranged scenario. On a number of occasions constituency meetings refused to register candidates who did not live and work in the area although this stipulation was illegal. In one Moscow district, for example, this was what happened to Vitali Korotich, the editor of the popular political magazine *Ogonek*, and the distinguished actor Yuri Nikulin.

All in all the constituency electoral meetings considerably 'thinned out' the lists of proposed candidates. In approximately 400 local and national constituencies there remained just one candidate. Many of the public organizations put forward the same number of candidates as the number of seats they had been allocated. The Communist Party Central Committee was an example of this, putting forward 100 candidates for 100 seats. The trade unions (114:100) and the Academy of Sciences (23:20) were not far behind. At the same time, in some constuencies up to ten or more candidates contested one seat. This made for very uneven competition in different groups of candidates.

A personal note can help to show the picture more clearly. The plenary session of the All-Union Council of Trade Unions voted down my candidature on the grounds that in 1986 I had supported retail price increases for meat and milk (the subsidy at present covering a third to a half of their cost of production). No account was taken of the fact that I had made the proviso that people should be fully compensated for the rise in prices by higher wages and pensions. The trade unions' negative attitude was not shared by the professional societies and associations. From an initial list of 50 candidates they elected 13 to continue the contest for 10 seats. I was one of the 13 they chose.

The two months that elapsed between the registration of candidates and the elections were extremely strenuous and exhausting. They were taken up with endless pre-election meetings which in extreme cases showed a complete lack of tolerance. All the walls in the Moscow Underground were pasted over with flyposters, appeals, and 'exposures', which were changed almost daily. Groups of people were busy canvassing for particular candidates. I had a difficult time, facing harassment by the notorious *Pamyat* ('Memory') Society. Members of that organization would come to every meeting where I was on the platform. They would wait until my turn to speak, interrupt with a lot of stupid questions as to why, for example, I 'had destroyed the Russian village' (!?), make other wild accusations and then leave before the end of the meeting. At the same time a scurrilous campaign was mounted against me in the newspapers *Literaturnaya Rossiya, Moskovskaya pravda* and *Moskovskii literator*. This took a heavy toll on my nerves. If I had known what it was going to involve, I would probably never have agreed to my name going forward as a candidate. And my 'election campaign' was not by any means the hardest.

Strong politically active groups of electors emerged during the course of this campaign, determined to keep a check on the whole election process and the counting of votes since it was known from experience that strange things can happen at such times. This kind of political mobilization was particularly strong in Moscow, Leningrad, Sverdlovsk, the capitals of the Baltic Republics and other cities.

And so, at last, the elections took place, most of the seats were filled and in those constituencies where nobody was elected (i.e. no candidate had received 50 per cent of the votes cast) a new round of elections was arranged. The publication of the main election results put new heart into people. They felt that in fact something did depend on them, that they were not just 'objects of administration from above' but subjects of political activity in their own right, capable of protecting their own interests. For this reason the second and third rounds of the elections were carried on more effectively and had better results. Deputies with radical tendencies were elected nearly everywhere.

Who finally formed the Congress of People's Deputies? Their composition differed considerably from that of the previous Supreme Soviet. The proportion of women decreased from 25–30 per cent to 17 per cent and the proportion of young people (30 years old and under) fell to 5 per cent. There were fewer workers and peasants and significantly more members of the intelligentsia. Far from declining, the proportion of Communist Party members grew to 87 per cent. The people thus showed faith in 'rank-and-file' Communists, but the Party functionaries had to give way. In such towns as Leningrad, Kemerovo and some others not a single leading Party official was elected. Even the absence of any opposition, when a single contestant had obligingly been put forward for the seat, was often of no help. People voted against. This could be said to be the first blow to the Party's monopoly position within the political power structure.

However, the Soviet Union is a large country and its Republics and regions are at different stages of political development. Whereas in Moscow, Leningrad and the Baltic Republics the elections did in fact take a new form, the same cannot be said for Central Asia and Kazakhstan. For example, at the Congress it was noticeable that the First Secretaries of all the 19 Party regional committees in Kazakhstan had been elected, which was clearly not the case in other Republics. The final result was that between 500 and 600 supporters of radical reform were elected and 1,600–1,700 supporters of a moderate approach to reform, if not its curtailment. This, then, is what the more-or-less solid majority of the Congress has turned out to be, which Yuri Afanasev was later to call 'aggressively obedient'. The description is fairly apt as this majority has obediently followed the 'conductor's baton' wielded by the chairperson while at the same time acting aggressively towards 'disobedient' ones, primarily the deputies belonging to what is known as the 'Moscow Group'.

The first session of the Congress of People's Deputies lasted more than two weeks, starting at 10 o'clock in the morning and sometimes not finishing before midnight. Everybody who could do so followed the proceedings on television. The great interest shown can be explained by the fact that, for the first time in their lives, people were witnessing a political forum, the course of which was not pre-determined and where a real political struggle was taking place. At times the struggle was fierce, and Mikhail Gorbachev had to exert all his expertise and talent as a politician to bring some order to the situation. There were particularly heated discussions on, among other things, the situation in the Baltic Republics, the secret pact between the Soviet Union and Germany in 1939, the events in Tbilisi on 9 April 1989 and the role of Soviet troops in Afghanistan.

The main issue before the Congress, however, was the question of political power or, to be more precise, the transfer to the Soviets of the supreme power that *de facto* is in the hands of the Soviet Communist Party. The supporters of radical restructuring demanded that the Congress declare itself immediately by special decree to be the country's highest authority. The other deputies took up a temporizing position on this issue. In the first days of the Congress the motions proposed by the radical wing were supported by between 400 and 600 votes; towards the end by up to 800. Although its supporters grew in number, however, the radical point of view did not win the day on a single issue. The conservative majority did not offer much argument in defence of its position but it did vote solidly against any motions proposed by the radicals. And it won.

What then were the main results of the Congress, what decisions did it take and what did it achieve?

To begin with, the Congress elected Mikhail Gorbachev as Chairperson of the Supreme Soviet, with A. Lukyanov as his deputy. Before his election Gorbachev gave detailed replies to many searching questions put to him by the deputies and his candidature was subjected to critical discussion. But there was no real alternative candidate for the position of Head of State. Only 87 (out of 2,250) votes were cast against him in the secret ballot. As for Lukyanov, he was subjected to much more criticism but in the end it was conceded that Gorbachev was entitled to choose a lieutenant who would have to work very closely with him.

A major part of the work of the Congress was taken up by elections to the Supreme Soviet, which consists of two chambers: the Soviet of the Union and the Soviet of Nationalities. The radical deputies opposed the motion on the procedure to be adopted because it in fact entailed not the election of the best of several candidates but rather a 'ratification' of proposed lists compiled on the basis of one candidate for each available seat. By secret ballot the Congress confirmed the composition of the Supreme Soviet as proposed to it by different regions of the USSR. The sole exception was the Moscow Group of deputies who put forward 55 candidates for 29 seats in order to provide some options. The vote by the Congress resulted in some particularly outstanding deputies being rejected while less well-known Muscovites were elected.

Personally I was not prepared to serve on the Supreme Soviet as my post as Director of the Centre for the Study of Public Opinion would not leave me the time needed to do so. By mistake, however, my name was included in the Moscow Group list. At a Moscow Group meeting I explained my unwillingness to stand for election, and my refusal to accept nomination was accepted. However, due to bad organization my name again appeared on the voting list, with the result that those voting against me included both those who did not want me elected and those who knew that I did not wish to stand, which produced a large negative vote. At the same time I was elected to the Congress's Committee for Social Problems.

The setting up of various commissions to study particularly serious problems must be considered a major positive achievement of the Congress. The first was set up to analyse the events in Tbilisi on 9 April 1989 when, in the course of troops 'clearing' the Main Square where a meeting was being held, 16 people died, 14 of them women. The task of the commission is to obtain a clear picture of what happened and to establish responsibility for the tragedy.

A second commission has been set up to study carefully the records concerning the secret pact concluded between Stalin and Hitler in 1939 and to draw conclusions as to the legality/illegality of the incorporation into the Soviet Union of Moldavia, the Western Ukraine and the Baltic Republics.

The aim of the third commission is an enquiry into the activities of former special investigators Gdlyan and Ivanov who for several years were working on the case of the Uzbek-Moscow mafia, which had made millions in illegal cotton deals. According to these two there were threads leading back from the crimes uncovered by them to the upper echelons of political power, including people still in high office. Those who took Gdlyan and Ivanov off the case claim that they had used illegal methods, forcing people to perjure themselves, make false confessions and implicate others. The commission is to establish who are the innocent in this case and who the guilty.

The Congress also elected a Constitutional Commission headed by Gorbachev. This commission is to perform the vital but complex task of producing either an amended version of the 1977 Constitution or a new Constitution to reflect the great changes taking place in our country.

A major part of the work of the Congress was devoted to discussion of the reports produced by Gorbachev and Ryzhkov on the country's socio-economic and political development. These critical reports dealt with a wide variety of problems and proposed a whole range of measures designed to improve the situation. About a hundred deputies took part in the discussion, most of their contributions being devoted to the serious problems affecting different social and regional groups – children, the handicapped, the aged, women, young people, workers, people living in villages, the populations of ecologically damaged areas, towns, etc. There emerged a broadly based picture of our social problems and difficulties.

These were the immediate results of the Congress of People's Deputies. Opinion polls have shown that 47 per cent of people regarded its work as successful, 27 per cent considered it unsuccessful, while the rest had difficulty in answering the questions or took a middle-of-the-road position. The relatively large proportion of people disappointed with the Congress can be explained firstly by the very high expectations of it and, secondly, by the fact that many people were in sympathy with the radical minority in the Congress which managed to achieve little in terms of direct results.

In my view, the work of the Congress has had some indirect but significant effects countrywide which may well be as important as the direct ones. These include:

i) The recognition by broad sections of people, i.e. industrial and collective-farm workers and the intelligentsia, that our society is in crisis – deep-rooted, extremely complex and, I would say, systemic – and that great efforts must therefore be made to overcome it.

ii) The growth in public political awareness, the awakening in many people, previously alienated from social problems and needs, of a lively interest in politics and, in particular, in the distribution and mechanisms of power. This is shown in the greater demands that the electorate is making on deputies, the floods of letters and telegrams demanding greater action on the part of deputies, and support for radical alternatives.

iii) A better understanding by deputies and the electorate of divergences in the interests of social classes and groups as well as the necessity and possibility of defending these interests on a political level.

iv) The 'discovery' by ordinary people (and by the authorities) of the existence of a whole host of young politicians with the education, commitment and civic courage to defend the interests of those who elected them in complex political struggle.

The Congress of People's Deputies was followed by the first session of the new Supreme Soviet, when the new government was formed. Impartial and detailed consideration of each candidate by permanent commissions and committees of the Supreme Soviet took place, during the course of which 9 out of 71 candidates were voted down. Deputies did not support the candidates for the posts of Minister of Culture, the Chairperson of the State Committee for Physical Culture and Sport, the Chairperson of the State Committee for Prices, the Minister of Water Resources, the Chairperson of the Commission for Purchasing Agricultural Produce, and others. A number of the successful candidates were elected by a small majority only. All this created an atmosphere demonstrating the high level of responsibility of ministers towards the Supreme Soviet and the Congress of People's Deputies. For the first time for many decades the elected Soviets were taking decisions, often against the recommendations of the Party, and thus confirming their status as the highest political authority.

In this session the Supreme Soviet also established a number of permanent commissions and committees, and scrutinized and enacted a number of laws.

Further results of the session include the fact that the deputies of the Supreme Soviet have begun to acquire the habits of parliamentary struggle; quite evidently, despite the none-too-democratic way it was formed, the Supreme Soviet is far from being 'Stalinist Brezhnevite', as it was angrily described by Yuri Afanasev at the Congress. Its members do in fact represent the views and interests of different social strata and also include a number of vivid personalities in their ranks. It is also worth noting that in the course of its work the Supreme Soviet gradually moved to the left, becoming more radical. A further improvement in the quality of its work and its decisions can be expected.

Soviet society is experiencing one of the most dramatic, complex and critical moments in its history.[1] The restructuring of social relations has broken through its original bounds as a purely economic reform and now encompasses international, social and cultural policies and matters concerning political power. In their effect on the different levels and areas of social affairs, current processes can be compared only to the October Revolution of 1917 and the counter-revolutionary reverses brought about by Stalin in the late 1920s.

In the first years of restructuring changes mainly affected the upper levels of government and administration. The reforming initiative displayed by those 'above' left most of the rest of society unmoved. From mid-1988, however, the changes began to cut deeper. Those 'below', who have become conscious of their interests and are prepared to fight for them, have now caught up with the initiatives of those 'above' and often overtaken them. As a result, political processes often develop not so much according to scenarios planned from 'above' but according to those imposed from 'below'. This was shown in the emergence of strong centrifugal national movements, the unusual upsurge of strike action, the emergence of alternative political organizations (for example, independent trade unions, independent writers' unions, workers' committees). For a different example, what else is to be made of the blockade of the Armenian Socialist Republic by the Azerbaidjan Socialist Republic, which does not allow trains carrying food, petrol and other essential goods to pass through its territory on its way to Armenia?

The first Congress of People's Deputies and the first session of the Supreme Soviet marked the beginning of the redistribution of political authority between the Party, which previously had supreme power, and the Soviets, which under the new conditions are now claiming it. It should be noted in this connection that opinion polls have shown that 90 per cent of the adult population consider that supreme power should be in the hands of the Congress of People's Deputies and the Supreme Soviet, and that only 10 per cent support the retention of the system under which real power remains in the hands of the Party and the state apparatus. However, in practice the previous power structures remain and it will be far from easy to change them. A resultant strange duality of power exists within the framework of which the Party subsystem relies on historical tradition and the Soviet one on the ideas of restructuring, the constitutional provisions, and the law. In these circumstances a political struggle takes place on almost every practical issue, which sometimes the party apparatus wins, sometimes the Soviets.

The steady if insufficiently rapid democratization of political power should make it possible to resolve the main issue – the democratization and 'de-etatization' of social ownership of the means of production. However, reforms in this area are not having an easy passage. They are encountering powerful opposition from the Party and Soviet apparatus, whose authority is based on its to-date monopolistic power over the state-owned means of production and output. The introduction of economic accounting in the regions and Republics, workforce contracts, leasing arrangements, the attempt to re-create a stratum of individual peasants, the growing economic autonomy of workforces and local communities – these are all ways of doing away with monopolistic state ownership of the major part of the wealth of society. Over the recent period a swing in the direction of more radical reforms has become apparent.

Taken together, the redistribution of economic ownership and political power gives a revolutionary character to the reforms which are being introduced. At the moment they are being stimulated in equal measure both from 'above' and from 'below'. At the same time, there is a noticeable tendency for an increasing role to be taken by those 'below', fully aware of their interests, having their own positions and an autonomous voice. If this process continues, i.e. the majority of working people embrace democratic values and identify with restructuring, it will take on a radical character as Soviet society emerges from the difficult period with the old social relations destroyed and a more effective path for economic development able to provide better social conditions for its members. If, however, our people do not display the necessary level of political activity, and the conservative apparatus gains the upper hand, half-hearted reform, incapable of bringing about substantial improvements, will occur.

There is a third possible variant of future development, i.e. a sharp swing to the right, the re-establishment of a Stalinist-like system with its 'iron' discipline, rigidity, the suppression of individual initiative and the political repression of dissidents. There are, unfortunately, quite a few supporters of this variant and they are biding their time. In my opinion, it is unlikely that this variant will come to pass but it would be wrong to consider it as out of the question.

To sum up, the essence of the period which Soviet society is going through at the moment can be described as the struggle of social forces to move in one or another direction of social development – the radical revolutionary, the liberal conservative or the patently reactionary.

I shall end at this point. It is impossible to keep pace with life in all its richness of new developments.

Today's hopes are accompanied by considerable anxiety. Encouraging changes in the political arena coincide with a serious lagging behind of our economy, with budget deficits, with insufficient resources for social needs and with the development of destructive processes in our society. We are embarking on the most complex period of restructuring – the old structures have been destroyed and new ones have not yet begun to operate. Life is becoming increasingly difficult. Nevertheless most people agree that there is no going back. All we can do is to summon up our strength to face and overcome the difficult times ahead. Indeed, there is no other way.

Notes

INTRODUCTION

1.   I have deliberately not included such criteria as strengthening national security, accelerating scientific and technological progress, increasing economic efficiency, securing an ecological balance, etc., since similar tasks are tackled by societies of varying socio–political types. The totality of these indicators at best reflects the preconditions, but by no means the outcome of the emergence and strengthening of socialism.

CHAPTER 1: BRIEF HISTORICAL BACKGROUND

1.   This had important consequences in my life: the question of payment for the labour of collective-farm workers occupied my attention for 15 years – until 1966.

2.   These phenomena were very well portrayed in the novels of Yuri Trifonov in *The House on the Embankment*, Yuri Bondarev in *Silence*, Aleksander Kron in *Insomnia*, and a number of others.

3.   Tsvetayeva's poems were not at that time being published and could only be recited by heart. Now, however, they are known to everyone.

4.   The principles of the organization of Stalinist society are splendidly exposed in Fazil Iskander's parable, 'The Rabbits and the Boa Constrictors' published in the magazine *Yunost*, No.1. One of the heroes of the parable is even called 'Wonderer'.

5.   A number of interesting examples of this way of thinking can be found in the readers' letters published in the highly popular magazine *Ogonek*.

6.   The only work of fiction to throw light on this migration process is a short story entitled 'The little golden cloud stayed the night', published in the magazine *Znamya*, No.3, 1987.

7.   Not surprisingly in the 1960s a whole number of brilliant works were written which, alas, did not become available to the reading public until the mid-1980s.

8.   *The Work-day and the Principle of Material Incentives on Collective Farms* (Gosplanizdat, Moscow, 1958), *The Present Collective-farm Economy* (Znaniye, Moscow, 1960), *Distribution According to Work on Collective Farms* (Ekonomika, Moscow, 1966). For the last book I was awarded the degree of Doctor of Economic Sciences, and in 1968 I was elected a Corresponding Member of the USSR Academy of Sciences.

9.   There is a large body of literature, not only abroad but in the Soviet

Union, concerning the unreliability of data published by the USSR Central Statistical Office over many years.

10.   A good example of organized crime can be seen in the activities of leading Party, Soviet and economic officials in Uzbekistan, described in an article entitled 'Cobras on gold' in *Pravda*, 22 January 1988. This was only one of many such facts.

11.   'Improving production relations and the social mechanism of economic development', Novosibirsk, 1983. Published in *The Washington Post*, 4 August 1983.

CHAPTER 2: THE SOCIOLOGY OF ECONOMIC REFORM

1.   In many enterprises the psychology of pilfering had become the norm of everyday behaviour. The following excerpts are taken from an article entitled 'All the passengers burst out laughing' (*Sotsialisticheskaya industriya*, 9 January 1988), which tells how the police carried out a check on a bus which was taking 36 workers and engineers from the Vorkutinsky Liqueur and Vodka Factory home after finishing their shift: '. . . the police found 48 bottles of vodka, a quantity of cellophane packets and other containers, also full of vodka and spirits. There was not even a pretence of shame on the part of those caught red-handed. Looking into the faces of the thieves . . . I was amazed – the factory workers were laughing and amidst the completely amicable laughter somebody called out: "Whose vodka is that?" Only three women did not manage to get rid of the stolen goods. The other workers managed to throw the bottles and bags on the floor and then they realized: "Not caught – not a thief." That is why they laughed so openly . . .' In the words of the deputy secretary of the factory party organization I. Shaposhnik: 'The factory workers cannot grasp the fact that the vodka is there but you cannot take it. This is what people's psychology is like. It will be a long and slow business changing it.'

2.   S. Andreyev: 'Reasons and consequences'. *Ural*, No.2, 1988, p.109.

CHAPTER 3: A SOCIAL POLICY AND ITS PROBLEMS

1.   Editor and compiler: Prof. V. Z. Rogovin.

2.   *Sotsialisticheskaya industriya*, 4 February 1988.

3.   *Pravda*, 2 February 1988.

4.   *Ogonek*, No.2, 1988.

5.   *Pravda*, 13 February 1988.

6.   Cf., for example, the article 'Licence for Sale' in the newspaper *Moskovskaya pravda*, 22 December 1987, the article 'Behind the Counter Incognito' in *Pravda*, 1 February 1988, and others.

7.   *Ogonek*, 1988.

8.   A. Nuikin, 'Ideals or Interests?', *Novy mir*, No.2, 1988, p.226.

9.   *Literaturnaya gazeta*, 10 October 1986.

10.   'The System within the System', *Literaturnaya gazeta*, 1987.

CHAPTER 4: THE SOCIAL MANAGEMENT OF RESTRUCTURING

1.   R. Yaremchuk, 'Rasstavayas s dogmami' ('Parting with dogmas'). *Pravda*, 21 November 1987.

2.   V. Romanyuk, 'Informatsiya k razmyshleniyu ili k svedeniyu?' ('Information for thought or for action?'). *Izvestiya*, 11 January 1988.

3.   E. Sazonov, 'Igra bez pravil'. ('Game without rules'). *Pravda*, 22 December 1987.

4.   V. N. Ivanov, 'Nashe sotsialnoye samochuvstviye' ('Our social self-awareness'). *Argumenty i fakty*, 1988, No.1.

5.   Zh. T. Toshchenko, 'V zerkale mnenii'. ('In the mirror of opinions'). *Sotsialisticheskaya industriya*, 9 February 1988.

6.   Cf., for example, Yu. V. Arutyunyan, *Sotsialnaya struktura selskovo naseleniya* ('The social structure of the rural population'), Moscow, Mysl, 1971; V. G. Venzher (ed.), *Sotsialno-ekonomicheskiye problemy perekhoda sovetskovo obshchestva k besklassovoi strukture.* ('The socio-economic problems of the transition of Soviet society to a classless structure') Economics Institute of the USSR Academy of Sciences, 1982, pp.7, 26–7; and many other works.

7.   Personally I do not agree with membership of the intelligentsia being defined in terms of degrees or diplomas, particularly since in the stagnation period they were very often awarded not as a result of students' hard work but because a college had to fulfil its 'gross output plan' or else were often simply sold.

8.   T. I. Zaslavskaya and I. V. Ryvkina, *Sotsiologiya ekonomicheskoi zhizni. Ocherki teorii.* ('The sociology of economic affairs. Theoretical essays') (forthcoming).

9.   Many Soviet agricultural economists (V. G. Venzher, A. A. Nikonov, L. V. Nikiforov, M. Ya. Lemeshev, A. M. Yemelyanov, I myself, and others) opposed the trend to turn collective farms into state farms, arguing that under socialism collective-farm production was more effective than that of state farms. The voices of these economists were drowned in the chorus of assertions that the collective-farm form of ownership was 'lower' than the state form and that it was therefore necessary to 'rub out the distinction' between collective and state farms at a more rapid pace.

10.   A. Gelman. 'Vremya sobiraniya sil'. ('Time to gather strength') *Sovetskaya kultura*, 9 April 1988.

11.   Ibid.

12.   Ibid.

13.   V. Yefimov and T. Kadyrov, 'Kolkhoz – assotsiatsiya kooperativov'. ('The collective farm as an association of co-operatives') *Izvestiya*, 5 April 1988, No.96.

CHAPTER 5: POLITICAL CONDITIONS FOR SUCCESS

1.   M. S. Gorbachev: Speech to the Joint Session of the CPSU Central Committee, the USSR Supreme Soviet, and the RSFSR Supreme Soviet in celebration of the Great October Socialist Revolution, 2 November 1987.

2.   M. S. Gorbachev: 'Restructuring – the Vital Cause of the People', Speech to the 18th Conference of Soviet Trade Unions, 25 February 1987.

3.   Prof. E. Ametistov, 'Yes, but these are the hands of the people', *Sovetskaya kultura*, 9 August 1988. In this section wide use has been made of the ideas contained in this article.

4.   Ibid.

CHAPTER 6: 1989 AS THE FIRST YEAR OF RADICAL RESTRUCTURING: A POSTSCRIPT

1.   This last section formed the core of a talk delivered to social scientists in Moscow in September 1989.

Index